The Language of Faith

Concilium is an international theological journal begun in 1965. Inspired by the Second Vatican Council and the spirit of reform and dialogue which the Council inaugurated, *Concilium* has featured many of the world's foremost theologians. The *Concilium Series*, published by Orbis Books and SCM Press, highlights the contributions of these distinguished authors as well as selected themes that reflect the journal's concern for the mystical-political meaning of the Gospel for our age.

Already published

David Tracy, *On Naming the Present*

Johann-Baptist Metz and Jürgen Moltmann, *Faith and the Future*

CONCILIUM SERIES

EDWARD SCHILLEBEECKX

The Language of Faith

Essays on Jesus, Theology, and the Church

with an Introduction by Robert J. Schreiter

ORBIS BOOKS

Maryknoll, New York 10545

SCM PRESS

Copyright © 1995 by the Concilium Foundation, Nijmegen, The Netherlands

Published by Orbis Books, Maryknoll, N.Y. 10545-0308, U.S.A., and SCM Press, London, England

Queries regarding rights and permissions should be addressed to: Stichting Concilium, Prins Bernhardstraat 23, 6521 AB Nijmegen, The Netherlands.

Manufactured in the United States of America

Library of Congress Cataloging-in-Publication Data

Schillebeeckx, Edward, 1914–
    The language of faith : essays on Jesus, theology, and the church
/ Edward Schillebeeckx ; with an introduction by Robert J.
Schreiter.
        p.   cm. — (Concilium series)
    Includes bibliographical references and index.
    ISBN 1-57075-017-3 (pbk.)
    1. Theology, Doctrinal.   2. Jesus Christ—Person and offices.
3. Church and the world.   4. Catholic Church—Doctrines.   I. Title.
II. Series: Concilium series (Maryknoll, N.Y.)
BX1751.2.S376   1995
230'.2—dc20   94-45065
                                                                        CIP

ORBIS/ISBN 1-57075-017-3   SCM/ISBN 0-334-02599-0

Contents

Introduction by Robert J. Schreiter   vii

1. The Church and Mankind (1964)   1

2. The Magisterium and the World of Politics (1968)   25

3. Some Thoughts on the Interpretation of Eschatology (1969)   43

4. The Problem of the Infallibility of the Church's Office (1973)   55

5. Critical Theories and Christian Political Commitment (1973)   71

6. The Crisis in the Language of Faith as a Hermeneutical Problem (1973)   83

7. The "God of Jesus" and the "Jesus of God" (1974)   95

8. Questions on Christian Salvation of and for Man (1978)   109

9. The Christian Community and Its Office-Bearers (1980)   127

10. Secular Criticism of Christian Obedience and the Christian Reaction to That Criticism (1980)   167

11. Christian Identity and Human Integrity (1982)   185

12. Eager to Spread the Gospel of Peace (1983)   199

13. Offices in the Church of the Poor (1984)   211

14. The Teaching Authority of All: A Reflection about the Structure of the New Testament (1985)   225

15. The Role of History in What Is Called the New Paradigm (1989)   237

16. The Religious and the Human Ecumene (1989)   249

Table of Original Publication   265

Index   267

Introduction

The journal *Concilium* and the name of the theologian Edward Schille-beeckx are inextricably twined. Schillebeeckx founded *Concilium* in 1965 along with Yves Congar, Karl Rahner, and Hans Küng. He served as its general editorial director and also as general editor of the Dogma section until well into his retirement years. But even more than this editorial guidance, the spirit of *Concilium* and the theology of Edward Schillebeeckx have gone hand in hand. In the very first issue, Schille-beeckx and Karl Rahner described the kind of new theology they hoped *Concilium* would communicate:

> . . . it is deliberately based on Scripture and the history of salva-tion. At the same time it has the humble courage to confront the new problems arising from the human condition of today. It seeks, on the basis of our contemporary situation, a better understanding of the Word of God for man and the world in our time.

This could also describe Edward Schillebeeckx's theological project.

Edward Schillebeeckx was born November 12, 1914 into a middle class family in Antwerp, Belgium. His parents and siblings had been evacuated to Antwerp from their native Kortenberg ahead of the advanc-ing Germany army. Within a short time they were able to return to Kortenberg, where Schillebeeckx grew up, the sixth of fourteen children. After completing secondary school with the Jesuits, he entered the Dominican Order at Ghent in 1934. He was ordained a priest in 1941.

It was already clear to his teachers and religious superiors that he was unusually gifted. The war prevented his undertaking further study at that time, and he was appointed to teach dogmatic theology to the Dominican seminarians in Louvain.

After the war, he went to study at the Dominican faculty in Paris, working especially with Yves Congar and M.-D. Chenu. He also attended lectures at some of the major educational institutions in the city. He returned to Louvain in 1947, continuing to teach the seminarians and completing a dissertation on the sacraments in 1951. He remained in Louvain until 1958, when he became Professor of Dogma and the His-tory of Theology at the University of Nijmegen in the Netherlands. He remained in that position until his retirement in 1983. Since that time, he has continued to live in Nijmegen, actively writing and speaking.

Schillebeeckx's own academic training represented the best of what could be obtained by a Catholic theological student in the 1930s and 1940s. To those coming to theology at the end of the twentieth century it is difficult to imagine how restrictive things were in those days. The study of Thomism was *de rigeur*; but it was a Thomism that largely departed from the vigor and challenge of that great thinker. Schillebeeckx was fortunate to have had Dominicus De Petter as his philosophical mentor in the 1930s. De Petter was a Thomist who also encouraged Schillebeeckx to read Kant and the phenomenologists, something ordinarily barred for seminarians. Under the tutelage of Congar and Chenu in Paris, Schillebeeckx was steeped in the *nouvelle théologie*. This approach ground the investigation of theological questions in the reading of patristic and medieval sources rather than the propositional theology that predominated at that time. Schillebeeckx's own dissertation was a testament to this regrounding of theology in the sources. It received considerable attention in Dutch and Flemish theological circles at the time, but hardly reached beyond the Low Countries because of the linguistic barrier. It was only with translations of a shorter work based on its conclusions, published as *Christ the Sacrament of the Encounter with God* (ET 1963), that it could come to the attention of a larger audience.

When Schillebeeckx moved to the Netherlands in 1958, he quickly became an advisor to the Dutch bishops. He accompanied them to the Second Vatican Council in 1962, but was denied *peritus* status by the Roman Curia. But he managed to have considerable influence despite this stricture through the theological lectures he gave in the evenings to groups of bishops. This also gave him international standing. The year the Council closed, Schillebeeckx, Congar, Rahner and Küng launched *Concilium* as a means of continuing the collaboration and the theological probing that had characterized the Second Vatican Council.

The conclusion of the Council also marked the beginning of an important development in Schillebeeckx's own theological direction. From the beginning he had been interested in making sense of Christian faith in a modern and increasingly secularized world. But the international experience of the Council had broadened his horizons considerably. This was to be followed by his first trip to the United States, where he encountered that secular reality in a different but vibrant fashion. At the same time, he began to read widely and deeply into the major intellectual currents coursing through Europe at that time: hermeneutical philosophy, critical theory, philosophy of language, and semiotics. The results of this can be seen in his 1972 collection of essays, *The*

Understanding of Faith (ET 1974). This complex of ideas was to form the interpretive foundation and framework over the next two decades. To these must be added Latin American liberation theology, an influence on his work that continued to grow from the late 1970s.

But alongside these interpretive efforts, Schillebeeckx also turned to the substantive matters of faith. Up to 1970, he had been known principally for his work on the sacraments; after *Christ the Sacrament*, he had produced volumes on marriage and on the Eucharist. But now he turned his attention to an indepth study of christology, since for Schillebeeckx the question of who Jesus Christ was for modern women and men was the most basic of all for Christian faith today. In 1974 he published *Jesus: An Experiment in Christology* (ET 1978), called by the American ecumenical weekly *The Christian Century* one of the ten most influential religious works of the twentieth century. This was followed by a second volume, *Christ: The Experience of Jesus as Lord* (1977; ET 1979), and then by *Church: The Human Story of God* (1989; ET 1990).

From the late 1970s into the mid-1980s he also wrote two books on ministry, focusing on the nature of priestly ministry and the right of the Christian community to the celebration of the Eucharist in light of the growing shortage of priests. This proved to be among some of his most controversial stands, generating itself a whole literature and an investigation by the Vatican Congregation of the Doctrine of the Faith.

Alongside these major works, Schillebeeckx has produced a host of articles, published homilies, shorter books, and two book-length interviews. On the occasion of his eightieth birthday in November, 1994, he published his "Theological Testament," summing up where he saw himself at that point, but warning his readers that this would not be the last word to be heard from him.

Edward Schillebeeckx stands as one of the greatest theologians of the twentieth century. He has engaged the issues of the possibility of belief, the liberation of humanity, and the reform of the Church as few have been able to do. He has struggled to take contemporary human experience seriously, and to craft a Christian response to that experience with the best resources of the Christian tradition. *Concilium*, both as a journal and a theological movement for the ongoing reform of the Church, has been a forum for the presentation and the development of Schillebeeckx's theological work. Thus a collection of essays from that forum gives a good insight both into the issues that have concerned him and the way his thought has grown over the years. The sixteen essays collected here all derive from that forum: thirteen from the journal itself, and two (nos. 8 and 15) from symposia sponsored by the editors of *Concilium*. One (no. 16) is an exception, but only partly so:

it was Schillebeeckx's contribution to a sixtieth birthday anniversary volume honoring Gustavo Gutiérrez, a longtime editorial director of *Concilium.*

The essays are presented in chronological order. The subtitle of this collection, *Essays on Jesus, Theology, and the Church,* captures well the major themes that run through the work. Although more than one of these themes can be found in most of the essays, these three themes can provide a way of getting an overview of what is presented here.

The Church

Issues surrounding the Church are the most pervasive in these essays. That should not be surprising, given both the purpose of *Concilium* and Schillebeeckx's central preoccupation as a theologian. It has been said that the relation of the Church to the world has been the principal motif of Schillebeeckx's theology. It was the topic he had initially hoped to address in his doctoral dissertation. The greater opening of the Church to the world happened at the major turning point in his own theological development at the time of the Second Vatican Council. And it has been the main theme of most of his writing in the 1980s and 1990s. Not accidentally, then, is this collection framed—in nos. 1 and 16—by the problematic of the Church in its relation to the world.

"The Church and Mankind" was written for the inaugural issue of *Concilium.* It represents the leading edge of thinking at the time when Vatican II was concluding: a commitment of openness to the world, an attempt to take the world utterly seriously, and a desire to become a dialogue partner with the secular world and not simply its opponent. Contrast this with no. 16, written some twenty-five years later: the boundaries between Church and world have become much more fluid. The Church must now deal not only with humankind in general, but with the many religious traditions through which humans seek salvation. This was already noted at the Council, but has taken on much greater urgency in the meantime. To speak of humankind at the end of the Council meant principally to grapple with secularization. The urgent task a quarter century later is the plight of the poor who constitute the majority of humankind. As the human face of the poor has found clearer configuration in Schillebeeckx's thought, his theology has taken on ever greater passion in protest against suffering and injustice. At century's end, increasing secularization remains an issue in the wealthy countries of the world. But the real threat of the perishing of the human itself poses an even greater challenge.

One can note a change in Schillebeeckx's language as one progresses through these essays. It becomes less ecclesiastical, and more passionate about humanity. "God's cause is the human cause," first echoed in the christology volumes of the 1970s, takes on an ever-more insistent tone thereafter. Essay 11, written in 1982, shows that juxtaposition of Christianity and humanity clearly.

Following that commitment to a new humanity and the role of the Christian in bringing that about, one can identify a group of essays that address aspects of critical involvement and political commitment (nos. 2, 5, 10, 12). "The Magisterium and the World of Politics" looks at the pastoral teaching of the Church and its binding character for the believer, especially in an increasingly complex and pluralistic world. It is a question that grew out of the Church's new relation to the world, and is one that has only grown in importance since that time. "Critical Theories and Christian Political Commitment" focuses explicitly on the praxis of the "critical communities," the politically committed base communities of Northwestern Europe. It is Schillebeeckx's single most important statement on base communities (although he returns to the theme in no. 14), and gives the reader a view of what the Church becomes when it engages itself for the sake of humanity. No. 10, which deals with Christian obedience, shows Schillebeeckx the historian at work (no. 9 is another example). While his presentation can be read in a private, spiritual sense, his discussion of privatization and authority toward the end of the essay casts it in another light. A continuing theme for Schillebeeckx has been the relation of the mystical to the political, a notion found here and in other essays. Finally, the essay on nuclear disarmament deals with one of the concrete political issues that face the Christian. The Cold War may have since passed, but the nuclear issue and the problems Schillebeeckx addresses here remain.

The new understanding of the Church's relation to the world opened up new horizons and generated tremendous energy and commitment. Schillebeeckx argues consistently out of this new ecclesiological vision of openness and engagement. Like many others, he hoped that the Church would revise its structures to carry forward this prophetic call. But such was not to happen. Essays 4, 9, 13, and 14 reflect the struggle to bring about change in Church structures of authority and ministry. "The Problem of the Infallibility of the Church's Office" was part of the intense questioning of how to understand papal infallibility. This doctrine had been proclaimed at a moment when the Church was set most resolutely against the world; what did it mean now that the Church had committed itself to a nearly complete reversal of that stance? The debate had been fueled especially by the publication of Hans Küng's *Infallible? An Enquiry* (ET 1971) and historical studies on the First Vatican Council. "The Christian Community and Its Office Bearers" was written as a concluding article to what may have been the most controversial of all numbers of *Concilium*. It faced squarely the growing crisis of Christians being denied the Eucharist because of a refusal to change rules as to who might preside. Schillebeeckx was to write two books and have a protracted contretemps with the Vatican over this issue. Essays 13 and 14 take up the meaning of Church office among the poor and the meaning of teaching authority in the emergence of the base communities.

Jesus

Research into the meaning of Jesus preoccupied Schillebeeckx through most of the 1970s. Essays nos. 7 and 8 were written during that time. "The 'God of Jesus' and the 'Jesus of God' " appeared at the same time as did his volume *Jesus*. It provides a good theological summary of the portrait of Jesus that Schillebeeckx proposes. His growing concern for the suffering of humanity and the power of "contrast experiences" as privileged moments of revelation in the world are echoed here. One finds also his description of Jesus as the "parable of God and the paradigm of humanity," a succinct presentation of the central aspects of his christology. "Questions of Christian Salvation of and for Man" appeared at the same time as the volume *Christ*, and provides a clear account of Schillebeeckx's theological anthropology or understanding of the human.

While these two essays deal most explicitly with his christology, nearly every essay thereafter is infused with the christology that had developed in those years. Schillebeeckx's thought is markedly christological in those ensuing essays.

Theology

All of the essays in this volume are about theology, of course. But three of them (nos. 3, 6, 15) address theology in a special way. In "Some Thoughts on the Interpretation of Eschatology" Schillebeeckx gives his single clearest understanding of eschatological language. Eschatology is an exceedingly important category in Schillebeeckx's thought, since hope for a new humanity is at the center of his theological vision. In this essay he lays out his understanding of history and the future. One gets glimpses too of his developing anthropology.

"The Crisis in the Language of Faith as a Hermeneutical Problem" continues a theme raised in no. 3: the nature of the language we use in expressing our faith. Schillebeeckx is insistent that theological language cannot be a ghetto language, to be understood only by a few. It must be intelligible to all who struggle for a new humanity, not just to the elect.

"The Role of History in What Is Called the New Paradigm" wrestles both with history and the so-called "new paradigm" of doing theology (the theme of a Tübingen *Concilium* conference). One finds in this essay the point to which Schillebeeckx's understanding of history has evolved—a central interest from his first published theological work in the 1940s. He has reservations about the language of paradigms, but is clear about the paradigm for which he opts: the paradigm of a new humanity.

All in all, these essays give a good view of both central themes in Schillebeeckx's thought and the evolution of how he has dealt with them. As one of the greatest theologians of the twentieth century, still firmly committed to the agenda of renewal of the Second Vatican Council and the journal it inspired, Edward Schillebeeckx's theological work stands as testimony to a theologian who continues to serve God's cause by promoting the human cause against suffering and injustice for the sake of a new humanity liberated and transformed in God's grace.

Robert J. Schreiter

The Language of Faith

1

The Church and Mankind

1964

The Problem

In our age we have become aware, more than in the past, that our salvation comes about within the one reality that is ours, within the scope of our own life in this world. Everywhere there is evidence of a reaction against any kind of religious practice which is alien to this world. Christianity had come to be regarded as something added on to life here on earth with its sorrow and joy, its fear and hope, its activities and moments of recollection. Many Christians used to practice their Christianity as a superstructure erected on top of their normal lives. Frequently they would look upon this life as merely matter, without religious significance in itself, for the occasional exercise of Christian virtues. Life's own significance had, in their eyes, nothing to do with Christianity.

Real religion, they held, was only practiced within a church edifice or by saying a few prayers at home—in other words, at the periphery of life. As a result, many Christians gave the impression that Christianity was an ideological superstructure, or a special department where people talked about forgiveness, redemption, the cross and resurrection, while life in this world waited outside. The human problems of life on this earth failed to get from them the attention they received from non-believers to the benefit of mankind.

At present, there is a strong emerging realization that adherence to faith is not a mere structure superimposed upon human and secular relationships, which would in fact be what they are, with or without Christianity, and so would be unaffected by faith. Consequently, reaction against ghetto-Catholicism and ghetto-Christianity is characteristic of present-day religious awareness among both Catholics and Reformed Christians. Service to a world which is growing into a closer unity; the ethical commitment imposed upon Western man by the advanced position which the West enjoys in contrast to the rest of the world, particularly the underdeveloped countries; the plans for a dynamic blueprint to set up a society upon earth that shall be worthy of men—all this is seen, also by the religious man of today, as the concrete, even the principal way in which he proposes to give form to his religion and to Christianity.

Hand in hand with this new religious awareness there is opposition to an exotic religious vocabulary. Religious ideas have to be couched in "profane" words, in language that springs from the profound realities of human existence. People want their Christianity to be less explicit and prefer it to work implicitly, almost incognito, toward salvation within their secular human relationships.

This current phenomenon, however, has one drawback. Many believers are at a loss as to what to do about the Church as an objective reality. Sociological researches draw attention to the fact that some kind of faith in God as the basis of all existence, and faith, too, in the Man Jesus, who by his life has shown the meaning of God's love for men, actually exist in persons who had "practiced" earlier in their lives but do not belong at present to any Church: they also show that precisely these persons no longer find any room in their belief for the "Church."

They could only accept the Church—and with enthusiasm—if Church meant no more than the establishment of a community among men, the real expression of the community that human fellowship ought to build up in the world. There is talk of "Christianity without a Church," a Christianity in which fellowship and brotherhood appear as the essence of Church.

The lines of our essay take two directions. We inquire first into the increasingly "ecclesial" tendency in the world, or rather in mankind; and secondly, we inquire into the tendency within the Church to sanctify the secular. On the one hand, the human fellowship in Christ is surely the heart of the Church as a phenomenon: St. Thomas calls sanctifying grace *gratia fraterna*, the grace that establishes brotherhood. On the other hand, as believers, we cannot help admitting that the Church is a community *sui juris*, or rather, *juris Christi*. But *ipso facto* we then create a certain distance between the Church and mankind. There are boundaries between the Church and humanity, and yet they are fluid, not hard and fast. Into the implications of this we now propose to inquire, for the sake of a mankind that grows away from the Church and for the sake of faith in the Church as founded by Christ.

The Unity of Mankind and the Communion of Saints

Mankind's specific unity from an anthropological viewpoint must formally (*formaliter*) be based, not on its biological substratum, but, by its very nature, on a community of *persons*, a *communio*. It can only be built on a value-appeal, the community-building force of truly human values. This means simply that human unity has its origin in oneness of vocation and destiny.

Communio among all men is the immanent human expression of this single vocation. Human unity in its essence is not a mere datum: it is a task to be carried out. This task, we know from revelation, is in fact the response to a free and gracious act of God. The *koinonía* or community which he wills is also his gift. By his absolute self-communication to men he at once reveals himself as their highest value and reveals mankind to itself as his People, the People of God. By the granting of his grace God constitutes mankind "the People of God." Communion among men is the reflection, immanent in mankind's history, of man's transcending communion with the living God: the God-willed unity of mankind is therefore nothing less than the *communio Sanctorum*, the community of mankind sanctified.

Not only is the fact of this community an undue gift to men, but the manner of producing it also has its origin in a sovereign, free act of God. The history of salvation in both the Old and the New Testaments, even though the outlook of the ancient Near Eastern peoples plays its role in them, makes this fact clear: God did not intend "abstract" fundamental values to be the basis on which human unity was to be realized. He intends to gather all men into a holy community of persons on the basis of values that were expressed in living persons as in prototypes.

Time and again someone is chosen from among ourselves to be the means of salvation in forming the "great gathering" of men from the diaspora, the People of God.[1] The manner, not due to men, in which God establishes a community among them is that of representative or vicarious mediation: for the sake of one man, whom God freely calls for the purpose, salvation—or destruction—is brought to many. In the Old and the New Testaments, time and again, the representative function whether of one man or of a limited collectivity is essential for salvation or destruction: Adam, Noah, Moses, the twelve Patriarchs, "Israel," the "King," the Servant of Yahweh, Jesus.

In the Bible the establishment of a community through mediation implies that election and universal mission coalesce into one. Thus, however gradually and hesitantly, Israel did at last become aware of her election to be an example to all peoples—of her election for the service of all men. In the Old Testament conception it is to Yahweh's redemptive covenant with Noah after the Flood that the totality of mankind throughout history owes its existence. And in connection with that covenant a catalog is drawn up of all the nations existing in the world as conceived by the ancients (Gen. 10).[2] Again, in Abraham "shall all nations be blessed" (Gen. 12, 3; 18, 18; 22, 18). His election, too, is God's ratification of universal salvation.

The notion of mediatorship shows us that men are dependent upon one another and that God in bringing his transcendent salvation means to preserve the structure of human fellowship. Through men he wants to bring salvation to men. The notions of "the first-born among many brethren" (Rom. 8, 29), which embraces prototypical religious fellowship, and of "God's first-born son" (Ex. 4, 22), in which divine choice and service to the neighbor are united, are led up to throughout the Old Testament. They suggest the fundamental notion that salvation is a gift conveyed through man's fraternal service to others according to God's election. Even Israel, the People of God, is, when chosen, "God's first-born son" (*loc. cit.*): Israel is personified, initially, in the vicarious figure of the King, who is therefore eponymously called "Son of God" (*e.g.*, 2 Sam. 7, 14; Ps. 2, 7), and ultimately in the figure of the coming Messiah and Son of Man, "the Son of God" *par excellence.*

Jesus is not merely one of us—he represents "Israel, the Son of God," but in an incomparably deeper sense: in a uniquely transcendent manner he is "the Son of the Father." Nevertheless, he is our fellowman "taken from among men" (Heb. 5, 1), "born of a woman" (Gal. 4, 4). Election and fraternal service, "Son of God," servant of God and men— these ideas find their highest fulfillment in Jesus. And so it is in him that the "great gathering" of all men around God, *he ekklesia toû Theoû* (1 Cor. 11, 22; 15, 9), is formed into a mutual *communio* of men with Christ as their center—a "Church of Christ," *hai ekklesiai toû Christoû* (Rom. 16, 16). Scattered mankind becomes in Christ unified mankind (Eph. 2, 15) founded on the "eschatological Man,"[3] the *eschatos Adam* (1 Cor. 15, 45). He is a vivifying Spirit (*loc. cit.*), not merely man, but a man who "gives life" to his fellowmen.

Mankind, then, has received salvation through the fraternal service of one chosen from among ourselves—Jesus Christ, the Elect of God, the Son of the Father. This fact of Christ, which took place in our history and in our secular and human affairs, has had a real effect on human history. Mankind's new fundamental but real unity and new structure as a community rests upon God's universal saving will. This will is not an actuality that is simply beyond history; it has manifested itself visibly within history in the "objective redemption," that is, in the personal life of Jesus, representative man, Son of God, appearing among us in our history.

In one Man—the *homo principalis,* as Irenaeus says,[4] *i.e.,* he who stands at the wellspring of the new mankind, which *ipso facto* he has gathered into a community—in this one Man all men have already ascended through the passion to the glory with the Father.

Thus the history of Israel, which is a component of, and imbedded in, human history, takes on a new meaning. For human history, wherever it is made, has in this manner found grace with the Father and is already conclusively accepted by the Father in the *Eschaton,* Jesus Christ. For the Father has established Jesus who humbled himself, as the glorified Christ, the "Son of God in power" (Rom. 1, 4) at his own right hand. Consequently Christ is at once the Alpha and Omega of human history in its entirety (Apoc. 1, 8; 21, 6; 22, 13). As such, he is the key to history, not only in an exclusively transcendent manner beyond time and space, but his humanity now glorified is a truly historical humanity that has reached its consummation at a real point in history. In Jesus, history is finally and conclusively perfected with that kind of perfect achievement that persists in eternity. As representative, first of Israel, and so of mankind, he is the prototypical moment of mankind's history; this moment has already been inserted in eternal glory. And so our Lord, although in a dimension that exceeds our experience, gives our human history its final immanent meaning. Every historical human event wherever occurring, even in areas called "profane," can thus be understood only through the eschatological Man, Jesus Christ.

Dialectical Tension between "Mankind" and the Church

Christ has bestowed a new religious meaning upon mankind in princi-ple and in the concrete (*i.e.,* integrated in our own history). Nevertheless, between mankind "gathered" into a collectivity in principle and its actual manifestation in Christ there exists a certain distance. This distance and tension are embodied in Christ's Church. For it is in the Church, by free assent to the grace of justification, by acceptance of God's Word in faith, and by admission to baptism in the name of the Holy Trinity, that mankind's new religious meaning takes on the form that estab-lishes an historical, visible, concrete community. When a man is incor-porated into the Church, Christ's triumphant grace becomes a plain, historical, recognizable fact.[5] The result is that, at least from the ascen-sion until the Second Coming, there is a certain distinction and dialec-tical tension between humanity redeemed in principle, at its source, and the Church.

In a series of articles of progressive subtlety, A. Vögtle, a Catholic biblical exegete, has demonstrated that Jesus, at least in his public teaching, nowhere manifests an intention of selecting from Israel a specific group of persons in order to form them into a separate community.[6] By his public preaching of God's dominion and by his call to repentance he plainly intended to gather not a remnant only but all of Israel and make of it the new Israel, the eschatological People of *God*. Sectarianism was alien to him. Radically he pursues the path of the history of salvation as Paul will afterward copy it: salvation is announced first to Israel, and then, according to the divine design, *via* Israel to the whole world.

Jesus' call of "the twelve" from among the group of disciples is clearly explained as a parable in action that his contemporaries could not mistake:[7] in "the twelve," the twelve Patriarchs of Israel are represented—a further proof of Jesus' purpose to win all Israel for the kingdom of heaven. Actually, however, all Israel does not adhere to his doctrine, but on the contrary, opposition to his activities grows ever stronger. Chiefly because of the massive dimensions the opposition assumed and as he sees the historical event of his death approaching and the violent form it is to take, Jesus begins within the limited circle of the disciples to interpret its meaning and to explain it in the light of the prophecy in Deutero-Isaiah: his death is to be an expiation "for the many"—that is, for all—and God has arranged it so beforehand. Not before his death and resurrection,[8] and only in connection with them, is he to speak to his disciples of "the Church which he is going to build upon the Rock" (Peter) (Matt. 16, 18f.; see John 21, 15–17).

This implies that the redeemed People of God will become after Jesus' death and resurrection an *Ecclesia Christi*—an historical, visible gathering or congregation of men around Christ, in visible communion with the "Rock" and the twelve apostles. This situation gives Jesus' community a special ecclesiastico-social structure, which as such does not coincide with the social structure of secular society.

We see, then, that on the one hand, in his public preaching Jesus never speaks of a Church with forms of organization, and that he lays down obedient acceptance of his message of salvation, here and now, in the *kairos* of the present moment, as the sole condition for entering the kingdom of God. And on the other hand, it is in the light of his death as an expiation for all men that he speaks of the founding of his Church. This he presents as a post-paschal event: "I *shall* build my Church." Holy Scripture, then, clearly connects the messianic suffering—Jesus' "going away"—with the post-paschal realization of the Church.

The Church is God's People with a special qualification: the People of God who through Jesus' death and resurrection become through the Spirit the Body of Christ—*soma Christoû*—the Body of the *Lord.* On earth this Body is built as "the Church" upon Peter, the Rock. The return to the Father—the vertical theme of Jesus' public preaching— becomes in the light of his death, explained to his apostles as reconciliation, after Easter and Pentecost also a horizontal theme: the building of a mutual community around the Rock. It becomes, consequently, a clear theme of a mankind redeemed with the purpose of an ecclesial brotherhood, a communal Church with its own initiation, its own cult, especially the sharing of the eucharistic table, a community guided and accompanied by a ministering office. Thus the death and glorification of Jesus, the Christ, have made access to this brotherhood, the sacramentally and historically visible Church, a condition for entrance into the kingdom of God.[9] The *communio* of believers gathered about its bishop (in communion with the Rock)—this *is* salvation, the Church of Christ. Precisely in this *koinonia* must the Father's absolute self-communication through the Son in the Holy Spirit find that historically visible realization, which is in truth the sign of all mankind's vocation. Hence the Church is not just a *koinonia,* a communion or sharing of grace with Christ, the fruit of his redemptive work, but it is also an institution for salvation to which the keys that make entrance possible into the kingdom of God have been entrusted. In contrast to Jesus' "Woe unto you, scribes and Pharisees," who bar the entrance to the kingdom (Matt. 23, 13), Christ gives Peter the keys that open the gates.

The Basis of the Dialectical Tension

There is, then, a distance or interval between mankind, fundamentally and historically redeemed, and the community of Jesus built upon the Rock, which is the Church or body of "practicing Christians." To understand this distance we must first remember the connection laid by Holy Scripture between the messianic death—Jesus' "going away"—and the Church, which is only post-paschal and therefore a new reality, new even in comparison with that universal reality which is the People of God.

From our point of view the death of Jesus is mankind's rejection of him: Israel's rejection through its representative, the Sanhedrin; the Gentiles' rejection of him in the person of Pilate, and even the rejection by the hierarchy of the future Church in the persons of the apostles who ran away, and of Peter, who denied him. In his death Jesus stands alone, crushed by "the sins of the world"; alone in his surrender to the Father for the service of his fellowmen. That which achieved this reconciliation was, therefore, also the cause of Jesus' factual absence—the absence, in other words, of the source of grace. From our point of view, the breach of the covenant of grace was made complete by his death: mankind has banished from the world "the coming of God's kingdom" in Christ and so has expelled it from the *communio* of men.

Every death, of course, means bodily absence and the breaking off of relations with the dead as fellowmen. In the case of Jesus, however, it is a matter of the death of the only one who could bring redemption. From our point of view, this removal of Christ, the Man of grace, is therefore irrevocable. For the renewal of his relations with us through the resurrection is certainly not owing to us, not even to Christ's humanity as such. Only by understanding the profound importance of his death can we fully appreciate the basic saving significance of his resurrection, which, on account of the sacrifice that had been offered, made possible the sending of the Holy Spirit and the building of the Church. In the resurrection, which was a grace of the Father, the redemptive work of Jesus triumphed. But this triumph implies that henceforth our salvation depends upon someone who is absent from our experience, Jesus Christ.

We may justly conclude from this that the final state of our condition as it was created by original sin is "a situation in which the *privation* of supernatural grace can *only be removed sacramentally*, a situation in which man found himself ever since, and, because of the breach of the covenant with God, was made complete through man's rejection of Christ."[10]

Jesus himself connects his going away with the coming of the Spirit and the building of his Church. In his Body, the Church, wherein the Holy Spirit dwells, he intends to remain as the source of all grace. Hence, this Body, the Church, becomes the condition or the embodiment of our restored relationship with Christ and our entrance into the kingdom of God. Christ, absent from the universal human community, is made present again through the resurrection in the Church, his Body on earth.

The weighty consequence of this fact is significantly expressed by St. Thomas: "The grace of Christ comes to us not through human nature but through the *personal action* of Christ himself."[11] In present-day terms this means that the source of Christ's grace is not fellow-creaturehood in and by itself, but fellow-creaturehood with Christ, who, while absent since his death from the horizon of our experience, means to remain present among us, but post-paschally, in virtue of the Spirit of God, in his Body, the Church.

As the Body of our Lord, the Church forms the living link with Christ—horizontally, with the Jesus of history, who arose and appeared to the apostles; vertically, with the Lord of glory, thanks to the Spirit that dwells in the whole community of the Church in its hierarchical function, its preaching, its sacraments. Because of Christ's fellowship with us the universal human fellowship, too, takes on a deepened meaning, and the boundaries between mankind and the Church begin to blur.

Fluidity of the Boundaries between the Church and Mankind

The history of salvation, then, deals with one covenant that has passed through two phases, or a twofold *dispositio.* An absolutely new situation has been created in the plan of salvation by Christ's death and resurrection. Now the further question arises: What is the relationship between the universal People of God, coextensive with mankind, and the Church, in which the People of God has become the Body of our Lord?

The *locus theologicus* of all reflection on the faith and, consequently, of the theology of the relationships between the Church and the world, is the historical advent of salvation in Jesus Christ: the man Jesus who is to us the absolute and gratuitous presence of God. (In Christ and through him, human existence has become the objective expression of God's absolute communication of himself to man and, by the same token, the objective expression of the human response to that total divine gift.) As a corollary of that fact, the human condition in its historical setting has become the concrete matter and space of the historical manifestation of man's God-related life in Christ. The human existence of Christ, taken with all its determinisms and all its human implications, is the *personal* life of God, the Son.

This means that the entire temporal dimension and the unabridged reality we call profane can be assumed into a God-related life, given that in the Son the eternal has presented itself personally within temporal and terrestrial realities. The very definition of the hypostatic union is exactly that. This also reveals the fact that thanks to Christ all of human history is swathed in God's love; it is assumed into the absolute and gratuitous presence of the mystery of God. The worldly and the temporal remain worldly and temporal; they are not sacralized but sanctified by that presence, that is, by the God-centered life of Christ and of his faithful.

(Everyone will agree that our human existence is immersed in unfathomable mystery, although the way of saying so may vary infinitely. In her revelation-through-the-Word, the Church merely clarifies for the benefit of all mankind the reality of the mystery's absolute presence in

Christ; it proclaims that this mystery has drawn closer to us) not only in some mystical and interior intimacy, but also through the medium of a palpable and visible historical reality. The whole kerygma and all of Christian dogma can be summarized in that fundamental affirmation: beginning with the Trinity, the incarnation, the life of grace, but also including the Church with her ministry, worship, preaching, sacraments as well as collective and individual eschatology.

Word-revelation, of which the Church is the herald, only unfolds the implications of that absolute and gratuitous presence which, as revelations-reality, is already present in the lives of men, even prior to their historical encounter with the phenomenon "Church." Moreover, the free acceptance of the mystery's absolute and gratuitous presence is the very substance of what we call theologal or God-related faith. To believe is to have confidence in this mystery thus present; it means trusting in him in spite of everything and under all circumstances. That affirmation strikes me as of the utmost importance because what is implied is that the acceptance of real human existence, concretely taken with all its responsibilities, is in truth an act of God-centered faith: for Christ has shown us, by living it, that human existence taken concretely—not in the abstract—was for him, precisely in his human condition steeped as it was in the mystery, the objective expression of his communion with the Father in the *dynamis* of the Holy Spirit and for the benefit of his fellowmen.

Here is what this brief analysis shows us:

1. Within the Church of Christ the absolute and gratuitous presence of the mystery becomes an explicit epiphany, historically and humanly observable—both as a reality and as a task to be accomplished.

2. This concentrated ecclesial manifestation of God merely explicates that which in fact and at its own level is going on in all of human existence, even if the subject is not aware of it, namely, the gratuitous presence of the mystery, which is an active, an operative presence.

From this viewpoint, the incarnation teaches us that the entire human reality may ferry divine grace and can be assumed into a God-centered life. Day-to-day human life with its worldly concerns for human advancement is the area wherein normal Christian life must develop; the explicit and ecclesial expression of that selfsame communion with God shall indeed be the fountainhead and the driving force of the expression of Christian life in the world. St. Paul told us as much in a masterful though negative manner: "Neither death, nor life, nor angels, nor principalities, nor things present, nor things to come, nor powers, nor height, nor depth, nor any other creature will be able to separate us from the love of God, which is in Christ Jesus our Lord" (Rom. 8, 38–39). What does it all mean if not that Christianity is upheld by faith in the absolute and gratuitous presence of God within Christ as well as by the fact that we must accept human history and our entire earthly life as a reality steeped and swaddled in God's love? Improving the world whenever we improve ourselves, we are always in the presence of and beneath the wings of the mystery who gives himself freely.

While respecting the worldly and earthly significance of the reality we call the world, this outlook gives it a profoundly theological meaning. This is what the world is: the profane, earthly and temporal reality with structures all its own, with its special and immediate end, but which, in Christ, is assumed into the absolute and gratuitous presence of God. In saying this one should beware of imagining the world as some static, immobile reality. Planet earth is the material given to man with which to fashion a human world, a dwelling-place worthy of man. Of course man's world has the mark of the creature upon it; moreover, as every-thing else common to man, it is a world wrought by sin. The construction of the world and the promotion of peoples remain a finite task, the work of men, and as such it shares in the ambiguity of all that is human. This world is creature, non-God. To say this is to affirm the secularity of earthly tasks. Indeed, creation is a divine act that situates realities within their respective spheres; and contrary to the mythological leg-ends held by the contemporaries of ancient Israel, the Bible refers to that divine act, in Genesis, as desacralizing and unmystifying the world, handing it over to itself, into the hands of man for God's glory. This means that as a result of the divine act of sustained creation, the history of mankind will assert itself as the progressive and prolonged desacralization of earthly structures and functions.

But that is only one facet of a far richer and more profound reality: since God created so as to bestow himself to man and to be, he himself, present in a gratuitous and redemptive manner, in our brother, Jesus the Anointed. This means that in the plan of salvation the concrete world, by definition, is an *implicit Christianity;* it is an objective, non-sacral but saintly and sanctified expression of mankind's communion with the living God; whereas the Church *qua* institution of salvation, with her explicit creed, her worship and sacraments, is the direct and sacral expression of that identical communion—she is the *separata a mundo.*

To speak of the relationships between the Church and the world does not mean therefore that a dialog is to be launched between the strictly Christian dimension of our human life and its distinctly non-Christian dimension; nor is it a question of conducting a dialog between the religious and the profane, between the supernatural and the natural or intra-worldly—it is rather a dialog between *two complementary, authentically Christian expressions* of one and the same God-related life concealed in the mystery of Christ, namely, the *ecclesial* expression (in the strict sense of the word) and the *worldly* expression of that identically same life, internalized within human life through man's free acceptance of grace. In other words, the *implicitly* Christian and the *explicitly* Christian dimension of the same God-related life, that is, of human life hidden in God's absolute and gratuitous presence.[11a] In that context, this is what is meant by implicit Christianity [it is the human, earthly and profane reality assumed in its secularity into the God-related life which it proceeds to express objectively, even when that God-related life remains anonymous and implicit.] Earthly reality will at the same time share in the first fruits of eschatological grace and in the advent of the kingdom of God. Within that God-centered life, albeit anonymous, the construction of the world and the promotion of peoples, those two great hopes of mankind on earth, become an activity which is not only intentionally but intrinsically relevant to the kingdom of God.

It is evident that the ultimate eschatological perfection of all earthly values completely transcends the temporal construction of this world, precisely because it is an absolute and gratuitous perfection; but nevertheless, by virtue of its assumption into God-related life, harbinger of the *vita venturi saeculi,* the world of earthly values will participate in that mystery of eternal life, as we are told by the dogma of the resurrection of the flesh and by the kerygma of the new earth.

Unequivocally, God loves man; and the being called man is not some abstract "human nature" but a flesh-and-blood being who, together with his fellowmen, takes the fate of the world and of mankind into his own hands; he is a being who, by humanizing the world humanizes himself. It is this historical, real being whom God loves. Every single human and worldly reality is therefore implied in God's absolute and gratuitous presence. This conveys a sense of the eternal and, therefore, of the irrevocable to the construction of the world and the promotion of the advancement of peoples.

Although it is solely due to his *capacitas gratiae* that man is the object of grace, the very being who, upon transcending his own self is assumed into theologal intimacy with God and shares in the eternal life—that being is none other than man, all of man as he really and historically exists, committed to this world.

In the past, a dualistic anthropological conception misled Christians into considering grace and redemption as a matter for God and the soul of man to deal with, so much so that the whole range of earthly life and of human responsibility for the terrestrial future of mankind seemed to be relegated to the fringe of Christianity; one ran the risk of disregarding the truly Christian value of building the world and of promoting the advancement of peoples, thereby relinquishing the chore to those who called themselves non-Christians. How easy it is to discern in that behavior one of the many factors through which the institutional Church alienated men from herself.

When we connect now the things which were said about the one signification of the Church with that which is called "implicit Christianity," we arrive at new explicitations concerning the relation "Church and World."

The acts of Christ in glory are the acts of the whole Christ, the integral Christ in and with his Body, the Church. Hence, what the Church as such does, is done also by the glorified Christ together with the Spirit, his Spirit. What is Christian, therefore, is also ecclesial: the qualifications are inseparably and organically united.

However much Jesus, as the Lord, transcends his Body, the Church, his immanence in the Church is coextensive with his transcendence. He transcends the Church through his immanence in it. That he transcends the boundaries of his Body, the Church, means that his free self-giving reaches out from within the Church to all who are not yet visible members of the Church. This implies that he is active among those who have not yet been historically confronted with the Church, but also that this activity of his is equally an activity of his Body, the Church. The bond with Christ, forged by this activity is, even when not explicitly seen as such, *ipso facto* an equally strong bond with the Church. Consequently, the Church represents the source of redemption also for that portion of mankind that has not yet experienced and availed itself of her in her peculiar historical form.

Seen in this perspective, the real interval separating the Church as such from mankind becomes less pronounced. The Church is actively present even where her adequate ecclesial form has not yet appeared. The contrast between the Church and mankind cannot be equated with an opposition between Church and non-Church. There is, moreover, much in her own life that is "non-ecclesial," just as in the collective life of mankind there is much that is ecclesial. In the strict sense, of course, the Church is mankind insofar as it willingly places itself under Christ's influence through faith and baptism, and "helps its unbelief" at the common table of the eucharist.

Perhaps it is better not to give the name "Church" to that portion of mankind that is anonymously Christian and in which the Church is anonymously present. This phenomenon might be called a "pre-Church"; but even against this, various objections might be brought. In the proper sense of the word, the Church is the saving revelation, the explicitly Christian realization of our Lord's activity among all mankind—the *koinonia* of men with one another in the acceptance of God and baptism in Christ, which is the efficacious sign of the call of those not yet in the Church.

On the other hand, anonymous Christianity—and its existence must be taken as a fact—not least because of its hopeful trust in the triumphant grace of Christ's redemption ("I have overcome the world") is an anonymity that inwardly demands a fitting sacramental visibility. Because the worldwide activity of Christ's grace is carried out in and through the Church, since his "going away" is related to the Church's post-paschal reality as the Body of our Lord, in virtue of the Spirit of God, this very grace is essentially "Church founding." Where the Church is at work as grace—and as such it is coextensive with mankind and therefore with universal fellowship—something of the *Corpus Mysticum* is brought to visible realization, though in a veiled manner. Because this grace takes on particular, historical, visible forms in the Church, its appearance bears witness to the fact that wherever it is operative (and that is wherever human history is in process of realization), it has an inward leaning toward historical manifestation, *i.e.*, toward ecclesial explicitness.

This process can be observed in human history. Beyond the pale of the concretely situated, real Church, this grace will express itself, as a result of the unrecognized bond with Christ and his Church, in widely varying human interpretations—whether in other religious forms, or in so-called "secular" institutions, whose explicit form is inadequate to express their true purpose. Failure to grasp the proper meaning of this deepest feeling latent in the restless life of mankind is no indication that the difference between mankind and the Church is merely one of "knowing explicitly" and "knowing implicitly." For it is only in self-expression that man reaches full self-consciousness. Whatever is experienced without being recognized is a fragile datum until it finds its way to authentic self-expression. And this is more than a question of mere knowledge.

Without the God-given ecclesial form and expression of this deepest core of life in Christ, this experience remains a "light hidden under a bushel," a flickering flame ready to be quenched by the weakest draught. The properly ecclesial milieu is where the word of God's forgiveness is heard, where baptism is administered and the eucharist celebrated, where there is the faith that nothing can separate us from the Lord and that for men there is no absolute solitude because God is with us. This milieu, which believers, the faithful, jointly constitute, is vitally necessary for the breakthrough of what grace effects silently and anonymously in human life. But the Church's special importance as a sign and revelation demands that she return again and again to the sources of biblical authenticity and show herself in forms that clearly and simply manifest her authenticity.

Thanks, therefore, to Christ's historical coming there is in living humanity a kind of built-in compass pointing to the Church. Her missionary activity is merely the counterpart of this. This pointing to the Church, or mankind's need of her in the concrete, and, on the other hand, her going out to mankind, are both visible forms of the one operative salvation which our Lord is in the Spirit of God, *Pneuma Theoû*. In both, Jesus the Christ visits his messianic community that he acquired upon the cross to prepare for himself his eschatological bride without spot unto the glory of God the Father.

The anonymous Church that is the work of Christ's Spirit and of his Body, the explicit Church vitally joined to him, will become manifest through the Spirit, as his Body, incorporated through baptism into his death and resurrection, as a visible sign both of the eschatological Man, Jesus Christ, and of what human life is concretely—namely, a deep and painful suffering, an existence ending in death, coupled with the unquenchable hope that this is not the last word about mankind. In Christ's *kenôsis* and *hypsôsis*, in his final humiliation and his exaltation, the destiny of human life is exemplified. The enduring struggle for life in mankind, hoping against all hope, is the nameless echo of this fact: there is here more than mere secularity, even though it is expressed perhaps in a purely secular fashion.

The boundaries between the Church and mankind are fluid not merely in the Church's direction, but also, it may be said, in the direction of mankind and the world. The present-day process toward desacralization and secularization points to the fact that what was earlier felt to be a specialty of the Church—helping those of slender means, works of charity and the like—has nowadays become "desacralized" as state relief measures for humanity within a secular vision, and is now an accepted feature of mankind at large. What had earlier taken the form of specific activities of the Church, in its precise sense, has now become in many ways an accepted expression of man's life in and for the world.

This osmosis from the Church to the world knows no final point on earth because here below the old aeon and the new continue to co-exist. The fact that the communion of men coincides with the communion of saints is, when manifest, a heavenly, not an earthly fact. The blurring of the boundaries between the Church and mankind can never abolish the dialectical tension between the two. This tension, however, does not destroy either the dynamic of the world's tendency to become ecclesial or the Church's tendency to sanctify the secular. The latter process, however, is a holy secularization arising from the transcendent community with God in Christ. Whoever forgets this would have the Church in the long run dissolve into something like the UN or UNESCO.

All this has been expressed by St. Paul in his own way and in the framework of his ancient world picture. Christ by his death and glorification has fulfilled "all things"—"all things in heaven and on earth," "visible and invisible," all created reality (Eph. 1, 10; Col. 1, 16–20). H. Schlier, the biblical exegete, in his commentary on Ephesians comments rightly upon this point: "There is no sphere of being that is not also the Church's sphere. The Church is fundamentally directed to the universe. Her boundaries are those of the universe. There is no realization of Christ's dominion without the Church or outside her, no 'fulfillment' apart from her. The way in which the universe grows toward Christ is the way the Church grows. There are areas, to be sure, that are opposed to 'fulfillment' through the Church; but ultimately the reason is that they are filled with themselves."[12]

St. Paul says this plainly: "God has placed all things under his feet, and has given him, exalted above all, as Head to the Church, which is his Body, the fullness of him who fulfills all in all" (Eph. 1, 22f.). It is through the Church that the fulfillment of all existence and all reality is achieved.[13] Eschatologically, Church and mankind coincide fully.

Unity of Creation, Redemption and Growth of the Church

The Church and mankind, then, are coming closer together; and yet the undeniable boundary remains between them because of Christ's post-paschal "building of the Church upon the Rock."[14] It now remains to clarify a dogmatic insight in which creation and the bestowal of grace, redemption and the building of the Church are all seen together in the sublime unity of God's covenant with men.

Grace is God's absolute self-communication to men; it is the personal sharing of life with God—Father, Son, and Holy Spirit. That even in the pre-Christian era grace could only be trinitarian, we only know in the light of the historical mystery of Christ. It is in him that this fundamental aspect of the whole life of grace first becomes explicit. There is a close connection between him and grace. The fact that the trinitarian character of grace, imparted before his coming, remained implicit and anonymous leads to the question whether the anonymous character of this trinitarian grace is not due to the fact that man's existence was originally orientated to Christ, and that this obviously had to remain implicit. An analysis of the trinitarian character of grace as well as of its postponed revelation in Christ shows that its original conferment and God's establishment of mankind as his People were the consequence of man's creation in view of Christ. "Adam's" creation was implicitly directed toward Christ, and because of this, grace was bestowed upon him.[15] In other words, human existence in the concrete is itself a messianic prophecy pointing to him who is to come. The task to form a true *communio* among men as the essential task of a community of *persons* is a prophecy of the coming of Christ's Mystical Body, the Church. Thus, by another and perhaps more radical way we come to a conclusion at least materially the same as Karl Rahner's who speaks of mankind in its entirety as the (faithful or unfaithful) People of God, and considers membership of this People a constitutive element of our concrete humanity.[16] Therefore, in the concrete, every free human act is one that works toward salvation or perdition. But it seems to me that the manner in which we arrive at this insight sheds a clearer light on mankind's objectively new situation since the death and resurrection of Christ.

Surely this new situation makes it obvious that salvation is conferred upon the People of God, not as such, but insofar as it has become the Body of Christ. This implies that since the appearance of the mystery of Christ in history at least the faithful People of God, in virtue of his sole saving power at work in his Body, the Church, becomes the expression of a *desiderium ecclesiae*. The basis of this should be clear from what has been thus far presented here, but it may help to clarify it further.

Creation in view of Christ, which includes the gift of grace, means that since creation all mankind carries within itself and anonymously this ecclesial orientation as a grace that is accepted or rejected. We may say, then, that it is always within and for a People of God that man's religious life is fulfilled, whether this People be mankind as yet unspecified or Israel, in which messianic humanity began to manifest itself more clearly, or the People of God redeemed by Christ, with its features sharply drawn and constituted as the Church.[17] The human community, insofar as it is created with this orientation toward Christ, is an early rough-draft of the Church that is to come. But it is no more than that. For the appearance of Jesus in history and his exclusion from the human community created a completely new situation. It is as the Risen One that he built his Church and set it visibly among men as a community with its peculiar sacramental community structure, with its hierarchical function, with its service of the Word.

This absolutely new fact in salvation history restricts the universal application of this reality of God's People as coextensive with mankind. On the other hand, this new fact lifts that reality into a new dimension and turns its implicit acceptance into a *votum ecclesiae*. The anonymously Christian portion of mankind now becomes for the first time a true *votum ecclesiae,* precisely because of Christ's universally operative action *in* the Church to the benefit of all mankind.[18]

Christ's Church, then, is not so much the last phase of the interior development of God's People as it comes into ever clearer view in visible form, although this aspect cannot be denied. Rather, Christ's historical redemptive work with its post-paschal fruit, the Church, recapitulates in his death and resurrection the People of God created from of old in view of him, and *constitutes* that People as the *votum ecclesiae.* Hence, we can say: *Extra ecclesiam nulla salus:* apart from Christ and his Body there is no salvation.

At the same time we must say that the Church here on earth has not yet reached the perfection of what she ought to be. This was acutely formulated by Origen: "*Ho kosmos tou kosmou he ekklesia":* man's world brought to actual perfection, to order—to peace and *communio*—this is the Church.[19] The Church carries within herself the principles and the incipient reality of this peace in virtue of the fact that she, the fruit of Christ's redemption, is his Body in this world.

In and through that Body he, now in glory, carries on his universal activity in the Spirit. The Church in human history, then, is, as token for all the world, the forerunner of eschatological salvation. Hence, her apostolic duty; hence, the constant demand daily to orientate herself anew at the wellsprings of Holy Scripture, especially at this time when the face of the world and of man is fundamentally altering.

The Church as Fellowship to Be Realized

The blurring of the enduring boundaries between the Church and mankind can also be explained more clearly through the Church's inner structure. In the one Church of Christ we may distinguish two different, though not opposed, dialectical aspects: the one, of the Church as a community guided by the Spirit of God active in the apostolic office of the episcopacy throughout the world; the other, of the same Church guided by the Spirit of God active in every individual's conscience.

This latter activity of the Spirit, and hence of individual Christians, also effects the building of the Church, especially in the midst of the world and of ordinary everyday things. This is where they are to be found who have not yet joined the Church community explicitly. Here, too, the building of the Church retains a kind of hidden character. Because this is a non-hierarchical activity, which is just as much the work of the Holy Spirit in Christian consciences, there really is an active building of the Church by her members in the midst of the so-called "profane" world, where the hierarchical Church is not present. A genuine, but even more veiled manifestation of this reality, moreover, is the genesis of the Church in the world that is Christian without the name. It can be recognized for what it is only in the light of Christ and the visible Church.

If, therefore, we would inquire into the pregnant characteristics that mark out the anonymously Christian Church which, because of what she is, longs for the moment when she can appear in her own ecclesial manifestation, we should not consider the fellowship or brotherhood among men in general, but with the special qualification which Jesus himself indicated. This qualification is love, a love that reaches out to the *mikroi*, the little ones, and to the *elachistoi*, the least of men, to help them for the reason that Jesus calls them "My brethren" (Matt. 25, 31–36). It is in respect to their practice of this love that Church members and non-Church members alike are to be judged at the end of time (Matt. 25, 35–45): "What you have done to the least of my brethren, you have done to me" (Matt. 25, 40). "I was hungry and you gave me to eat; I was thirsty and you gave me to drink; I was a stranger and you welcomed me" (Matt. 25, 35f.). "What you have failed to do for the least of these, you have failed to do for me" (Matt. 25, 45).

In modern terms this might be expressed thus: Your failure to help the underdeveloped countries is failing Christ himself. The help you extend to them, not from political motives, but out of pure brotherhood and fellowship, is authentic Christianity. Self-sacrifice to the extreme was the messianic act by which Christ founded his Church. Where men follow in his footsteps on the way of self-sacrifice, without even knowing perhaps whose steps they are, they are working to establish the Church, the community in Christ. The parable of the Good Samaritan teaches us, with a certain amount of sarcasm directed at those who are "in the Church," that everyone who assists anyone whom he finds in need and helps him superabundantly, with the luxury of extravagant love, is actively establishing the *koinonia*. He makes of the man he helps, his neighbor and brother.

The activity that establishes the Church which is, even without the name, Christian, goes outside and beyond the limits of the official Church, which is sociologically situated and clearly visible in history—the Church of those who acknowledge Christ and share the table of the eucharist. This activity exceeds the official Church's limits even in such a way that this superabundant love, however clearly visible in the Church's saints, is not, historically and *per se*, necessarily realized by practicing Christians. And yet the Church is truly established only where love makes men brothers, because the active love that establishes her is the core of her being. It was to preserve that core that Christ established an official hierarchy, which he assists in a special manner in order to preserve his People in one community of love and hope founded upon one faith in him. Ultimately, however, the Church is not a matter of this hierarchy but of the People of God and the active love that establishes her. And for her, the hierarchy, although in the *modus* of Christian authority, has a function of service.

Outside the visible community of Jesus, then, the establishment of the Church is accomplished primarily by surrender to one's fellowmen in unselfish love. Concretely, our fellow-creatures are a token of God's grace, a sacramental sign of his saving will. Such they are only because created in Christ and for the sake of him who is the constitutive sign of God's saving will. The universal sacramentality of fellow-crea-turehood is not destroyed because of the perfect sacramental form of Christ's fellow-creaturehood, nor is it, so to say, translated into the formal structure of the visible Church. On the contrary, because of the appearance of the Man, Jesus Christ the Son of God, in history, the sacramental power of the grace of fellowship can be realized in its full meaning now for the first time. It is realized in him and for him. The general sacramental feature of fellowship is made concrete only in the community that is called the Church. And the seven sacraments, the preaching, the worship, the hierarchy's guidance—all these are but the highest point of crystallization of the stake the Church has in our fel-lowmen.

The Church, therefore, will appear as a sign among men, actually drawing and inviting them, only when the love of her members for humankind becomes concretely and historically visible here and now, and is no longer confined to those particular climactic moments in which at present Christ places his grace in a concentrated manner. It is just during the Second Vatican Council that out of the deliberations on the nature of the Church there has come a desire to include in the schema a consideration of the active presence of church members in the world. The schema which is shortly to become the Constitution, *De Ecclesia,* cries out from the heart for schema xvii.

On all these grounds we cannot relegate the Church's significance for the unchurched to some kind of "representative function" that would dispense them from the superabundant love and redeem them by "sub-stitution," that is, by the overflowing love which is at least present in Christ's Church. In an authentically Christian perspective, vicarious-ness and mediation never stand for substitution, but for a prototypical reality which gives of its abundance *in order that* others, by virtue of the grace they have received, may be enabled themselves to achieve what had already been done by the prototype. In this sense the Church exists in the strength of Christ's Spirit for the good of all men. But equally, the operation of Christ's grace among men through the Church must retain a visible form, especially in its apostolic activity. In the Church's confrontation with mankind in history her members must be living examples and "types" of this overflowing love and manifest their willingness to give up their personal lives in the service of others.

Secular and Sacral Realization of the Church's Holiness

The problem posed at the beginning of this essay has found some answer, it is hoped, in the course of our investigation. There is obviously going on throughout mankind a process of bringing things into the Church, and in the Church, correspondingly, there is a process of secularization that conveys sanctity. Within the inviolable limits set by the Word, the sacrament, and the office—and all those are forms of *service*—the boundaries between the Church and mankind are blurred. It is in the positive encounter with Christ in his Church that the most complete form of Christianity that may be realized is objectively offered to us.

The Church, then, must be a really habitable home, and her mission is to bring this to pass in every age in ever differing ways. Complete religion has an explicitly Christian and ecclesial practical expression. Because of this, Christianity, however involved it is in our everyday cares and tasks and all our secular activity, has a special sacral space set apart from secular developments and from culture, within which we grow in intimacy with God. Here we are simply together with God in Christ. Now, on a merely human level silence forms a part of discourse and social intercourse, though in and for itself it has no meaning; it has meaning only as a function of fellowship. It is necessary in order to make contact between men human and to keep it so—to humanize it. It is silence that makes speech personal. Without it, dialog is impossible. But in a revealed religion, silence with God has a value in itself and for its own sake, just because God is God. Failure to recognize the value of mere being with God, as the Beloved, without doing anything, is to gouge the heart out of Christianity.

Our whole immersion in the world of men and things penetrates also into our communion with God, not as mere distraction, but essentially. We cannot tell God that we love or desire to love him except with words, concepts and pictures taken from our human environment. Moreover, our communion with God is not individualism, for our prayer would be insincere—not prayer at all—if we did not pray: "Our Father, . . ." or if in our prayer we forgot God's kingdom and our fellowman.

Christianity means not only communion with God in the concrete milieu of Christ in his Church, but also *working* with the living God, with the Father "who is ever active" (John 5, 17) both in the Church and in the world. Religion is primarily personal intercourse with God— the living God, who is the Creator of men and things, all of which he offers to us for humanization. Therefore, our living relationship with our neighbor and with the world is not only cultural, but also religious.

Agape embraces God and men. Love of God cannot and must not be separated from love of men. Christian love for the neighbor means that we—God and I—love *my* fellowman. While in natural human love, God is present only in silence as the transcendent Third, my Christian *caritas* toward my fellows is just as much love, but a love lived in communion with God. And so the Christian loves his fellowman with the same love as that with which he loves God and with which both he and his fellowmen are loved by God. In Christ alone do we learn the proper meaning of "being a man for the sake of others," although secular and human experience will teach us how we must express this fellowship in concrete situations.

But, however ecclesial the explicit expression of religion and Christianity may be, the working out of our Christian character must needs take shape in the ordinary daily dealings in and with the world and our fellowmen. The sincerity of our personal dealings with God, of our Christianity and ecclesial status must therefore be tested constantly by the authenticity of our fellowship, our genuine love of men. The source of this Christian love of the neighbor, however, lies in our personal assimilation of those ways of dealing with God which Christ himself has given us: hearing the Word of God, familiarity with Holy Scripture, the common celebration of the Church's sacramental liturgy. In our world, then, authentic Christianity has both a *sacred* and a corresponding *secular* milieu. In everything he does, by acceptance or refusal, man brings about salvation or perdition.

We must be close to God, not merely in church, in prayer and the sacraments, in Scripture reading—in a word, in the sacred forms of religion—but also in our secular and human relationships and in our everyday tasks. Then we may say with serenity that there are different ways of being Christian. Some will bring their interior relationship with God to fulfillment chiefly in sacral forms, thereby stressing the fact that the Church is "not of this world." Others will express their Christianity particularly in secular activities, in "secular sanctity," and so will stress the fact that the Christian faith is not an ideological structure superimposed upon human life.

But these are emphases of the one Christian life which is immanent in this world precisely because it is transcendent. For what has been said here about the universal relationship between mankind and the Church is also valid for the individual Christian. The unrecognized genuine witness of the Christian in this profane world finds the source of its strength in that explicit Christianity which is shaped by active participation in the life of the Word and of the Sacrament of "Christ's Church."

Translated by N. D. Smith

NOTES

1. See J. Scharbert, *Heilsmittler im Alten Testament und im Alten Orient* (*Quaest. Disp.* 23, 24, Freiburg im Br., 1964).
2. See G. von Rad, "Das z. erste Buch Mose" in *Das Alte Testament Deutsch*, 2 (Göttingen, 1949), pp. 119ff.
3. See among others E. Peterson, "Die Kirche," *Theologische Traktate* (Munich, 1951), pp. 409–28.
4. Irenaeus, *Adv. Haereses* V.21.1 (*PG* 7.1179). *Principalis* (*archaios*) in *Adv. Haer.* means "standing at the point of," and is used in connection with Irenaeus' theory of Recapitulation. Christ stands at the new beginning of all things.
5. See among others K. Rahner, "Kirche und Parusie Christi," in *Catholica* 17 (1963), pp. 113–28.
6. A. Vögtle, *Das öffentliche Wirken Jesu auf dem Hintergrund der Qumranbewegung* (Freiburger Universitätsreden, N.F., 27, Freiburg im Br., 1958, pp. 5–20, esp. pp. 15ff.); "Ekklesiologische Auftragsworte des Auferstandenen," in *Actes du Congrès internationale catholique des sciences bibliques à Bruxelles* (1959), pp. 892–906; "Jesus und die Kirche," in *Begegnung der Christen*, ed. Hoesle-Cullmann (Frankfurt am Main, 1960), pp. 54, 82; "Der Einzelne und die Gemeinschaft in der Stufenfolge der Christusoffenbarung," in *Sentire Ecclesiam*, ed. Daniélou and Vorgrimler, (Freiburg im Br., 1961), pp. 50–91; see also "Die Adam-Christus Typologie und der Menschensohn," in *Trierer Theol. Zeitschrift* (1951), pp. 209–28. See also footnote 7 below.
7. See A. Vögtle, *Das öffentliche Wirken Jesu*, p. 15; F. Braun, *Neues Licht auf die Kirche* (Einsiedeln, 1946), p. 71; A. Friedrichsen, "Messias und Kirche," in *Ein Buch von der Kirche* (Göttingen, 1951), p. 33; see K. Rengstorf, *Theol. Wörterb. z. N.T.* (Teil 2), pp. 321–28, s.v. *dodeka*.
8. See A. Vögtle, "Messiasbekenntnis und Petrusverheissung," in *Biblische Zeitschrift*, N.F. 1 (1957), pp. 257–72 and 2 (1958), pp. 85–103. The connection between Peter's confession at Caesarea and Christ's promise of the *Ecclesia* is called secondary, *i.e.*, it is an "arrangement" of Matthew or of the Matthew tradition.
9. Mark 10, 40 and Matthew 20, 20–23; Mark 14, 25; see Luke 22, 16, 18.
10. P. Schoonenberg, "Natuur en zondenval," in *Tijdschr. v. Theol.* 2 (1962), pp. 199–200; see also E. Schillebeeckx, *Christ, the Sacrament of the Encounter with God* (New York, 1963), pp. 40–46.
11. *Summa Theologiae*, III, q.8, a.2, ad 1.

11a. It is obvious that in so saying I speak of the state of implicit Christianity as such, realizing that the individual can shut himself away from grace. God is the sole judge of man's conscience. One does not therefore affirm that all non-Christians are by the mere fact implicitly Christians, just as one does not maintain that every member of the Church is an authentic Christian. Nevertheless the redemptive grace of "Christus Victor" is more powerful than the fragility of human freedom.

12. H. Schlier, "Die Kirche nach dem Briefe an die Epheser," in *Die Zeit der Kirche* (Freiburg im Br., 1956), p. 69.

13. Schlier has the following acute comment on this passage in Saint Paul: "The Church is the *Pleroma* of Christ. This means the plenitude, fulfilled by him and in its turn fulfilling, of him who has fulfilled all things and continues to do so. In her (the Church's) plenitude, all is enclosed and so this all becomes itself that plenitude which is the Church" (*ibid.*, p. 170).

14. The thought of this article will be taken up again in CONCILIUM and applied to the problem of membership in the Churches, in connection with the pluralism of the Christian Church communities.

15. I have attempted to develop this in detail in "Die Heiligung des Namen Gottes durch die Menschenliebe Jesu des Christus," in *Gott in Welt* (Festgabe für K. Rahner, Freiburg, 1964), esp. pp. 73–90.

16. K. Rahner, "Die Gliedschaft in der Kirche nach der Lehre de Enzyklika Pius XII, *Mystici Corporis*," in *Schriften zur Theologie* 2 (Einsiedeln, 1955), pp. 7–94.

17. E. Schillebeeckx, *Personale Begegnung mit Gott: Eine Antwort an John A. T. Robinson* (Mainz, 1964), pp. 78f.

18. Be it noted that I do not claim that *all* those who do not belong to a church are *per se* anonymous Christians, just as we do not maintain that all church members are authentic Christians. I only say that such an anonymous Christianity is a genuine possibility, and, considering the abounding power of grace, a reality in the case of many. We do not wish, nor are we able, to affirm their number. We know well the essential ambiguity of human freedom: it is a potentiality for good and for evil. But our confidence in God is greater than that ambiguity!

19. See A. Auer, "Kirche und Welt," in *Mysterium Kirche* II (Salzburg, 1962), pp. 492f.

2

The Magisterium and the World of Politics

1968

Recent actions and documents of high ecclesiastical authority, such as Paul VI's address to the United Nations, the encyclicals *Pacem in Terris* and *Populorum Progressio*, and for a large part also the Constitution *On the Church in the Modern World*, have created a problem: what is the nature, the bearing and the binding character of such statements by the magisterium? For such statements are not directly based on the data of revelation but are also dependent on a good (or not so good) analysis of the actual situation within human society. Such statements by the magisterium are therefore also determined by non-theological information. And this raises certain issues for the theologian.[1]

Two Invalid Objections

1. One cannot maintain that Pope or Council was not aware of the fact that these questions belong to the sphere of historical and contingent actualities. The Pastoral Constitution says explicitly that it appeals to the conscience of all "in matters that are subject to constant development."[2] The magisterium knows therefore that in this field it speaks more or less hypothetically, that is, given that this is the situation of man and society.

2. The second objection is far more tenacious. Some feel that, although at long last Christianity has become unpolitical in the sense of having got rid of ecclesiastical politics, and although the world's own secular character has been recognized and confirmed as such by the Christian

25

faith, Council and Pope are, in a roundabout way, again "dabbling in politics" and exceeding their competence.

I do not deny that the gradual and rightful recognition of the world's autonomy has led many Christians to a kind of "political liberalism," a taking refuge in what is "spiritual"; religion is a private matter, the world and politics belong to the world as such, while the Church's place is in man's heart, in one's private social ambiance, in the sacristy and the church of stone and bricks. So Christians were not interested in politics and took part in it at the most in order to secure as many advantages for the Church as possible. On the other hand, this same "political liberalism" caused Christians to fight each other in political conflicts, convinced that in political matters Christians are wholly free, as if it does not matter whether political affairs are conducted according to the demands of the Christian message or not.

In its doctrinal section the Pastoral Constitution, which recognizes the world's autonomy, has nevertheless denounced the schizophrenic situation which separates *life in the world* from *Christian life*.[3] It stresses that the Christian message concerns man as a whole, also in his personal relationships, whether private or public, and in his labors to make this earth more habitable and worthy of man: "the Church's religious mission is by the same token a human one"[4]; "the Church is charged to show forth the mystery of God, man's last end; simultaneously she shows man the meaning of his existence, the intimate truth about himself."[5]

The eschatological expectation is therefore not a brake on this building up of a human world but rather the fulfilment of it by adding new motives;[6] it is a more intensive stimulus towards this building up of the world and this promotion of all nations[7] because the "eschaton" stimulates us to bring about a better earthly future.[8] The Church has therefore "to serve the general welfare of all."[9]

The doctrinal part of the Constitution in particular contains striking statements which are the more remarkable if we remember the history of what happened before the Council. It says that, although we cannot identify the humanization process of this world with the growth of the Kingdom of God, these two are very closely intertwined in so far as a better ordering of the human community contributes towards this Kingdom.[10] Several Council Fathers protested against a radical separation between the future of this earth and the Christian expectation, and this led to a change in the original text. The *expensio modorum* (reasons for accepting an amendment) rightly explains that in so far as laboring for welfare on this earth is an aspect of care for the brother, an expression of love, this commitment to a better future on this earth cannot be adequately distinguished from a commitment to the Kingdom of God.[11] Just as typical is the modification of the original text from: "The form of this world, distorted by sin, *will pass* away" to "*is passing* away." What was meant here is that in the world's progress towards a better future through care for the brother the *eschaton* itself is already shaping history,[12] obviously not automatically, but through the commitment of love which demands justice for all, and this is impossible, given the human condition, without a concrete social and political order.

This shows that the very process by which Christendom is being extricated from an entanglement which tied ecclesiastical structures to political ones (caesaro-papism, papal caesarism, all kinds of "theocracies" and the harnessing of the Church to particular regimes), has now made it possible for Christians to be involved through a genuine, Gospel-inspired commitment to the realities of the world of politics.

Evangelical Inspiration and the "Signs of the Times"

From what has been said it is clear that when the Church's magisterium speaks about social and political issues, it does so by virtue of the Church's specific mandate to proclaim and promote the *salvation* of the *concrete human person*. The Church therefore speaks out of her own historical responsibility for man.

It is precisely this claim which creates problems. It hardly needs demonstration that, just as all fundamentalism is abhorrent in the interpretation of the Bible, so a biblical fundamentalism in political matters would have disastrous consequences. The Christian message does not provide us directly with any concrete program for political action. On the other hand, one cannot maintain that the choice of a particular social policy is an open question for Christians. Between the message of the Gospel, therefore, and the concrete historical political decisions some decisive element must intervene. This was clearly seen in the Pastoral Constitution: "To carry out this task the Church must *continually examine the signs of the times* and *interpret them in the light of the Gospel.*"[13] In other words, the Church cannot directly rely on revelation in these matters. It is here that human experience and "non-theological" factors play a very important part. Can we analyze the structure of this?

A General Structure

There is no need to insist here on the fact that if in this field the Church cannot fulfil her mandate except through dialog with the world, this is by no means an exceptional case. The Church does not speak *in spite of* but precisely *because of* her claim to exclusiveness (*Ausschliesslichkeitsanspruch*): she *never* speaks exclusively from revelation, but is essentially a Church of dialog, even in the witness to and proclamation of the Good News. The actual situation, as the hermeneutical situation, exercises an essential influence on the *contemporary* proclamation of the *total* evangelical message.[14]

I only recall this point in order to make clear beforehand that the contribution of non-theological information to the Church's magisterial pronouncements cannot be the immediate reason for the specific character of such ecclesiastical pronouncements about political matters. The same happens, for instance, in a dogmatic definition where the Church tries to express this particular message in other than purely biblical words and concepts. The Church and the magisterium can never live *exclusively* on "data of revelation." The relation of the Church to the world is not simply one of a "teaching Church" to a "listening world," but an exchange, a dialog, where contributions are made from both sides and both sides listen to each other, even in the authoritative proclamation of the Church's unique message. There is no need to develop this further.[15]

In the case of a magisterial pronouncement on political matters, this dialog character of the Church stands out because here directives are given for right conduct in *the field of the world as such*, and not merely because the world is used to express possible truths of revelation in conceptual form, as is the case with doctrinal definitions. In this field the Church takes up a position with regard to the world precisely as worldly. And this she does because of her function of service with regard to mankind's salvation. For instance, she demands, or recommends, agrarian reform. Here she can obviously not draw directly on revelation. This revelation does indeed impose on her a constant care for the brother. But this care must be expressed in terms of concrete history. That this expression of care demands here and now this particular measure and not another (for instance, whether she should emphasize the right to property or rather the need for fair distribution and socialization), makes one wonder where the magisterium obtains this kind of knowledge, and on what the binding character of such directives would be based.

The Particular Structure of such Decisions of an Ethical and Historical Character

1. I have already pointed out that it is impossible to derive any concrete political plan of action *directly* from the Gospel message. Some think that this is possible when we combine this message with a scientifically

conducted analysis of our present society. On the other hand, one may say that even such a scientific analysis still leaves a wide choice of alternative measures, and does not imply that only this or that political measure is ethically binding here and now, whether for a region or for the whole world. Often a number of possibilities arise which then usually give rise to different answers according to different social tendencies, organizations or even political parties. And the fact is that, except where room is left for various solutions, the papal documents referred to, and the Pastoral Constitution, often refer to one particular concrete option. And here the problem becomes pressing: how can the Church justify an authoritative demand for specific options in political matters in such a way that, given the necessary conditions, it is no longer an open question for the Christian but requires him to act?[16]

Without denying the charismatic assistance of the Spirit in the teaching, sanctifying and pastoral function of the Church, but rather accepting it fully, I nevertheless cannot see in this charismatic assistance the immediate explanation of the final concrete choice made in such ecclesiastical pronouncements. For this might create the impression that we invoke the Spirit on those difficult points which we cannot explain and that we try to bridge the unbridgeable distance between general Christian principles and the many-faced concrete situation by appealing to an intervening impulse from on high which would decide the definite choice from among the many possible ones. The Spirit of God does not work as a stop-gap, but in and through man himself. In this sense we may say that an appeal to the Spirit cannot *explain* anything, whilst, on the other hand, we emphatically maintain as believers that we see the charismatic assistance of the Spirit become historically manifest precisely when we have analyzed the inner structure of such a concrete decision by the magisterium and have made it intelligible (*in so far as* free human decisions can be penetrated intelligibly). Thus the factual analysis of this inner structure is also homage to the Spirit.

2. Here we must discuss a general problem of ethics. Many people start from a certain "duality" in ethical norms because they *proceed from* an abstract and theoretical morality. They therefore talk of abstract norms that are generally valid and concrete norms that refer to a "precise situation." And so they draw the conclusion that general principles of ethics can never lead to a concrete situation by simple *deduction.* They are inevitably confronted with the question of how to bridge the gap between the abstract and generally valid norms and the increasingly complicated human social situation which can, as such, usually call forth a variety of possible human solutions and reactions.

Moreover, while in some cases it may be of little importance what particular solution is found, there are many cases where only one particular answer is capable of promoting human dignity here and now and for that reason truly morally binding.[17] If, therefore, on the one hand, the general principles cannot provide us with a concrete solution and, on the other, even a scientific analysis of the situation cannot give us an unambiguous and clear solution, it follows that, in the opinion of those dualists (general norms *and* strictly situational norms), there must be somewhere an unknown third factor to act as a catalyst and to release the one proper and obligatory option from among the many. This catalyst would then *either* be a "supernatural" one, the guiding power of the Spirit, which breaks through the ambivalence of the problem, *or* some human, irrational factor such as intuition, or an unrationalized sympathetic hunch, an imaginative sense of history, etc.

One may ask whether the starting-point of such reasoning, the abstract norm *and* the concrete norm, is the right one for this problem. I do not deny the significance of abstract, generally valid norms in the total context of human life. The question is, however, whether we place them in the right context and see them in their proper function in such a way that they show at the same time that a mere situational ethics would provide no solution. I cannot deal fully with this here and if I did, there would not be enough space left for the real problem. Some points have to be mentioned, nevertheless.

Abstract pronouncements cannot seize hold of the reality, simply *by themselves;* they nevertheless derive a realistic value from our total experience of reality. For instance, "to be human" is not a part of the real, that is, individual and concrete human person *side by side* with another part which would constitute the individuality; for the individuality determines "being human" *from within.* Only and exclusively as intrinsically individualized is "being human" a reality and can it be the source of moral norms (which, in religious parlance, we can rightly describe as the will of God).

There is therefore only one source of ethical norms, namely, the *historical reality* of the value of the inviolable human person with all its bodily and social implications. That is why we cannot attribute validity to abstract norms *as such.* Moreover, no abstract statement can produce a call or invitation. The abstract and general nature of the norms simply shows up man's inability to express the concrete reality exhaustively. These abstract concepts appear in fact only as a "moment" of a more integral human awareness of experience in which they obtain, due to the concrete existential contact with reality, the value of an inner objective reference to this experienced reality: only in that direction, indicated by the abstract conceptual pronouncement, lies the concrete reality, and in no other. But for the rest the abstract content cannot determine this direction in the concrete.

These abstract, generally valid norms are therefore an inadequate yet real *pointer* to the one real, concrete ethical norm, namely, this concrete human person living historically in this concrete society. Ethical norms are requirements made by reality, and of this the so-called abstract general norms are but the essentially inadequate expression. It is, therefore, not the inadequate expression which constitutes, by itself, the ethical norm, but it is a pointer to the one and only norm: these persons who must be approached in a love which demands justice for all. The abstract expression can only indicate in a vague and general way the content of this one, concretely determined reality as it calls on me; therefore I can never see in an abstract norm what I must do or not do here and now. For the same reason, namely, because these general norms express, however inadequately, at least something real about the concrete reality, my concrete decision must never fall *outside* the direction indicated by these norms (if, of course, correctly formulated). These general norms are directives, derived from earlier experiences and indicating a moral appreciation of basic human values without which human life would simply become absurd. And thus we overcome a morality which is either purely abstract or mere situation ethics.

If, then, for all practical purposes, the problem is not one of a confrontation between general norms and strictly situational elements but one of respect for and the promotion of the concrete human person in his concrete society, the question is still: how do we know, or how does the magisterium know, what should be done in practice within present society in order to contribute as a Christian to an existence that is more in line with man's dignity? How does such a constructive ethical investigation proceed?

3. The Pastoral Constitution says we must "examine the signs of the time and interpret them in the light of the Gospel"; that means, we must interpret the concrete reality of society as the expression of a moral demand made on the Christian conscience. But human history shows that this is not primarily a matter of finding a *theoretical* interpretation of these "signs of the time," because when we do that the prophetic voice of a new moral imperative is usually heard too late. Elsewhere the Pastoral Constitution speaks more realistically about a concern with urgent problems "in the light of the Gospel and of *human experience*" (46).

The past has shown that, long before the Churches had analyzed the social problems, there were people who, in their commitment and in a pre-analytic dialog with the world, had already reached the moral decision that fundamental changes were required. New situational ethical imperatives have rarely or never been initiated by philosophers, theologians, Churches or ecclesiastical authorities. They emerge from a concrete experience of life and impose themselves with the clear evidence of experience. Theoretical reflection comes afterwards, and so do the critical examination and rationalization, the philosophical or theological and official formulation. And so, after the event, such imperatives are put forth as "generally valid, abstract norms." All this brings out the essential need for a "living presence in the world." The Church cannot fulfil her prophetic task with regard to the worldly problems of man and society simply by appealing to revelation, but only by listening very carefully to that "outside prophecy" (*Fremdprophetie*) which appeals to her from the situation of the world and in which she recognizes the familiar voice of her Lord.

When we listen to and analyze this voice of worldly prophecy we discover that moral historical decisions and the initiation of new moral imperatives and directives are in fact *not born* from a confrontation between general principles and the result of a preferably scientific analysis of the social situation but usually (though not necessarily exclusively) from those concrete experiences which may perhaps best be described as "contrast experiences."

There are hundreds of such cases. The contrast experiences of the two world-wars, the concentration camps, political torture, the color-bar, the developing countries, the hungry, the homeless, the underprivileged and the poor in countries where there is so much potential wealth, and so on—all these experiences make people suddenly say: this should not and must not go on. And so develops the protest against war, social injustice, racial discrimination, the ownership of vast properties, etc. In our present society moral imperatives and historical decisions spring, moreover, particularly from the experience of a *collective* evil, such as the inadequate income of certain sections of society, colonial exploitation, racial discrimination and other injustices.

When we analyze these contrast experiences for what they can tell us about possible new ethical imperatives, we find that these negative experiences imply an awareness of values that is veiled, positive, though not yet articulate; that they stir the conscience which begins to protest. Here the absence of "what ought to be" is *experienced* initially, and this leads to a perhaps vague, yet real, perception of "what should be done here and now." This experience is, of course, but the preliminary stage leading to the proper reflection of both a scientific analysis of the situation as of a new assessment of principles gained from experiences in the past. Yet, without this initial experience, which evokes a prophetic protest, neither the sciences, nor philosophy nor theology would have been stirred into action. (Such experiences often lead even to new sciences such as polemology [problems of war and peace] and the sociology of religion.) Through these experiences man begins to realize that he is living at a level *below* that of his basic potential and that he is kept at this low level precisely by the pressure of existing social structures to which he is subject.

In the past such contrast experiences led conscientious people to the ethical imperative of charitable deeds in the private sphere of immediate inter-personal encounter (Vincent de Paul, Don Bosco, etc.). Today, in contrast with "medieval" man, we know that the social "establishment" is not a divine creation, but a cultural and man-made situation which can be dealt with and reformed.[18] Historical imperatives emerging from such contrast-experiences then tackle the reform of the existing society itself. In other words, this type of contrast experiences now leads to the moral imperative of decisions in the social and political field. This shows once again that the new moral imperatives, based on negative experiences, are part of human history; the science of ethics then begins to reflect upon this and in the course of time a whole framework of generally valid principles (basic and detailed) is built up.

It is therefore not this ethical thematization which is either the most important or the most decisive. And this makes it still clearer that the concrete ethical decision is not a mere "moral case" of a generally valid abstract norm. For these contrast experiences show that the moral imperative is first discovered in its immediate, concrete, *inner* meaning, before it can be made the object of a science and then reduced to a generally valid principle. For that reason there is no need for an appeal to a "third" factor which some want to introduce in order to bridge the gap between the "general norm" and the "strictly situational element." The initial creative decision which discovered the historical imperative directly in its *inner* meaning in the very contrast experience *is*, for the believer, at the same time the charismatic element of this whole process. The general norms, on the contrary, are the mapping out of a long history of experience (full of contrast experiences) in search of a society more worthy of man, and doing so precisely on the basis mainly of these negative experiences.

This should make it obvious that a Christian's life is not very much helped by the magisterium proposing merely "general principles" for social and political issues because in that case the Church lags by definition behind the historical situation since such principles are the tail-end of a preceding history, while the history of the future must be prepared by historical decisions and moral imperatives. To have seen this constitutes the real contribution made by such encyclicals as *Pacem in Terris* and *Populorum Progressio*. They deal really with moral "historical decisions" (though obviously against a background of basic principles already gained from past experiences).

So far I have tried to analyze the concrete origin of moral historical decisions. There remains the specific Christian aspect to be dealt with in all this. Does the experience of our human existence guarantee that we *can* make life more worthy of man in a meaningful way? Does this not founder on man himself? Moreover, if a better future is the norm, does this belief in a better future allow us to sacrifice human beings in the present in order to achieve this better world in the future? The Gospel can indeed bring some clarity into this.

The heart of the message of Jesus' death and resurrection unto eternity lies in the proclamation that, by virtue of the Christ event, it is indeed possible to build up humanity and that this is not a labor of Sisyphus. In biblical terms this possibility is maintained, over against all human despair, when we say that this is the grace of God's kingdom being achieved in man's world; it is a kingdom of justice, peace and love, a kingdom where there will be no evil, nor mourning, nor crying, nor pain (2 Peter 3. 13; Apoc. 21. 4). Christian hope knows that this possibility is given to man as a grace, and so the Christian lives in the conscious faith that his faithful commitment to a better temporal order is *not in vain*, although he does not see *how* this temporal order which is not yet the promised kingdom, can be the obscure beginning of the *eschaton*. The hope of this radically new and final kingdom stimulates him never to rest satisfied with what has already been achieved in this world. Historically we can never say: *this* is the promised future. The Gospel called the one who said that "anti-Christ."

I agree with P. Ricoeur, J. B. Metz and J. Paupert[19] that the evangelical message gives us no direct program of social and political action, but, on the other hand, is socially and politically relevant in an indirect way, namely, in a "utopian" sense. But how should we understand this? The Gospel message of Christian expectation offers the stimulating possibility constantly to overcome the limitations of any present "establishment." It contains a permanent criticism of the actual situation: secular institutions, social structures and their dominant mentality. It urges constant improvement, and above all, it brings the firm conviction that this building up of a more human world is genuinely possible.

We should not be afraid of the word "utopia" here as it refers to the perspective from which we can criticize society. It is moreover an historical fact that most of the "rights of man" which are now accepted (at least in principle), were initially considered by all well-thinking people as unrealistic and utopian dreams of peculiar individuals. The pressure function of a "utopia" is indeed an historical factor: mankind believes in what is humanly impossible. Moreover, the future with which we are concerned is not a mere accumulation of vague wishful thinking but something that was promised in Jesus Christ and becomes real, through grace, in history, and so possible for man. From the point of view of life in a political society the Christian expectation and the Sermon on the Mount play the part of an effective "utopia" which will keep on exercising an ever-present pressure on all social and political matters.

When we allow this Christian factor to play in human experience, particularly in what I have called contrast experiences whence the new moral imperatives arise, it becomes clear that the protest prompted by these negative experiences ("this cannot go on") is also the expression of the firm hope that things *can* be done differently, *must* improve, and *will* get better through our commitment. The prophetic voice which rises from the contrast experience is therefore *protest,* hope-inspiring *promise* and *historical initiative.* To put it more accurately still: the possibility and condition of the protest and the historical decision lie in the actual presence of this hope, for, without it, the negative experience would not prompt the contrast experience and the protest. Thus the negative experience itself shows the primacy of this hope of a better future.[20] Is the history of these contrast experiences not the *historical* soil on which the profoundly human and religious notions of *salvation* and *disaster* could grow? It is moreover only when people become *aware* of the fact that a better existence than the "established" one is possible, and seen indeed as realizable, that protest appears and the need for historical decisions is sensed. Is it not this awareness, for instance, which has created a pre-revolutionary situation throughout Latin America?[21]

Because of the continuity in man's consciousness, where pre-reflexive experience and reflexive analysis meet in a complex unity, we can roughly distinguish two phases in these contrast experiences: first, that of the negative experience itself, where the "utopian" urge of the Gospel provokes the prophetic protest against man's misjudgment of the possibilities of his own existence, and where the moral demand for changes and improvements develops, with the result that in a vague way some concrete moral pointers begin to stand out; secondly, the phase where the message of the Gospel matures through a combination of theology and the scientific analysis of a particular situation into a responsible and more concrete plan of social and political action. In this way the message of the Gospel becomes indirectly relevant in social and political matters.

I agree, therefore, with J. B. Metz that we can truly speak of two functions of the Church, one that criticizes society and one that applies the "utopian" view to society.[22] And this should be understood in the sense that it is its "utopian" view which is the standard of its criticism.

This holds for the Christian Churches as such, and therefore for all the faithful and particularly for the ecclesiastical authorities who, through their service, are responsible in the Church for the world. That something of this sense of responsibility *begins* to find a clear expression in such documents as *Pacem in Terris* and *Populorum Progressio* shows the beginning of a new self-awareness in the magisterium which no longer merely registers the historical past in general principles but means to give a lead in those moral "historical decisions" that are opening up the future.

In *this* sense we may call the Church (as *sacramentum mundi,* or *sacramentum historia,* in so far as she serves God's kingdom, since we now see the historical dimension of the world as implied in the primacy of the future) the institutionalized "critical function" with regard to the temporal order, a function based on a divine charisma. This is based on the prophetic character of the Church and so on her hope of that promised future which starts modestly in the history of this world as salvation history, and this means as the gradual *redemption* of *history* itself. It is this Christian expectation which itself creates history, in and through the commitment of the believers.

This new self-awareness of the magisterium is the more valuable today as our present society with its indispensable involvement in rational planning urgently demands *collective* historical decisions in social and political affairs. That is why non-Catholics, too, watch these ecclesiastical decisions: Church and world are more and more convinced that they need each other's contribution for the sake of the one, communal, overall welfare of all mankind. Perhaps this new self-awareness demands that this critical function be better organized while individual Christians themselves (nourished on this "utopian" and "critical" contribution) should not withdraw from concrete social politics but join in with all men of good will (but this, too, is an historical decision which affects the concrete situation).

The New Testament criticism of emperor-worship, together with its confirmation of the real and proper authority of the emperor, is already a symptom of this "utopian" and "critical" function of the Church with regard to society, and provides an authentic biblical foundation. This critical function can only be exercised through a genuine "presence in the world," through experiences where God so to speak inserts the world and history between himself and us as the perceptible *expression* (or "translation") of his call on us here and now. They are also the *medium* in and through which the Christian is made explicitly aware of this call. Lastly, they are the *sphere* within which he must embody his response to that call in his life.

Thus the world and history teach the Christian explicitly the concrete content of this call from God with regard to what happens in society. It is there that the Christian should be first of all the active *prophet*, not of what can be achieved by power politics, but of that Christian "utopia" which brings about the *totally new*, all that is radically worthy of man, through his care for the brother. This "utopia" is the permanent source of criticism of all life on this earth, but attacks particularly the existing situation in so far as it pretends to be already the realization of the "Christian order." This is not to deny the importance of a policy based on the balance of power during a given period of time. But it *does* mean that precisely in this case the Church and the individual Christian must continue to exercise a critical function, and that therefore the element of prophetic "unrest" must be kept alive. Eschatological hope makes the commitment to the temporal order *radical* and by the same token makes any already existing temporal order *relative*. Thus the Christian's social and political commitment, rooted in his care for mankind, is the hermeneutic of his faith in the Kingdom of God's promise. The Church's critical function is not that of an outsider, pursuing a parallel path, but rather that of a critical involvement in the building of the world and the progress of the nations.

The Morally Binding Force of the Church's Magisterium in Social and Political Matters

The specific nature of statements by the magisterium on political, economic and general cultural issues can only be understood in the light of what has been said so far in this article. I presuppose here that we are dealing with statements where the magisterium pronounces directly on the *doctrinal* background of a moral, historical decision in the field of politics. For we are concerned here with the theological value of the "historical decisions" contained in such documents, in other words, with the value of a non-doctrinal, somewhat "hypothetical" pronouncement by the Church's highest authority, Pope or Council. The words "somewhat hypothetical" refer to the fact that such texts also depend on non-theological information and speak of a contingent secular reality. This is the same as saying that such a pronouncement can only have value in so far as a condition is realized: "given this particular historical situation of society." The concrete indications are therefore not, by themselves, valid for all times, nor even *everywhere* here and now, since the situation may differ fundamentally from one place to another.[23]

Given the pace of development in today's society, these official documents may therefore be soon out of date, so that to keep on appealing
to such concrete historical indications might soon become reactionary
in the future. This is implied in the very definition of an "historical
decision." Therefore, apart from possible inadequacies with regard to
the analysis of the situation and past principles, social and political
encyclicals appear in relatively quick succession and there are striking
differences in their moral indications. The Pastoral Constitution says
therefore quite rightly that the signs of the times must be *continually*
examined. In the meantime, *this* specific pronouncement will hold *here
and now* for the ecclesiastical community.

Basically, and first of all, the obligation lies in a demand addressed
to all Christians and arising from a real situation, in so far as it is seen
as inhuman and unchristian. This situation ought to stir the Christian
conscience even before any official pronouncement. The Church's intervention merely confirms this. The specific character of such an intervention lies in the fact that this demand is formulated in a clear, precise,
concrete and definite sense (*e.g.*, in this situation the breaking up of
vast landed properties by expropriation is morally necessary).

Although in many cases the concrete demand is meant to be understood as "illustrative" and leaves room for other possibilities,[24] occasion-
ally such an official document puts forth a decisive choice in a way
which rules out other measures. And history has shown *after the event*
that among various possible measures only *one* proved to be objectively right.

And so we are faced once again and yet more urgently with the question: does the magisterium provide us, believers, with a guarantee that
its specific indication is the only right one among many others? It seems
to me that this can never be maintained in an *absolute* sense because
"historical decisions" in the field of politics can never have that kind of
guarantee, not even when they proceed from ecclesiastical authority,
although we believe nevertheless that it stands under the charismatic
guidance of the Spirit and that it functions in and is borne by the whole
community of the Church. We may say that this gives the Christian
confidence (within the limits of the "hypothetical" element referred to
above) that whoever acts accordingly will really act more in line with
what the situation demands, and that the Christian can therefore face
the consequences of such an action more confidently, even if it should
lead to trouble. All this, indeed, is not so much directly concerned
with obedience to the Church's teaching authority as with her pastoral
prophetic function. This function does not have the same precision
but a more powerful prophetic ability to "call forth," to stimulate a
continuous search, and no Christian can close his ears, his heart and

his inventive imagination to that. And this leads us to the specific nature of the obligatory quality of these official directives. Because the concrete moral imperative grows mainly out of contrast experiences, it has a primarily and principally *negative* character: "this cannot go on." What, for instance, *peace* may mean positively, when we reject cold or hot wars, nobody knows. The Christian only has the vision of the "eschatological peace" (and even that he is only able to describe negatively). But in the experience of the concrete "non-peace" both our will to overcome *this* situation and the inventiveness of our informed love seeking means to achieve justice for *all*, will grow apace.

And so this, perhaps somewhat abstract, yet significant analysis (so it seems to me) leads us to the conclusion that the obligatory character of a magisterial pronouncement on political and social issues lies rather in the "negative" aspect (this *must* change) than in something positive, although the specific obligation contained in this positive element *shares*, in a contemporary and prudent manner, in the absolutely obligatory character of the negative experience. The "negative theology" in speculative matters shows us here the way to a "negative theology" in practical matters, in which the eschatological vision of the future is the positive, "utopian" and "critical" norm for this particular concrete and changing situation. A Christian, therefore, who has read, for example, *Populorum Progressio*, without any noticeable change in his day-to-day life, is guilty with regard to the prophetic voice of this papal document. He is guilty particularly with regard to mankind and God because he obviously accepts the existing order which the Bible qualifies as disorder, an order which will remain subject to the criticism of the biblical message for as long as history lasts.

Translated by Theo Westow

NOTES

1. This problem was studied by K. Rahner, "Over de theologische problematiek van een 'Pastorale Constitutie,' " in *Vaticanum II*, n. 2, *De Kerk in de wereld van deze tijd* (Hilversum, 1967), pp. 315–38. I do not intend to repeat what he has said but rather to approach the issue from another angle without implying any criticism of Rahner. It is rather a *complementary* view.

2. Art. 91. Also, *Peace on earth*, art. 154.

3. Art. 43. P. Tillich says in the same sense: "The existence of religion as a special realm is the most conspicuous proof of man's fallen state," *Theology of Culture*, New York, 1964, p. 42.

4. *Loc. cit.*, art. 11.

5. Art. 41.

6. Art. 41.

7. Art. 39 and ch. 4 and 5 (pt. 2).

8. Art. 43, also 34, 36 and 41. Cf. E. Schillebeeckx, "Christelijk geloof en aardse toekomstverwachting," in *Vaticanum II*, n. 2, *De Kerk in de wereld van deze tijd* (Hilversum, 1967), pp. 78–112.

9. Past. Const., art. 42.

10. Art. 39.

11. *Expensio modorum*, in cap. 3, pars I, p. 236.

12. Past. Const., art. 39 (with corresponding *Expensio modorum*).

13. Art. 4.

14. I have tried to explain this in: "De Kerk als sacrament van de dialoog," in *Tijdschrift voor Theologie*, VII (1967), n. 4, and specially in: "Naar een katholiek gebruik van de hermeneutiek," in *Geloof bij kenterend getij, Festschrift voor Prof. W. van de Pol* (Roermond, 1967).

15. The Council admitted this: "The Church does not ignore how much she has received from the history and development of humanity" (Past. Const., art. 44), and it applied this explicitly to the way in which she expounds her unique message (art. 58).

16. The immediate obligation lies with the ecclesial community as such, and therefore on the "faithful at large," not simply on its individual members. Not every *individual* faithful is, for instance, called upon to go to a developing country, nor need he be a theologian although there must be theology in the Church. I am taking this point for granted.

17. The question is not that there is something relative and imperfect in *all* human decisions, also those of Church authorities. This is the mark of the human condition. I am referring here to the problem that specific historical decisions, however imperfect, can carry a moral obligation.

18. See among others, H. Freyer, *Theorie des gegenwärtigen Zeitalters* (Stuttgart, [2]1963), who, in 1955, was one of the first to analyze the tractability of the world and of society.

19. P. Ricoeur, "Tâches de l'éducateur politique," in *Esprit*, 33 (1965), n. 340, pp. 78–93, esp. 88 f.; J.-M. Paupert, *Pour une politique évangélique* (Paris, 1965); J. B. Metz, "Epilogue," in *From Anathema to Dialogue* by R. Garaudy, K. Rahner, J. B. Metz (London, 1967), pp. 109 ff.

20. I do not consider here the question how and how far it is possible, outside an explicitly Christian conviction, to have the firm will to construct a better world for all men, either as based on a positive reality which we, Christians, can *interpret* as an anonymously "Christian hope" (clarified through revelation), or as based on false ideologies, although this question is not without importance, also politically.

21. See C. Furtado, *La pré-révolution brésilienne* (Paris, 1964).

22. Cf. J. Moltmann, *Theology of Hope* (London, 1967); J. B. Metz, *loc. cit.*, and "The Church and the World," in *The Word in History*, St Xavier Symposium (London, 1968), pp. 69–85; P. Ricoeur, *l.c.*, and "Le socius et le prochain," in *Histoire et Vérité* (Paris, 1955), pp. 99–111.

23. See the qualification mentioned in art. 16. Moreover, the condition "given the generally described situation" remains always valid here. Because of the unification of the world and the consequently greater solidarity of

people and of Christians, a given situation may well hold elsewhere though not in one's own country. The obligation is therefore influenced by all kinds of modifications.

24. This is why the Pastoral Constitution speaks of "searching out solutions of so many involved questions" (art. 46).

3

Some Thoughts on the Interpretation of Eschatology

1969

The Christian believes that the living God showed the uniqueness and power of his unconditional love for man in Jesus Christ, and thus revealed himself as man's salvation. The first Christian generations confessed this event and expressed this confession in many varied ways in the books of the new testament. These books, therefore, give us interpretations of the Jesus-event against the background of the old testament sphere of understanding.

The dialectic of the development of dogma or tradition shows that, in order to be faithful to the original event, the church was constantly obliged to give a fresh interpretation of this apostolic interpretation. This problem became acute for the first time when Christianity with its Palestinian culture and corresponding interpretation was transplanted to an environment with a Hellenistic culture and mentality. The new testament still shows clear traces of the difficulties experienced in this 'translation.'

An Interpretation of an Interpretation

We listen to this message now, in our own age. And this means that in our different situation and our different sphere of understanding we react to this Christian message with constant questioning. The relevance, therefore, of the message concerning the ultimate things, the *eschata*, or the final and definitive salvation of man, implies the need to analyze our own sphere of understanding, not only from the point of view of the sociology and philosophy of our own culture, but also theologically. But, precisely because our modern self-understanding carries our whole past with it, we cannot grasp our present sphere of understanding if we do not take equal care to understand our own past. To try to assimilate the eschatological message of the bible today without a critical understanding of what theology made of it in the many centuries of its past, with a constantly changing understanding, would be wholly inadequate. A first glance at this process shows clearly that the constantly renewed assimilation of the Christian message is connected with the common expression of changing views on man and the world, and formulated by a succession of philosophical schools. To examine the differences in understanding that succeeded each other in the church's two-thousand-year-old tradition is therefore a hermeneutic requirement in the interpretation of the Christian confession of the *eschata.*

But this same investigation must penetrate into the depths of the old and new testament origins of this eschatological confession. This process shows that different cultures clash with each other and inspire different kinds of question. It also shows that, while becoming aware of all these differences, the believer is really trying to interpret and reflect on the meaning of that phase in history in which he himself lives. The old testament is then seen as the key source for the explanation of the life and death of a people who became aware of being God's people, just as the new testament became the key source for the explanation of Jesus' life and death. Both the old and the new testament have an interpretative function: up to a point they interpret their own content; they are hermeneutics in action. But for us this collection of writings is itself something in need of interpretation. And so hermeneutics becomes the interpretation of an interpretation.

Although, then, the problem of interpretation is itself already one of the facts of the bible, it has become more acute today than ever before, and this for two main reasons. First, we no longer belong to the same culture, no longer have the same mentality or the same outlook on man and the world, as those that prevailed in the days when the original and the later interpretations of the Christ-event were formulated. The distance in time makes our problem far more difficult. The culture of the Semites and that of Hellenism at least shared a common 'antiquity.' Yet a modern translation is possible because the ancient self-understanding of man is one of the elements that has shaped our modern self-understanding. Pluralism is never absolute. Although there is no identity, there are always channels of communication between the various interpretations. Secondly, we belong to an age which acknowledges the demands of textual and historical criticism, an age which considers it immoral to surrender oneself unconditionally to something without some rational justification: all people, including those of good will, reject *a priori* a kind of blind faith which has no human and genuine intelligible basis. Even with our unconditional obedience of faith we can no longer avoid the need to make the eschatological dogmas intelligible and in some way understandable. Today faith insists that the believer pass through the ordeal of a new interpretation of his faith if he wishes to be faithful to the message of the gospel.

History and the Future

Today we observe a basic shift in the way man looks at history. The more or less explicit identification of history with the past, which dominated the writing of history since the beginning of its modern phase, is now yielding to a view which sees history more as events in the making, events in the process of arrival, and therefore as happenings in which we ourselves play an active part. The future is of primary importance in what we call 'history.' So the concept of man's earthly future begins to exercise a kind of polarity in man's thought, and knowledge, whereas in the past—at least in the West—the future dimension of history was almost only considered as a matter of the *finis ultimus*, the ultimate end of man, beyond and after this earthly life.

Since the rediscovery of man's true historicity as a creature of time, that on the basis of its past sets its course of life in the present towards a future, eschatology is seen as a question which lies embodied in man's existence. Man's experience does not simply run on in time, with an undercurrent of 'becoming,' but implies an element of time-consciousness. This does not allow him to escape from time but it allows him in a certain sense to transcend the lived time (*le temps vécu*), although he cannot put this time-transcending permanence into words, at least not positively. This time-consciousness which makes man reach beyond experienced time into both the past and the future makes man's questioning about the beginning and the end particularly relevant.

It seems to me, therefore, that to inquire after the future is a natural process, and fundamental to our human condition. Although caught up in time and never outside it, man is not the prisoner of time in his historical growth; he transcends time from within. That is why he can never feel satisfied. Within this time-condition man is therefore free to achieve a certain openness with regard to time. He can do so because he can also indulge like an epicure in the short-lived joys of the temporary condition in which he lives. But if he takes this time-consciousness seriously, he cannot avoid facing the question of the meaning of human history. For every moment of his free existence implies present, past and future. His freedom indeed is exercised in the present but only in so far as this present sets its course towards the future. The pure present is always on the point of sliding into the past. Man's future-building freedom thus essentially presupposes an open eschatology, an expectation of the future, a will towards the future which, in itself, slips into the ambiguity of all history-making freedom.

The Future as Transcendence

When in our old culture, mainly concerned with the past, we thought and spoke about God's transcendence we almost naturally projected God into the past. Eternity was something like an immobilized or immortalized past—'in the beginning was God.' We knew of course quite well that God's eternity embraced man's present and man's future; that God was both first and last, and as such also a present that transcended our human present. On this point the older theology developed marvellous insights which have by no means lost their relevance. In a culture which constantly looked towards the past there existed obviously a powerful mutual attraction between 'transcendence' and eternity on the one hand and an immortalized 'past' on the other. Today, however, our culture is firmly turned towards the future as something that our culture itself must build. So the Christian notion of transcendence, supple and capable of more than one meaning, has to go through the same process. The meaning of 'transcendence' comes therefore closer to what in our time-bound condition we call 'future.' If divine transcendence transcends and embraces man's past, present and future from within, the believer will preferably and rightly link God's transcendence with the future as soon as man has recognized the primacy of the future in our time-bound condition. So he will link God with the future of man and, since man is a communal person, with the future of mankind as a whole. When we once accept the reality of a genuine belief in the invisible reality of God who is the true source of our understanding of God from within this world, this new understanding of his transcendence will lead to the new image of God in our culture.

In this cultural context the God of the believer will manifest himself as 'He who comes,' the God who is our future. This implies a far-reaching change: he, whom we formerly saw as the 'wholly other' in our old outlook on man and the world, is now seen as he who is our future and who creates anew man's future. He shows himself as the God who gives us in Jesus Christ the opportunity to build the future, to make all things new and to rise above our own sinful history and that of all mankind. Thus the new culture becomes an inspiration to rediscover as a surprise the good news of the old and the new testament, the news that the God of promise has put us on the way to the promised land, a land which, like Israel of old, we ourselves must claim and cultivate, trusting in his promise.

God's Faithfulness

In order to avoid hasty conclusions one should not lose sight of the biblical basis of what I have called this new understanding of God. The new culture is but an occasion and stimulus to rediscover the living God as our future in the old and the new testament. But according to the bible the basis of the eschatological expectation of the future is the certainty, in faith, of an actual relationship with God. This actual relationship with the God of the covenant, which makes the past present again, must not be sacrificed to the primacy of the future. The basis of our hope is therefore our faith in Yahweh who reveals himself in both past and present as the living God of the community.

This is understandable when we realize that the present and its past are the only basis on which we can build a future, otherwise we simply land ourselves in futuristic fantasies. The past belongs essentially to our human condition which in its present is orientated towards the future. And the interpretation of old testament history shows that the past only becomes clearer in the present when again and again it is seen in the light of the future. In the bible the interpretation of a past event always coincides with the announcement of a new expectation for the future. The past is 'read again' in a manner which makes it once more actual, and thus it becomes a guarantee for the hope of a new future. Embodied in the scriptural canon, the traditional material which voices future expectations is raised above the level of its original intent, and in this dimension of its own future the past remains for ever actual. The etiological explanation of the present from the past is at the same time a confession that new salvation is dawning. Thus the critical analysis of the old testament theme of taking possession of the land shows that its connection with the theme of fulfilment and promise is a theological reflection on the *actual* possession of the holy land. Here we have therefore a theological view of history arising from actuality and providing an interpretation of the past as well as a pointer towards the future.

If we want to understand Israel's history as a promise, we shall find that this promise is not an absolute starting-point without a prehistory, as if it were a kind of word of God which promised Israel a new future out of the blue and from on high, and drew a picture of it with all its future and observable features. On the contrary, Israel only began to understand its own history as a divine promise when it looked back from its present to its own past and recognized God's faithfulness, a faithfulness which naturally means an expectation of future salvation for man through history and therefore looks towards the future. Looking back, we see Yahweh's faithfulness as promise; looking ahead, we see it as an expectation and continuous fulfilment, and on the basis of this faithfulness our expectation constantly opens up a new future through a history which stretches beyond us. It is therefore through the historical development of its tradition that Israel began to understand what was meant by God's promise. Because Israel remembered certain meaningful events from the past and associated them with new events of the present, both past and present illuminated each other, and thus it experienced and interpreted its history as the gradual fulfilment of a divine promise. Within this concept of history the present itself was seen as a new promise, a new door opening to a new future. And ultimately the whole earthly history becomes the unfolding of an eschatological expectation.

It is therefore a lived tradition, a history of the transmission of traditions, which underlies the Israelite's interpretation of history as a divine promise, as God's saving activity, as covenant and, implied in all this, as revelation. An event experienced by the community is handed down to future generations only in so far as, and because, it has a special meaning for that community. And the community discovers the meaning of this event because it has passed through a particular history which carries traditions and insights with it. The past event only reaches us, therefore, with the meaning it had for that community and never without it or outside it. The history of the transmission of traditions thus reveals the gradual unfolding of the meaning of the event to future generations, with all the additions and corrections which the constant reading and re-reading of the event have brought to it in the further development of history. We can only discover the meaning of a past event for us now by taking into account also the history of traditions without arbitrary interpretations. We see here the principle of hermeneutics. Only when we understand history as a critically examined history of traditions can we understand it as a promise that was lived in Israel and received its first definitive fulfilment in Jesus Christ.

If we see biblical history as an event handed down to us in a believing and critical interpretation, we can also see that the reference to the future is contained in the present of the people of God as it lives within the context of this history of traditions. 'Future' is an intrinsic dimension of present, is related to what must still happen in time without allowing us to see its future shape at present. This biblical structure of the prophecy of the future which sets the present within a living history of traditions rejects on the one hand any 'de-eschatologization' of time (there is no room for a radical eschatology of the present) and on the other hand demands a rejection of all apocalyptic elements from the expectation of the future (apocalyptic thought thinks from the future to the present).

Because of man's essential historicity, 'future' means a future starting from the present and therefore from the past. Although its actual shape remains hidden, the future is an intrinsic element in man's self-understanding. This hidden reality is therefore intrinsically related to the actuality. This has been insufficiently understood by Jürgen Moltmann.

In this sense there can be no true eschatology of the future without a certain eschatology of the present. Although the future has an element of 'not yet' in it we cannot neglect the element of 'already.' In fact, only the 'already' allows us to say anything meaningful about the still unknown future. It is therefore typical that the old testament never describes the unknown future in totally new and unexpected terms. Hope always looks for some ideal restoration, the particular features of which are supposed to be known from the past. The total picture, however, is always new. Expectation is not a state of hoping for a simple re-shaping of the past. Israel hoped for the fulfillment of what Yahweh had already done in its desire for the total achievement of it all. The re-actualization of the past in the present with an eye on the future makes Israel expect with increasing tension that future which only Yahweh can bring, and which then will be definitive, once for all. Such an expectation has nothing to do with crystal-gazing or an unveiling of the future. It is rather an insight of faith, gained by the knowledge of God's dealings with his people. Only the unconditional surrender to Yahweh's faithfulness and the living traditions that are related to it can bring any certainty about the future. In terms of man's historicity Yahweh's faithfulness is expectation of a future, certainty about the goodness of the plan of creation which is both the beginning and the *eschaton*, the ultimate end. It is 'very good' (Gen 1:31). In other words, man's future as seen by God (the bible puts these words into Yahweh's mouth), is 'very good,' a future of salvation. The lack of salvation, temporary or possibly final, is of man's own doing. It is interesting here that biblical thought about the beginning ('protology') is intertwined with eschatological thought. This protology, as formulated in the final draft of the creation story in Genesis, can only be understood on the basis of actual experience of God's faithfulness with its consequent eschatological expectations. The story of creation is therefore also an eschatological statement.

Eschaton and Future

What, however, is the connection between future and *eschaton?* O. Procksch, G. von Rad and T. Vriezen rightly maintain against V. Maag that in the old testament the belief in God's dominion is not identical with the kingdom of God in the eschatological sense. Moreover, for centuries Israel practiced its religion without expecting a hereafter. Apart from the late apocalyptic eschatology in the old testament, expressions such as 'the last days' do not refer to an existence beyond this earth, beyond history, but to a future within this world. The *eschaton* is marked by newness and universalism but it is all in a concept of history which remains on this side of the beyond. To this Ezekiel and Deutero-Isaiah add the idea of an approaching nearness. Throughout the prophetic tradition the picture of God's day of judgement is thrown on to the screen of earthly history; it is the picture of an expectation of a future in this world, this history. Only in Daniel and the very latest apocalyptic insertions into earlier prophetic traditions does the day of Yahweh put a full stop to history. The *eschaton* then refers to a situation beyond this earth, or at least to the time immediately preceding the end of time. But even in the probably late apocalyptic passage in Isaiah 24–7 the last days are still seen within the reality of the history of this world: the old people of God is then given its final eschatological status without mentioning whether history will still go on after that. Not until the book of Daniel is there question of a transcendent eschatology and is there talk of a post-historical existence, expressed in the powerful religious symbol of resurrection. That there will be a future for the historical past, and even for the dead, appears only very late in the old testament.

For centuries, therefore, the belief in Yahweh could be practiced meaningfully without the assertion of a transcendent, post-historical and final fulfillment. This development in revelation shows that one does not live religiously for the sake of the hereafter. The development of Israel's faith shows that the unquestionable value of the covenant, the actual relationship between the historic Israel and God, provides the hermeneutic context for a belief in a transcendent eschatology. The 'setting in life' of the eschatological expectation beyond this world is the temporal all-surpassing meaning of the actual relationship with the living God. This conceals the hidden urge towards a transcendent future. For some time devout Israelites had already had some inkling of the idea that even death has no power over him whom God loves. Most powerfully perhaps in Psalms 16, 49 and 73 that spiritual experience of relationship with God is expressed which would sooner or later destroy the idea of the state after death as one of excommunication from life, from life in this world with one's fellows in communion with God, and so pave the way for a transcendent eschatology. In these psalms Yahweh's faithfulness fosters the idea that love must be immortal and definitive, that through this love we know that we are in God's hand not only *in* but also *after* death. Beyond this vague hunch the psalmists had no appropriate terminology to express the certainty of this spiritual experience, and the concept of resurrection provided the first suitable formula.

The present, then, understood as the actual relationship with God and experienced historically as God's dealings with man, is not only the hermeneutic principle for the interpretation of religious expectations of the future, but also the principle which links the future of this earth with the transcendent *eschaton*. The bible gives us no anticipatory historical report on this *eschaton*. We know nothing about the transcendent last things—judgement, Christ's return, heaven, hell, purgatory—except in so far as they are already indicated in the course of historical events expressing the actual relationship between the God of the covenant and mankind, particularly in Christ, 'the last Adam,' or 'man of the *eschaton*' (1 Cor 15:45). Eschatology, therefore, does not allow us to withdraw from earthly history, because only in the depth of this history can eternity begin to take shape. The post-terrestrial *eschaton* is but a question of the manner in which what is already growing in the history of this world will receive its final fulfillment. This analysis seems to confirm Rahner's position: 'To speak from the present to the future is eschatology; to speak from the future to the present is apocalyptic.' Eschatology is the expression of the belief that history is in God's hands, that the history of the world can reach its fulfillment in communion with God and that it will be brought to this fulfillment in Christ who embodies God's promise. Eschatology does not allow us to cash in on the hereafter, but it is something to be achieved responsibly by all the faithful within the framework of our terrestrial history. Faced with the real evil existing in history, eschatology expresses the belief that the true faithful can and must bend this history into the salvation of all. This must be done within the perspective of present world history, in newness and in the context of universality. This salvation must already be achieved now in our history, in this world, and so this history becomes itself a prophecy of the final and transcendent *eschaton*. It is the promise of a new world, a powerful symbol which sets us thinking and above all acting. The credibility of this promise lies in the renewal now of our human history. Through their justification the faithful themselves become responsible for the newness of this human world whose dimension in depth will be perpetuated into eternity. For this eternity does not come after our time or our history, but is both the transcendent and the intrinsic ultimate fulfillment of this history itself.

All exegetes accept that the biblical words about the kingdom of God are connected with Jesus' own message. In Jesus the world is given the last promise. But in Jesus of Nazareth we see that the *eschaton* is a post-historical event about which we can only speak from the angle of a history understood in the terms of faith. The raising of Jesus to the status of Lord is a saving act of God which, at a point of time, turned the history which ended in his death into a fulfilled history. That is why it touches our own terrestrial history. We are faced here with a real event which is embedded in history and yet is not historical but eschatological. While the apocalyptic approach puts the *eschaton* at the end of the history of this world, Christianity has put it within history itself. Because of the ambiguity of human freedom this history remains open to the future; on the other hand, it already carries the judgement within it. For in the man Jesus the future of mankind has been revealed to us: the fulfillment of the life of Jesus himself, in both its individual and collective-social aspects.

The new world, in Jesus Christ, irrevocably promised and actually on its way, is therefore not a prefabricated reality but is coming into being as an historical process of acting-in-faith in this world. In its present realization this history is a prophetic pointer to the final fulfill-ment which can no longer be achieved or expressed in terms of terres-trial history. It does not end this terrestrial history by leaving it behind but by bringing it wholly to its fulfillment. That is why we can only speak haltingly about the final eschatological kingdom and mainly in images and symbols that have grown out of contrast experiences (the 'this-situation-should-be-changed' type) in our still growing world: 'there shall be neither mourning nor crying nor pain any more' (Rev 21:4); 'new heavens and a new earth in which righteousness dwells' (2 Peter 3:13). In the concrete the hermeneutics and exegesis of the final kingdom therefore consist mainly in the stressing of the actual commit-ment of the faithful to the renewal of this human history of ours. Only this constructive Christian activity provides a credible exegesis or inter-pretation of what we believe when, as the people of God, we confess: 'I believe in eternal life.' In other words, I believe in an earthly, historical life that is truly *life* and that is stronger than death for him who believes in the living God, who gave man the final promise of his faithfulness in Jesus Christ 'for ever and ever' and to the end of time.

The fact that transcendent eschatology arose very late in the history of revelation defends genuine religion against Freudian or marxist criti-cism which maintains that belief in the hereafter is by definition projec-tion and alienation. The joy of being able to serve Yahweh has made the believer in God's revelation keep silent about the hereafter for centu-ries in spite of the pressure of opinions that were current in neighboring cultures. Israel's greatest tragedy was that it had to make up its mind about its ideas of death, in other words, about the experience of the fact that death still snatched this living-with-God away from God's sovereignty (Deut 30:19–20). But in the end, this living-with-the-living-God on this earth had to yield its secret: such a life makes even death a relative event, it is stronger than death. There is no trace of a natural immortality of the soul in either the old or the new testament. But we do find there the primacy of the actual covenant relationship with the living God who is faithfulness and therefore also future, even for the faithful who have died. The kingdom of Yahweh cannot be reconciled with being dead. In its cultural and religious history Israel had already passed its peak before it realized—in fact, only two centuries before Jesus came—the genuine eschatological implications of its old faith and saw that history, seen as the dealings of God with man through his covenant, contained far more than could be related in a purely historical fashion. In its historicity history is a prophecy which points beyond the historical events to the transcendent *eschaton.* This means that only an analysis of the way the Christian lives in this world can tell us something in very sober terms about the great eschatological themes, resurrection, judgment, the *parousia,* the fulfillment of a bodily mankind in full communion with God, in short, about what we call 'heaven,' a reality which only man himself can twist into a negation, a self-built hell, the rejection of that love which is the foundation of this total communion.

On the basis of these few hermeneutical principles theology can be seen as the rational and meaningful unfolding of what shows itself in history. It is not the only possible rational interpretation of reality, but it can show that in its affirmation of reality the Christian faith gives a humanly meaningful, intelligible and responsible interpretation of man and his world. Thus it can enter into a genuine dialog with the many other interpretations current in this world—for the good of all.

Translated by N. D. Smith

4

The Problem of the Infallibility
of the Church's Office

1973

Man's Answer in Faith Belongs to the Content of Revelation

If it is true that an historical event can be so decisive that it has to be expressed in the language of faith, then this speaking about God's activity in history can only be meaningful if man's interpretative understanding of this in faith belongs to revelation itself. Revelation and man's interpretative understanding of revelation in faith are correlative. An historical event cannot be recognized as a decisive act of God unless it is understood and accepted on the basis of a definite experience as *de facto* determinative for our understanding of ourselves and of the whole of reality and especially of our life in practice. This is the meaning of the rather vague formula "Jesus is Lord." The Christian reply to any question about the determinative factor in their lives is to point to Jesus of Nazareth, confessed as the Christ, the only-begotten Son.

Revelation, then, is God's saving activity in history experienced and expressed by believers in answer to the question about the meaning of life. It is a reduction to call the mere fact of God's activity revelation in itself, without interpretation, or to call this interpretation as such revelation, in which case faith would be no more than a subjective view of history. Revelation includes both these aspects and, because it is only fulfilled *in* man's response, it can never be discussed in a completely objective, scientific or historically critical way.

In its aspect of knowing, faith is, moreover, an interpretative knowledge; in other words, theology as interpretation is not only valid as a reflection about faith and its content, but is also valid *in* the content of faith itself, as expressed, and *in* revelation itself, also as expressed. This interpretative—in other words, theological—aspect of the reply given by believers belongs essentially to the *content* of revelation and of faith and dogma, both in the case of the central content of faith and in that of the peripheral aspects of faith graded according to a "hierarchy of truths,"[1] and not simply to the way in which revelation and faith are expressed. The whole of revelation and of faith and dogma are *in* history. There is no zone that is immune from the storms of man's history, no zone of pure theology. God's saving activity is only formal revelation so long as it is expressed in faith, on the basis of living experience, by men who are *in* history. This makes it more difficult for us to speak about an identity of Christian faith, because that identity is so interwoven with man's history, his redemption and his integrity.

The Promise of God's Help

In itself, the Church is not able to remain faithful to this identity in an historical event, but is, as the product of men who want good but often do evil, ambiguous. The Church's faith and proclamation of that faith will not, however, cease, according to the promise expressed in the gospel of Matthew, which begins with the confession of Emmanuel, God with us (Matt. 1. 23) and ends with Emmanuel, God with us in Jesus Christ: "I am with you always, to the close of the age" (Matt. 28. 20).

The structure of the ancient covenant was basically "I shall be with you—you will be with me," yet, despite the difference between and the deep continuity of the Old and the New Testaments, the promise of this covenant is not an automatic or purely juridical guarantee of success.

In the first draft of the Constitution on the Church, the biblical mystery of the "community of the Christ" was identified simply with the Catholic Church, but in the definitive text the wording is more sensitive and finely shaded: "Haec ecclesia . . . *subsistit in* ecclesia catholica."[2] This "subsists in," meaning "is present in a veiled form," does not have any specifically scholastic significance. On the contrary, it is clear from the *acta* of the Council that the words were deliberately chosen in order to dilute the first and stronger expression of the Church's exclusive identity: "Haec ecclesia . . . *est* ecclesia catholica."[3] The commission commented: "This empirical Church reveals the mystery (of the Church), but not without shadows . . . although this lack of lustre does not make the manifestation of the mystery completely impossible" (*op. cit.*). The manifestation of the Church thus becomes manifest—or recognizable—*in* the Catholic Church "in sin and in purification."[4] Weakness and sin can only be overcome "by the power of Christ and by love" (*op. cit.*), so that it may be said that this Church is called to be "sancta simul et purificanda"—"at the same time holy and always in need of being purified."[5]

This applies to the whole Church—there is no part of its concrete life where this is not so. The Church's "remaining in the truth" and remaining perfectly faithful is made possible by the promise and the call "never to cease to renew herself."[6] Far from being triumphant in this claim to "indefectibility," the Church manifests a weakness in which only God's grace is triumphant.

This indefectibility is, moreover, not a static, "essential" characteristic of the Church, but something which involves the Church's dynamic and existential faith in the promise. The truth of revelation is a truth of witness, in which the bond between the person and message is always present. The promise of indefectibility is made *interior* in the Church itself in and through faith, hope and love which always urge the Christian to *metanoia* and renewal. This promise is not merely juridical and without historical form. In the Constitution on the Church, this indefectibility is attributed to the constant activity of the Holy Spirit: "so that . . . moved by the Holy Spirit, (the Church) may never cease to renew herself."[7] The Holy Spirit, the *telos* or End of the Trinity, brings, as a gift to the Church the Church itself to the End.

All this is said of the Church as a whole, before any distinction is made between the community and its office-bearers; the promise applies to both. The indefectibility of the Church is faithfulness expressed in a history, not only of human attitudes, but also of grace itself, going before man, so that the Church, in its concrete historical form, is always limping behind it. The real history of the Church, then, is a history of constant decline and renewal. What can and what cannot be reformed are always so inextricably interwoven that the Church cannot always distinguish them. By virtue of grace, the Church is at the same time both *metanoia* and self-correction and subject both to the promise and to the New Testament warning, "judgment begins with the household of God" (I Pet. 4. 17–18).

Indefectibility of Office

After outlining the ecclesiological background to the problem, we must now turn to the concept of the infallibility of office as expressed in the papacy and the Church's councils. All the Christian denominations believe, after all, in God's promise of help to the "communities of God," that the message of the Gospel will never cease to be heard and that this lasting quality implies a "remaining in the truth."

These two aspects are inseparable—the "Church" that no longer "remains in the truth" is no longer a "community of God" or "of Christ." The context of the Matthaean logion, "I shall be with you," is Jesus' speaking, about the "baptizing" and "teaching" Church (Matt. 28. 18–20). The promise is made to the Church's *confession* in both functions. It is hardly possible to accept, from the ecclesiological point of view, that the Church, in its confession of baptism, can "remain in the truth" if there is no promise that its teaching will have a similar lasting value. The Church's "remaining in the truth" implies faithfulness in the teaching Church.

The same "presence in a veiled form" (*subsistere in*) of the biblical mystery in the Roman Catholic Church applies not only to the community of God as a whole, but also to the Church's confession in the teaching of those holding office. There is, in other words, no simple identity between the dogmatic confession of faith and the Word of God. Before discussing what is meant by the dogma of infallibility, however, I should like to outline the context within which this pronouncement ought to be examined if its significance is to be properly understood and it is not to contradict all the concrete facts of human experience and thought.

The Perspectivism of Every Assertion of Truth

An assertion may be both true and untrue according to the sphere or context of questioning and understanding in which it is situated. This has been said often enough by linguistic analysts and, in a different context, by Hans Küng[8] and now Bernard Lonergan has written that the relativists make three basic premises. The first is that the significance of every assertion is relative, that is, it is related to its context. The second is that every context is subject to change and is situated within a process of development and/or decline. Thirdly, it is not possible to predict what the context will be in the future.[9] He then goes on to say that these premises are, as such, correct. It does not, for example, follow from the first premise that the context cannot be replaced. Within the replaced context, a correct assertion is recognizably true and cannot at the same time be untrue. With regard to the second premise, it may happen that an assertion which was true in its own context will be incorrect in a different context. The fact that it can be proved by an historical reconstruction of the original context that this assertion was true in that context means that we can recognize the truth that was originally intended.[10]

Truth can only be attained from an historically situated perspective—it is not itself "perspectivistic," but absolute, yet we can only possess it in an historical, perspectivistic or relative way. The historical sphere or context of questioning within which an assertion provides an answer also determines the truth of that assertion. The interpretative question is the real crux of the whole process of interpretation and of the answer or interpretative assertion, especially if interpretative knowledge is sought. The "hermeneutical situation," the situational context from which the interpreter questions what is to be interpreted, is historical and therefore variable. All these components of the "context" are concentrated in the questions that are asked of what has to be interpreted and this marks off the "sphere of understanding" or background to the interpretative question which guides the whole process of understanding.

G. Vass rightly insists that one aspect of every question is orientated towards the object, so that the situation within which it is asked has a fundamental significance with regard to the answer that will be given.[11] The question anticipates *possible* alternatives and the verifiable certainty of the preferred alternative. Without this orientation, it is meaningless or else impossible to ask an interpretative question. If the answer is already known, the question is unreal and a question cannot be asked unless possible alternatives are anticipated in it—this is a *necessary* condition for any search for truth. What is more, the possibility that there are sufficient reasons for one of the possible alternatives to be preferred as an answer must also be anticipated. In a word, what is contained within the norm of what is to be interpreted and within the framework of the questioning and its anticipations is "interpretative knowledge."

With regard to the truth of an interpretation, we are clearly wrong to call a conclusion true or false, thus paying attention *only* to the "answer in itself," that is, to the final assertion, without taking into consideration the questioning within its historical context. In *interpretative* knowledge, the ultimate assertion is only true or false within the context of questioning and understanding. In other words, the whole historical context of the questioning itself is an integral part of the whole interpretative truth. I would therefore agree here with Lévi-Strauss when he insisted that the wise man is not the man who gives true answers, but the man who asks the right questions.[12]

This is not a form of relativism, but a recognition that coming to the truth is a continuous historical process. It would undoubtedly lead to relativism if the problem of truth were regarded as finally settled, in which case truth would be the correct answer to correct, historically determined questions and would no longer have any universal significance. In that case, "true" is what provides the most coherent answer to a contingent questioning. Truth is thus an inner coherence between question and answer, on the one hand, a discovery of a certain historical situation which is expressed in a certain form of questioning as a problem and, on the other, the most suitable answer given to that questioning.[13] The ultimate answer to the question of truth cannot be found in this correlation because truth is orientated towards a universal consensus. The correlation between a correct question and a correct answer is not the universal truth towards which man consciously tends, but man who lives in history cannot dispense with historical perspectivism.

This means that truth, which is always sought within a constantly changing situation of question and answer and a basically historical contingency, is never found only in *my* interpretation of reality, but only in my going beyond my own historical answer. In other words, the historically situated answer is only "true" in so far as it is included in a continuous historical process. Within the current of history, each human being has here and now, that is, "perspectivistically," a place where he is invited to ask a question that no one else can ask.[14] However historically determined my question and my answer may be, my fundamental need is to say something that is valid here and now and at the same time universal. It is, in other words, only when my truth is played off against the other person's truth in dialog that we are really *on the way towards* the truth in history. Each man needs the other person's truth both of the past and of the future in order to come to the fullness of truth; as Paul Ricoeur has said, the truth is the *magnet* of our articulations. A true assertion is the result of our seizing hold of the correct perspective of truth within an historically determined situation of question and answer.

The Perspectivism of the Articulations of Faith

As I have already said, revelation is God's saving activity in human history experienced and expressed by the community of believers who interpret it. In that case, the Christian confession of faith comes within the category of interpretative knowledge and shares the historical nature of the situation of question and answer.

Dogmatic definitions have at times been put forward by the Church as an expression of authentic Christian faith, whereas at other times this literal articulation has been condemned by the same Church. A few examples of this may show how the historically determined situation of question and answer and man's seizing hold of the correct objective perspective which transcends that situation are both fundamental to the Church's definitions of faith. The early anti-Pelagian pronouncements can be contrasted with the Church's condemnation of the teaching of M. de Bay, Jansen and Quesnel to provide a good illustration of what I mean. Both in the early documents (the *Indiculus Pseudo-Caelestini*, DS 239, which is of doubtful dogmatic value, the Second Council of Orange, DS 383, and the Synod of Quiercy, DS 622) and in the more recent texts (condemning the reformers and the Jansenists, DS 1515 and 1388), the Church's attitude towards the effect of sin on human freedom is made clear. In the first case, the Church declares that man's freedom is lost through (original) sin, whereas in the second case the false teachers are condemned for asserting that man's freedom is lost through (original) sin. The same articulation or statement thus expresses Christian faith in the first case and false teaching in the second. Other examples are the early and medieval Church's condemnation of the teaching that man could do good without grace (DS 240, 242, 243, 244; 379, 390, 392, 393, 395; 725) in contrast to the later Church's defense of this statement against de Bay and the Jansenists (DS 1927–1930; 1937, 1965, 2308, 2438–2442) and the early Church's defense of the assertion that sinners and unbelievers could only perform sinful actions (DS 392) as against the later condemnation of the same statement when it was made by the Jansenists (DS 1925, 1927, 1935, 1938, 1940; also Trent, 1557).

This problem can be solved if we bear in mind that the same statement may be materially both true and false according to the historical context of question and answer within which it is placed. The early texts express a reaction against the Pelagian optimism of natural ethics, whereas the later assertions are a reaction against the pessimistic view of corrupt human freedom. What is more, a different understanding of freedom is reflected in each case. The early Church saw freedom as "freedom to good" and sinful action—in modern terminology, a free self-determination to evil—as an absence of freedom and slavery.[15] Later, however, the Church integrated Aristotle's anthropological concept into its earlier Augustinian view of freedom, so that what was correctly defended by the early Church was also correctly condemned by the later Church. The Augustinian approval and the Aristotelian disapproval do not formally apply to the same assertion, because both statements were made within different historical contexts of understanding. The same distinction applies to what is materially the same assertion that there cannot and that there can be ethically good actions without grace. The early Church had a specifically Christian view of ethical goodness as a human action measured against its saving aspect. The later Church, on the other hand, was aware of the anthropological aspect of the goodness of human activity.

Any scandal caused by such antithetic statements made by the Church can be overcome by bearing in mind that they were made in an historical situation of question and answer. In condemning Jansenism, however, did the Church sufficiently respect the Jansenists' Augustinian and therefore conservative context of questioning and understanding in the light of its new and so to speak progressive understanding? One of the chief causes of polarization in human communications is the existence of radically different spheres of understanding at one and the same period. The Jansenists can rightly be accused of "conservatism" in their strict adherence of the literal teaching of Augustine and the early Church and their blindness to the contemporary historical context. What we cannot, however, say *a priori* is that their assertions, situated within a context of understanding which had become antiquated, were *per se* incorrect precisely within that context. It is clear that some awareness of the reason for this mutual lack of understanding was present in the Church, since the general condemnation of Jansenist teaching was modified from "heretical" to "offensive to ordinary believers" (*offensiva piarum auriculorum*).

I have deliberately chosen examples of the Church's condemnation of "conservative" teaching, not because I wanted to contrast "conservatism" with "progressivism," but because I wanted to draw attention to the question of *creative faithfulness* to the Gospel, a faithfulness which is only possible in a changing and developing history. Furthermore, there is sufficient evidence in the life and practice of the Church to show that the same assertion may be both true and untrue according to the context of understanding and to semantic usage. The consequence of this is that it is not possible to speak in advance about the "irrevocable" character of certain pronouncements made by the Church's teaching office if the historical context of questioning and understanding and the changing semantic usage of language are disregarded. If the charism of infallibility is to be at all meaningful, it must have a special function within this context. What is more, it is not possible for the teaching Church to speak of "heterodoxy" without having previously examined its own context of questioning and understanding and without having ensured that it is not projecting its own questions into the mind of the author whose work is being examined. The teaching Church may, on the other hand, well have a pastoral duty to draw the attention of believers to the possibility of misunderstanding to which certain writings may give rise.

A Legitimate or a Necessary Process?

Another very important question has, however, to be answered before we can discuss the First Vatican Council's dogma of infallibility—is the interpretation that has been practiced throughout the Church's history a *necessary* process, in view of the origins of the Christian Church, or is it simply a *legitimate* process, in view of the historical contingency of the questions?[16]

If our human affirmations of truth are conditioned by the historical situation of question and answer within which these affirmations are made, we must, on the basis of this historical contingency, consciously admit that our articulations of our knowledge of truth, in so far as they are true, are legitimate but not necessary. Dogma might, for instance, have developed along entirely different lines if the historical models of interpretation had been different. But, even within a "system immanent" development, new experiences exert pressure on earlier models, in which case we have to choose between two possibilities. We may leave the earlier model unchanged and try to let it absorb the new experiences. In this case, new "system immanent" difficulties, which can only be dealt with by applying very subtle distinctions, accumulate until the earlier model is broken open. The alternative is to replace this earlier model by a perhaps provisional model which will enable the new experiences to be better accommodated and understood.[17] This second model gives us the key by which legitimate differences between many of the interpretations of the Eastern churches and many of those of the Latin Church can be explained. "Remaining in the truth" is a concrete historical reality, not a supra-historical reality for the churches.

Infallibility

The dogma of infallibility, as defined by the First Vatican Council, must now be considered within the historical context of question and answer if it is to be at all meaningful. It is clear from recent controversy that the term "infallibility" as applied to the Church's "remaining in the truth" is widely regarded as unsatisfactory. Many Catholics are uncertain as to the precise scope and meaning of the dogma itself and Walter Kasper has undoubtedly expressed, in the introduction to his critical defense of Hans Küng's argument, what many Catholics believe.[18] Other Christians sometimes have the impression that Catholics have to "pretend" that papal infallibility is virtually all-embracing[19] and the Church has never officially protested against this very non-Catholic idea.

Infallibility as such is an attribute of truth; they have virtually the same meaning. Since the time of Descartes, the question has already been, however, how can we be *sure* that we are "in the truth"? In Christian terms, the question is whether "infallibility," as a form of the

Church's "remaining in the truth" can be localized. All Christians confess the infallibility of the universal Church, but both Luther and Calvin restricted this to the Word of God, believing that the universal Church, as a "creature of the Word," could not err in its confession of faith, but at the same time that it was possible to verify jurisdictionally the Church's infallible pronouncements.[20] Most Protestants would insist that the concrete infallibility of Roman Catholic teaching cannot be verified, because God's promise is grace, not something at the "disposal" of any body such as the Church. The community of believers as a whole is infallible in its confession of faith, but the presence of the Church's "remaining in the truth" can never be guaranteed—it surprises us by its presence. It is only in Scripture that there is, according to the reformed churches, any verifiable authority of the Church's infallibility and Luther himself insisted that if there were no articulations of faith there could be no real confession of faith.[21] It is clear, then, that Protestantism is, like Catholicism, challenged by the difficulties presented by linguistic analysis to the concept of infallibility.

According to the Roman Catholic view, the Church's "remaining in the truth" is above all an interiorization of God's promise of grace in the Church. Nonetheless, the presence of infallibility in all believers as a surprise, in the Protestant sense, is also a fundamental aspect of the Catholic view of infallibility. The whole "body of the faithful, anointed as they are by the Holy One, cannot err in matters of belief," the Second Vatican Council declared.[22] The Holy Spirit is always present in the whole community's confession and practice of faith, the truth surprising us by being present not only in the official Church. The so-called Protestant view, then, is really a universally Christian *consensus* and it is this fundamental form of the Church's infallibility that provides the key to all other forms, including the dogma as defined by the First Vatican Council (DS 3074).

In universal consensus with all the Christian churches, then, the Roman Catholic Church goes on to speak of the "infallibility of office," the subject of which is, on the one hand, the world episcopate in unity with the Pope and, on the other, the Pope in communion with the world's bishops and the universal faith of all Christians. According to the definition of Vatican I (DS 3074), infallibility is not so much concerned with the material content of the articulation of faith as such as with the meaning of the statement by the Church's teaching office (DS 3020). Certain acts or judgments by certain persons or authoritative bodies are called "infallible" when they are made *ex cathedra* and this term is more precisely defined as concerning the Pope when he speaks as the pastor and teacher formally of *all* believers in defining what is expressed as *revealed*.[23] The First Vatican Council did not *define*, however, if there is a papal—or conciliar—definition *ex cathedra*.[24] In one of the official *Notificationes* appended to the Constitution on the Church of the Second Vatican Council and answering a question about the "theological qualification" to be attached to the constitution, the commission of theologians declared: "As is self-evident, the Council's text must always be interpreted in accordance with the general rules which are known to all."[25]

The statement made in this *Notificatio* confronts us with the very real and difficult problem of the "meta-language," in other words, the statement about a statement. If an "infallible" statement is made, we can only be certain about the infallibility of that statement if we are told at another time in an infallible way that it is an infallible statement. Otherwise, we can, according to the rules of the meta-language, only know in a fallible way whether the concrete statement is intended by the Church to be infallible. Expressed in this way, of course, the problem of infallibility would seem to be insoluble. Vatican I was, however, not aware of this particular problem—it lay outside the historical context of the Council's questioning and understanding. For the time being, we may say that later history has shown clearly enough that, whatever the significance of Vatican I may have been, it did not or could not answer questions that are now, a century later, extremely important.

Since Vatican I, Heidegger's "truth does not originally reside in the *statement*"[26] inevitably reminds the Catholic theologian of Thomas Aquinas' "the act of faith is ultimately directed towards what is expressed (the *res*), not towards the formula itself (*enuntiabile*) in which it is expressed."[27] This extremely "modern" statement of the medieval theologian has often been quoted, but usually outside the context in which it was originally made. Thomas wrote with two contemporary ways of thinking in mind—illuminism, which stressed man's wordless approach to the mystery, and "rationalism," which emphasized the articulation of truth. His own position was between these two extremes: "secundum aliquid *utrumque* est verum";[28] in other words, there is an element of truth in both ways of thinking, and neither should be lost. It is above all a question of the mystery itself, but, Thomas insisted, this mystery has to be approached through the medium of historical articulation, in which the *res* itself is, imperfectly perhaps, expressed. Through our relative historical articulations (*enuntiabilia*), we reach the truth (*attingere veritatem*), which is never possessed, but only "aimed at" and which is a *docta ignorantia*, a "negative theology" or conscious unknowing which is only possible on the basis of a "positive knowing" that is non-explicit but indirectly expressed in negative dialectics. It is this that bears all knowledge of the truth.[29] In this sense, all judgment of the truth has an irrevocable element, but it has it in a revocable manner.

The Judgment of Truth in a Context of Faith

We can never reach the Absolute *directly* in our consciousness-in-the-world, but we are given it *directly*, as a mystery, in God's revelation of himself, experienced and expressed in the history of the Christian faith, although this gift is made thematically or explicitly only in an *indirect* historical expression. On the basis of this new situation, however, this indirect "secular" expression is qualified inwardly, by virtue of the "light of faith," by the fact that the Absolute is given *directly*. Because of this special event *in* ordinary human structures, the pure conservation of this eschatological content of faith "calls" for the charismatic help of the Spirit.

I would, on this basis, venture to suggest a rather complicated formulation which, I believe, both guarantees the real *meaning* of the dogma of infallibility in a completely *Catholic* way and at the same time also does full justice to the *historicity* of the Christian confession of faith. It is this. In its offices or ministries (the papacy, the episcopate, etc.), the Church is able, at a given moment and within a concrete historical context of understanding, to express the Christian confession of faith *correctly, legitimately, faithfully* and with authoritative *binding* force. It can do this even though such concepts as "infallible," "irrevocable" and *ex sese* are disputable as historically situated terms implying a certain view of truth and belonging to a certain ecclesiological context. It can also do it although no concrete formulation or articulation (*enuntiabile*) can claim to stand up to the test of time.

If the promise of God's help is to be at all meaningful in history, those holding office must therefore have authority to define Christian faith *here and now*. The articulation of this judgment will, however, always be conditioned by history. We may go further and say that the mystery of Christ will also usually be expressed in a negative, indirect way, at any given moment in history, that is, by the exclusion of a concrete alternative, although this generally takes place through the medium of a concrete affirmation of another alternative.

An example of this is the Tridentine definition of original sin, which says that all men sin "not like Adam" or "not by imitation of Adam," but "by reproduction" (*generatione*) from a sinful human race (DS 790; see also DS 418, 102, 103a). The statement "not by imitation," taken together with the statement "by reproduction," which was, at the time of Trent, all that was considered important, does not *per se* exclude other alternatives which were at that time not envisaged for anthropological reasons. It is clear that "by reproduction" was also intended by the Tridentine dogma on the basis of what was primarily intended, namely, "not by imitation." Since dogmatic statements are expressed in universally human concepts that are not in themselves dogmatic, it is, in a later situation of changed anthropological attitudes, where, for example, the "not by imitation" can be safeguarded by other meaningful models and the "by reproduction" is no longer required, possible for the articulation of a dogma to be discarded without any necessary denial of the dogma itself.

This is a clear indication of the fact that even a so-called infallible definition is an *historical* event in the Church and that it is, precisely as an historical event, subject to the "official charism of the truth" (DS 3071). Not to choose one of the implied alternatives in the historical question about the content of faith at a given moment in history, when faithfulness to the Gospel is at stake, might be tantamount to failing to give an historically faithful answer to the meaningful question: "But who do you say that I am?" (Mark 8. 29; Matt. 16. 15; Luke 9. 20). This is inevitably reminiscent of Paul Ricoeur's comment on the painful necessity to choose, in the vicissitudes of history, the positive in the sadness of the finite. There is no absolute way of answering this question and, because the relationship with the present context of understanding is also *co*-determinative with regard to the faithful answer to the question, no answer in its materially literal sense, that is, outside its context of questioning, is irrevocably the ultimate answer that will be valid for all time. On the other hand, as a faithful answer at a given time and within a given context of understanding, the dogmatic answer is certainly our model, our norm when we attempt to give an answer in a different historical situation.

If, then, God does not help those holding office in the Church to express, within a concrete historical context of understanding, the Christian confession of faith correctly, legitimately, faithfully and with binding force, his promise that the Church will "remain in the truth" will remain empty. It is in connection with this kind of judgment borne by the full charism of the Church's office that the Roman Catholic Church has used the term "infallibility," which is ultimately the infallible guidance of the Holy Spirit manifested in an imperfect historical objectivization in the Church. It would, I think, be much more suitable now, in a different historical context of understanding, to speak of a correct, legitimate judgment concerning faith which is faithful to the Gospel and ultimately binding on all believers. This concept would be more acceptable than the term "infallibility," which is surrounded by ideological and sociological difficulties that seem almost insoluble. The significance of a statement about faith is, after all, partly determined at least by how it functions in practice and a correct dogma may well function wrongly in the life of the Church.

What, then, is its concrete value as truth? (I use the word "concrete" advisedly here and am not referring to its "abstract" truth.) The unity of theory and practice therefore needs to be reformulated if a dogma is to function correctly and this only happens when the dogma is subjected to the criticism of the totality of faith within the whole of history.

Two factors need to be preserved in the reformulation. On the one hand, the lasting confession of faith of the universal Church contains a dogmatic judgment about faith on the part of those holding office. (This aspect was called "infallibility" by the First Vatican Council.) On the other hand, this "infallibility of office" and the "indefectibility" of the community of believers form a structural and organic unity but are distinguished from each other, despite the fact that the "consensus of the Church" itself is expressed in the judgment of those in office. The Pope and the bishops are, in this, subject to the Word of God and to the norm of that Word from which the whole community of believers lives.[30]

Two factors are similarly present in the Catholic hermeneutical circle. On the one hand, dogma is interpreted with Scripture constantly in mind. This means on the one hand that Scripture always forms part of the context within which any given dogma is understood. On the other hand, Scripture is at the same time always brought into relationship with dogma. Every dogmatic definition has therefore to be interpreted not only by using the method of historical and literary criticism of the text and its historical and social context, but also within the unity of the total history of faith beginning with Scripture. If it is not clearly appreciated that dogmatic definitions are conditioned by this non-dogmatic context of understanding which is neither revealed nor "infallible," the purely material repetition of an early dogma can result in a complete misunderstanding of the teaching that the Church at that time wished to safeguard.

Translated by David Smith

NOTES

1. Decree *Unitatis redintegratio* on Ecumenism, II.
2. Constitution *Lumen gentium* on the Church, 8.
3. "Loco *est* dicitur *subsistit in*, ut expressio melius concordet cum affirmatione de elementis ecclesialibus quae alibi adsunt" (*Relatio de singulis numeris, Relatio* in n. 8, p. 25).
4. *Op. cit.*, p. 23.
5. *Lumen gentium*, 8.
6. *Op. cit.*, 9.
7. *Op. cit.*, 9.

8. *Infallible? An Enquiry* (London, 1971).

9. B. Lonergan, *Doctrinal Pluralism* (Milwaukee, 1971), p. 10.

10. *Op. cit.*, pp. 10–11.

11. G. Vass, "On the Historical Structure of Christian Truth," in *The Heythrop Journal*, 9 (1968), pp. 129–42, 274–89; Vass's answer to the question of truth is, in my opinion, insufficient.

12. *Mythologiques*, I (Paris, 1971), p. 19.

13. P. Ricoeur *Histoire et vérité* (Paris, 1955), p. 52.

14. *Op. cit.*, pp. 54–5.

15. In the Middle Ages, we find Thomas Aquinas accepting this Augustinian concept of freedom, but at the same time linking it with the Aristotelian concept; see *De veritate*, q. 22, a. 6.

16. This has been most clearly formulated as a *question* by M. Wiles in *The Making of Christian Doctrine* (Cambridge, 1967), pp. 1–17.

17. In this context, B. Welte has rightly spoken of a sensational age in man's thinking, of periodic cracks appearing in the mind of the Christian community; see H. Schlier and others, *Zur Frühgeschichte der Christologie* (Freiburg, 1970), pp. 100–17.

18. W. Kasper, "Zur Diskussion um das Problem der Unfehlbarkeit," *Stimmen der Zeit*, 188 (1971), pp. 363–5.

19. I have even met Catholics who thought that the nomination of a bishop by the Pope was an "infallible" act.

20. See, for example, E. Jüngel, *Unterwegs zur Sache* (Munich, 1972), p. 195.

21. *De servo arbitrio*, 1225 (WA 18, 603, 28–9).

22. Constitution *Lumen gentium* on the Church, 12.

23. I agree with G. Thils that the Church's definitions, with or without an *anathema*, about truths that are *not* revealed are not included in the statements which the First Vatican Council *intended* to be regarded as *ex cathedra;* see G. Thils, *L'infaillibilité pontificale* (Gembloux, 1969), pp. 234–46.

24. See W. Kasper, *op. cit.* (footnote 18), p. 368.

25. *Constitutiones, Decreta, Declarationes* (Conc. Vat. II) (Vatican City, 1966), p. 214.

26. *Vom Wesen der Wahrheit* (Frankfurt, 3rd edn., 1954), p. 12.

27. *Summa Theologiae*, II–II, q. 1, a. 2, ad 2.

28. *Op. cit.*, a. 2, in c.

29. See my article, "The Value of our Speech about God and of our Concepts of Faith," in *Concept of Truth and Theological Renewal* (London and Sydney, 1968), pp. 5–29.

30. Dogmatic Constitution *Dei Verbum* on Revelation, 10.

5

Critical Theories and Christian Political Commitment

1973

The questions that I have to try to answer in this article are these. Have the contemporary emancipation movements had any influence on the critical attitude of Christian communities? What impulses can possibly emanate from the so-called critical theories and what effects do they have on praxis in the community? Finally, are there any limits to this?[1]

Emancipation Movements and Critical Theories

1. Under Roman law, man's legal status in the establishment was either that of mancipation, in which case he was made a slave by the symbolic act of "taking by the hand," or that of manumission, when he was freed from slavery, or symbolically "sent from the hand" of his master. In the Enlightenment, this emancipation was based on man's courage to "use his intellect without the guidance of others" and the emancipated, free man was one who "uses his intellect publicly at all times."[2]

We have in recent years become aware of the possible obstruction of the hermeneutical process and of mutual understanding among people by the structures of society, giving rise to a political dimension in the process of discovering the truth. What is more, the need to change structures that have become repressive has similarly become an essential aspect of the process of universal understanding and a prerequisite for mutual agreement among men.

One of the most important consequences of this movement of emancipation, which began with the Enlightenment and has continued unabated ever since, has been that authority together with all traditions, institutions and norms can no longer be justified simply by the fact that these already exist in society. They can only be justified in the light of human reason. Enlightened reason has become the principle of non-violent, free communication, which rejects everything that is repressive or oppressive in society and provides the means of solving all human conflicts and contradictions. The Enlightenment initiated the modern movement of emancipation, with the criticism of established religion, the abolition of slavery, the creation of parliamentary government and the struggle for civil rights in the West. What is more, the Christian critical faculty was developed not directly from the Bible or theology, but indirectly, via human reasoning.

2. In the past decade, our attitude towards this movement of emancipation which was initiated by the Enlightenment has undergone a certain change. We recognize, for example, that, during the Enlightenment, the tendency towards freedom was subject to different historical conditions from those prevailing today. In the past, God was held responsible for the evil conditions in the world that he ruled in his providence. This earlier theodicy ("justice of God") has now been replaced, since, with the Enlightenment, man has come to be regarded as the subject and the producer of his own history, by an "anthropodicy" ("justice of man"), a concrete criticism of man in society.

The advocates of these modern critical theories are without any doubt following closely the tradition of the movement towards freedom that began with the Enlightenment. They approach it, however, as twentieth-century liberals or socialists and above all as men liberated from the tutelage of religion. The most important of these critical theories relating to the movement of "emancipative freedom" have been elaborated by Ernst Bloch, who has criticized socialism for having neglected the "warm current"—the utopia—of Marxism, Herbert Marcuse, who has accused modern society of being "one-dimensional," and the members of the so-called Frankfurt school, Max Horkheimer, Theodor Adorno and Jürgen Habermas.

Following the rational principle of the Enlightenment, the industrial countries of the West have developed science and technology to the point where they have become indispensable factors in the process of emancipation. The originators of the contemporary critical theories, analyzing the positivist assumptions underlying modern society with the conscious aim of furthering this process, have exposed certain alarming side-effects resulting from the "one-way traffic" of a society so firmly based on science and technology. One obvious result is that there is no possibility of an alternative way of life, nor is there much chance that true humanity or what Kant called the "good life" will survive. As Adorno has said, "the consequence of the rational and systematic control by industrial society of man's whole being, even his inner being, is that it is not really possible for any man in the modern world to live according to his own decisions."[3]

This tendency in industrial society has caused the emancipation movement of the Enlightenment to peter out and concern on the part of very many members of society for the welfare of all men to dwindle away. Almost all decisions concerning society are now in the hands of a few technocrats or politicians, usually in sharp competition with each other for ultimate control, while most people remain silent and indifferent. The main concern is that the social system should function more and more perfectly in all its sub-divisions, while questions such as "why?" or "where is it leading" are lost in the shadows. We are constantly confronted with the image of "a comfortable, smooth, reasonable, democratic unfreedom,"[4] an anonymous compulsion of which many people are barely conscious.

It cannot be denied that Christians who are attempting to adapt the Church to a modern society which they have not yet subjected to critical scrutiny have much to learn from these critical theories, which have brought to light so many new forms of inhumanity caused by the present social system. The Church should above all pay attention to the just criticism that these uncritical attempts are in fact a legitimation of the *status quo* in society.

It is also remarkable how many of these originators of critical theories have come from Judaism and are therefore in the now secularized prophetic and critical tradition of the Old Testament and of the hope of the coming of a new, free, humane and just Kingdom of God. Even those who are not themselves Jews are influenced by the Jewish leaders of the movement, Horkheimer, Adorno and Bloch. What is more, the original "emancipative" inspiration of the Enlightenment is clearly reflected in a new form in this modern movement.

Marcuse, for example, cannot find any meaningful way out of the inner contradictions inherent in modern society. The will to renew society must come from inwardly renewed man, but a vicious circle exists because certain outward factors which are favorable to the renewal of society are also necessary for this inner renewal.[5] The only meaningful action that is possible in such circumstances is the "great refusal." This includes, on the one hand, a utopian element, a refusal to forget that it could be different, and, on the other hand, an aspect of contestation, a refusal to join in the game and a permanent criticism of the established order.[6]

Habermas is clearly dissatisfied with the model of interpretation used, not only by Marcuse, but also by Marx and Max Weber and has insisted that the concrete form of modern society is determined by the relationship between work or technical interest and communicative action or hermeneutical interest. In modern capitalist society, there is a constant danger that rational, systematic action—what Horkheimer has called "instrumental thought"—will become completely autonomous and that society will be disposed of in a purely material way, becoming a self-regulating system governed by the new "substitute ideology" of technocracy.[7] Emancipation from nature is obstructed by this process and nature itself is excessively exploited with a resulting disturbance in man's environment. It also causes a disruption of communication between men and this in turn gives rise to repression and oppression in society. On the basis of this progressively rational and systematic activity, there is an increasing danger that man himself will become a piece of "manipulable technique."

Habermas believes that these side-effects of the emancipation movement that had its origin in the Enlightenment principle of rationality can only be overcome if we return to the fundamental inspiration of the Enlightenment itself. "The basis of the Enlightenment," he has asserted, "is that science is bound to the principle that all discussion must be free from established power structures and to no other principle."[8] This is why he is convinced that there can be only one way of achieving in complete freedom a "universal consensus" about what is true and good for man, and that is by theoretically anticipating an "ideal" situation in which dialog is mature and free from coercion.[9]

Habermas' critical theory is indissolubly linked with a "revolutionary praxis," but he takes care to make a distinction between theory and praxis here: "The consequence of the systematic unity of theory and praxis is not a unity of scientific analysis and direct preparation for political action. This is why an appeal to the unity of theory and praxis cannot form the basis of a demand for an institutional unity of science and preparation for action. It is necessary to separate both spheres. . . . Between science and planning for action are structural differences, which call for a clear institutional division between the two. If they are identified, both are harmed—science is corrupted under the pressure of praxis and political action is led astray by a pseudo-scientific alibi."[10] This is one of the reasons why the "New Left" in Germany dissociated itself from Habermas and it is a clear indication of a loss of solidarity among the members of the so-called "Frankfurt school."

Have These Critical Theories Influenced the Politically Committed "Critical Communities"?

To my knowledge, there is no reference at all to these critical theories in Dorothee Sölle's "political evening prayer" at Cologne, which is the document of one of the most outstanding politically committed "critical communities" of our times.[11] This shows, I think, how careful one has to be not to speak too soon of a direct influence of these critical theories on critical Christian communities. During a four-month lecture tour of American universities early in 1971, when I came into contact with many critical groups of politically committed Christian students, I met no one who had even heard of Habermas.[12] What is more, it was only among similar students at Berkeley in California that the Frankfurt school was known and then only indirectly.[13] There were, however, active groups and a professor, who had participated in the ecumenical celebration during the student uprising in Paris in May 1968, told me that, apart from two leaders of the uprising, none of the politically committed students had at that time read any of the critical theories, although most of them had heard of the theories of Marcuse. Finally, it is certain that politically committed parishes, like Don Mazzi's in Isolotto, have no direct or indirect relations with any critical theories.

What is quite clear, however, is that, partly because of the influence of the speed of modern information services, which expose abuses in any part of the world to people everywhere, the spirit of contestation has become very widespread in recent years. We have become very conscious of the contrasts in world society—between groups in our own countries and between the prosperous and the underdeveloped countries. There have also been popular scientific prognoses concerning the year 2000 and the urgent need to take counter-measures now to avert disaster. Finally, there is a general anti-institutional and anti-ideological feeling resulting from a meaningless suffering imposed by bureaucracy. All these phenomena have given rise to a widespread malaise in society, a malaise made more acute by the fact that so many young people—"hippies" and others—have opted out of a society that seems to them to be meaningless.

Signs of a "counter-culture" and a "new consciousness," an "anti-history" existing alongside the "official" history, indicate clearly enough that our society has in a sense reached a dead end. Criticism of this society in a spirit of sharp contestation has led to the development, at the level of systematic thought, of critical theories and, at the level of Christian praxis, of politically committed critical communities.

Whereas the Church has, until quite recently, been judged only according to evangelical or theological criteria, it has now come to be regarded as one part of the whole complex establishment of society and as such subject to the same criticism as such institutions as parliament, the legal system, state education, and so on, all of which share in the evils of society. All these structures are so closely interrelated that, in remaining aloof from political contestation, especially in the case of any struggle between those in power and the "poor," is in fact a pronounced favouring of those in power. It is above all this situation which has made many Christian communities critical not only of society as a whole, but of the institutional Church in particular. To regard this as an infiltration of un-Christian, even demonic elements into the Church is to be blind to the "signs of the times" and is attributable to a false ideology or to wrong information.

The specifically Christian aspect of this criticism of the Church and society comes from a new understanding of Jesus of Nazareth and the Kingdom of God, often stimulated by study at various levels. Although some recent popular works have provided an exaggerated and historically distorted picture of Jesus as a revolutionary engaged in political contestation, others are exegetically more sound in their presentation of the political relevance of the appearance of Jesus as a political figure.[14]

Because of the present historical situation and a new understanding of the historical Jesus, these critical communities on the one hand long for freedom, humanity, peace and justice in society and, on the other, resist the power structures that threaten these values by repression or oppression. What J. Jüngel has called "a Kingdom of God mindful of humanity," a rule that has been handed down to us in the tradition of the Old and New Testaments, inevitably makes Christians feel at one with the contemporary emancipation movements, although they have a critical attitude towards their violent and one-sided tendencies and subject them to the criterion of the "life praxis of Jesus."

It would be quite wrong to accuse these Christian critical communities of being inspired by Marxist infiltrators, above all because there is so much Marxist criticism of the Marxist system and because there are social evils in Marxist communist societies just as there are under capitalism. What Christian critical communities have derived from Marxism are very valuable aids to the analysis of society. The Marxist system, however, is subjected to sharp criticism. It cannot, of course, be denied that there are Marxist-Christian student cells in many countries. It would, however, be a mistake to think that all student and other communities are of this kind and, especially in the case of Latin America, where all freedom movements are labeled as communist, it is important to take this idea of Marxist infiltration with a grain of salt.

Christian Limits and Corrections

1. In contemporary society, it is impossible to believe in a Christianity that is not at one with the movement to emancipate mankind. The reverse is also true—Christianity has also become incredible to those who, against all Christian reason, persist in maintaining their established positions in society. This is a distinctively modern form of the stumbling-block of Christian faith, the direct cause of which is not Christianity itself, but the evidence of these privileged positions of power that are accepted without question.

If this Christian solidarity with the modern critical emancipation movements is not to produce a replica of what is being done elsewhere in the world by Christians simply as men and by many others, then the Christian promise that inspires this solidarity has to be expressed and celebrated. The Church is, after all, the community of God called out by Jesus Christ and its message is both promise and criticism—criticism and political commitment on the basis of God's promise in Jesus Christ.

The question that arises in this context is this—is the freedom which these emancipation movements are seeking a utopian ideal without a definite direction, postulated as correlative with the contrasts in the world? Is there any basis for any definite expectation? We have seen that Marcuse was unable to answer this question and continues to believe in a utopia that cannot be realized and that Habermas believes in an ideal community in which dialog is free from coercion as the norm for all attempts at emancipation.

How, then, can this postulate be justified and can the dialectical tension between "institution" and "freedom" ever be resolved? Is it perhaps not true to say that being man is simply a permanent attempt to become free within this tension? The expectation of a utopia that can never be realized rules out the possibility of provisional, theoretical and practical solutions. It always contains the threat of totalitarianism, of a betrayal of the truly human quest for freedom, of an ultimate withdrawal from the struggle because of impotence with regard to the provisional renewal of society or even of a final resorting to violence.

This belief in a utopia is also based on the assumption that man's release from institutional structures will automatically bring about more freedom and humanity. "Radical negativity," however, may cause more unfreedom and inhumanity than the structures of society. Man can never be completely identified with his own products—either his good structures or his bad ones. Marcuse has drawn attention to a vicious circle in the dialectical tension between the need for man to find a "new heart" and the necessity for good structures which make him free but at the same time "institutionalize" freedom itself.

The Christian community therefore has the task of considering whether faith in the redemption, with its negative aspect of original sin, can provide a perspective which will have the effect of bringing freedom here and now in the light of the Christian promise. During a congress at Nijmegen University, L. Kolakowski, who is clearly disillusioned with all systems, declared that he does not expect Christians to do what Marxists have already done better, but hoped that they would let the special contribution of the Christian tradition be heard. (I would add that they should do this in conjunction with what the Marxists have done.) Kolakowski was thinking especially of the Christian doctrine of original sin in this context, not of the positive doctrine of redemption.

It is possible for a critical community to be politically committed, but to fail to provide this distinctively Christian perspective and to celebrate the promise in the liturgical language which prayerfully expresses the transcendent element. Such a community might achieve very fruitful results, but it would not be acting as a Christian community. It would be in danger of becoming a purely political cell without evangelical inspiration—one of very many useful and indeed necessary political pressure groups, but not an *ecclesia Christi.*

2. Elsewhere, Kolakowski has said that, in order to solve the conflicts in human history, man has to depend on an arsenal of means "which can only be found in human traditions."[15] Paul Ricoeur too has often drawn attention to the fruitful practice of critically remembering human traditions in a society such as ours, which has lost its historical roots and has come to depend on scientific planning and prognosis of the future. A true revival of the principle of the Enlightenment cannot take place either by rejecting all traditions or by making them all hermeneutically present. It can only be done by a critical remembrance of certain traditions. It was precisely in this way that the Western movement of emancipative freedom came about. We internalize the past not in order to make it present here and now, but rather to save for the future certain values which might otherwise have been lost in the past. An option for the future thus always mediates the critical remembrance of the past. This remembrance therefore is an eminent factor in the human process achieving freedom, which in turn always tends to be one-dimensional.

The Christian memory contains much more, of course, than a concrete remembrance of "critical theories," which is basically no more than a recollection of rationality as the Enlightenment principle of freedom. Generally speaking, as Habermas has pointed out, our critical remembrance of the traditions of the great religions of the world is of great importance in the process of achieving freedom and in the search for a truly human identity.[16] In this, we are faced with the irreducible contribution made by the non-scientific freedom movements, which in many respects go further than the rational principle of the Enlightenment on which all the modern critical theories are based. These non-scientific religious traditions provide the concept of "emancipation," which is in itself abstract, utopian and without content, with a very concrete content, which is in turn able to give a positive orientation to the movement of emancipative freedom, not, however, without the mediation of human reason, which is both analytical and interpretative.

Within this remembrance of varied religious inspiration, Christians find, in the life praxis of Jesus, that is, in their remembrance of his life and of his death and resurrection, both the basis of the promise and the criticism which comes from this and at the same time an orientation for their action in making the world free.[17] Jesus the Christ is, in other words, the norm for the Christian's emancipative interest. The Christian does not regard the perspective of the Kingdom of God, of the human freedom for which he is looking, as a utopia. For him, this is something that is already given—it has already been realized in a concrete historical form in the life praxis of Jesus, whose proclamation of the Kingdom of God is the thematization of this praxis. Habermas speaks of a purely theoretical anticipation of the ideal of a "good life" lived in a community in which communication is free from coercion. The Christian, on the contrary, in his practical anticipation, follows Jesus in his activity in bringing about freedom. Jesus' motivation in this praxis of life led in the service of freedom to be found in his relationship with God, his Father, who set him free to identify himself with all men.

The principle of rationality ultimately comes to grief because of its concept of freedom itself—even in an ideal community, we are confronted with the freedom of our fellow man, who may freely reject the principle that all conflicts in society can be resolved by communication which is free from coercion. This at once gives rise to a dilemma—should our fellow man, whose freedom is differently orientated, be coerced?

The Christian who remembers critically the religious traditions of mankind will know that the only justified basis for the freedom movement is a religious redemption, the freedom of God's forgiveness, which has to be given form in man's history. All Christian praxis is founded on faith in God and the critical community that does not express and celebrate this faith liturgically is cutting itself off from the source from which it draws its strength to live and work for freedom precisely as a Christian community. In that case, it may, even if its inspiration is very humane, ultimately pursue a very inhuman policy—"created in the world, five Vietnams, three Bangla Deshes and Biafras, and the system *will* collapse." Although he has lost his lustre, man still has enough humanity to be able to take that. A Christian community that is critical has, however, to be constantly alert to temptations of this kind, which sacrifice people to a better system—Max Horkheimer, for example, has spoken of man's "longing that the murderer should not triumph over the innocent victim."[18] The Christian critical community must always be conscious of the limits to man's critical reason. It should also be critical of the ideological distinction between "faith" and "religion," that is, its own religion. Finally, it should remain rationally open to the mystery of Christian life which cannot be manipulated—*intellectus quaerens fidem.* These and other conditions must be fulfilled if the Christian critical community is to be truly human and truly Christian.

3. I should like to conclude with a few words about the "deprivatization" of human subjectivity. There has been a good deal of criticism in recent years both of the privatizing tendency in the middle-class idea of man as a subject and of the opposite tendency to eliminate the subject. In this, the Christian critical community will recall the implications both of Jesus' message concerning the people of God and the Kingdom and of Jesus' life praxis as directed towards the individual. The Christian deprivatization of the subject is clearly to be found in mutual recognition of man as a free subject situated within (changing) structures. Without the recognition of and respect for the personal freedom or subjectivity of the individual, criticism of social or political action is hardly credible.

The critical community must therefore be bold enough to risk involvement both in action to achieve freedom and to change society and also in counseling and consoling individuals who have got into difficulties, even if these Christian therapeutic functions at the same time tend to justify the existing social structures. The promise of salvation here and now extends to all men and, even if the structures of society still cannot be made more just, this salvation can be brought to individuals here and now. The Christian may be committed to the task of bringing salvation to the whole of society in the form of better and more just structures for all men, but, until these structures have been created, he cannot and should not, in the meantime, that is, during the whole of the eschatological interim period, overlook one single individual fellow man. Many contemporary expressions of Christian charity have social and political dimensions, but inter-personal charity practiced by politically committed critical communities of Christians is still relevant and meaningful even if it has been thrust into the background of the community's activities.

Precisely because it claims to be Christian, no critical community can ever become an exclusive "in group" refusing membership to others who think differently. It must remain open and reject discrimination. In the inevitable case of structural difficulties, it will always be necessary to seek provisional solutions, which will be plausible in the Christian sense and even officially recognized by the Church. The critical community must, moreover, never forget that, in imitation of Jesus, it is seeking freedom not so much for itself as for others.

Jesus' apparently vain sacrifice of love arose from the contrast between his experience of the living God and his memory of the accumulated suffering of mankind. Yet this sacrificial death seems to contradict the message of the Kingdom of God that Jesus brought to man and the praxis of the life that he lived. None the less, his death on the cross is justified by God, in the prophecy of the Christian community, concerning Jesus' resurrection, as the norm for the "good life" lived in freedom and seeking freedom for others.

Translated by David Smith

NOTES

1. These questions have been prompted by my recent article on "Kritische theorie en theologische hermeneutiek," in *Geloofsverstaan: Interpretasie en kritick* (Bloemendaal, 1972), pp. 186–216.

2. I. Kant, "Was ist Aufklärung?," W. Weischedel, ed., *Werke,* vol. 9 (Darmstadt, 1968), p. 53; W. Oelmüller, *Die unbefriedigte Aufklärung* (Frankfurt, 1969); idem, *Was ist heute Aufklärung?* (Düsseldorf, 1972).

3. T. W. Adorno, *Erziehung zur Mündigkeit* (Frankfurt, 1970), p. 151.

4. H. Marcuse, *One-Dimensional Man* (London, 1964), p. 1.

5. *Idem, Das Ende der Utopie* (Berlin, 1967), pp. 40–1.

6. *Idem, Triebstruktur und Gesellschaft* (Frankfurt, 1965), p. 148.

7. J. Habermas, *Technik und Wissenschaft als "Ideologie"* (Frankfurt, 1968); *Erkenntnis und Interesse* (Frankfurt, 1968); *Zur Logik der Sozialwissenschaften* (Tübingen, 1967); *Theorie und Praxis* (Neuwied, 3rd edn., 1969); *Strukturwandel in der Öffentlichkeit* (Neuwied, 4th edn., 1969).

8. J. Habermas, *Protestbewegung und Hochschulreformen* (Frankfurt, 1969), p. 245.

9. See the controversy between H. G. Gadamer and J. Habermas, in *Hermeneutik und Ideologiekritik* (Frankfurt, 1971), especially pp. 57–82.

10. See J. Habermas, *Protestbewegung und Hochschulreformen, op. cit.,* pp. 246 and 248.

11. See D. Sölle and F. Steffensky, eds., *Politisches Nachtgebet in Köln,* 2 vols. (Stuttgart, 1970–1971); id., *Politische Theologie* (Berlin, 1971).

12. As far as I know, Habermas was first introduced to American Christians in the theological journal *Continuum* in 1971.

13. Despite the fact that many members of this school found refuge in the United States during the Nazi regime.

14. See, for example, R. Pesch, *Von der "Praxis des Himmels"* (Graz, 1971); O. Cullmann, *Jesus und die Revolutionären seiner Zeit* (Tübingen, 1970); H. W. Bartsch, *Jesus. Prophet und Messias aus Galiläa* (Frankfurt, 1970).

15. L. Kolakowski, "Der Anspruch auf die selbstverschuldete Mündigkeit," in L. Reinisch, ed., *Vom Sinn der Tradition* (Munich, 1970), p. 3.

16. J. Habermas, *Philosophisch-politische Profile* (Frankfurt, 1971), p. 35.

17. In addition to R. Pesch, *Von der "Praxis des Himmels,"* *op. cit.*, see also H. Kessler, *Erlösung und Befreiung* (Düsseldorf, 1972).

18. M. Horkheimer, *Die Sehnsucht nach dem ganz Anderen* (Hamburg, 1970), p. 62.

6

The Crisis in the Language of Faith
as a Hermeneutical Problem

1973

The Historical Contingency of the Language of Faith

Since the Christian revelation is God's saving act as something experienced and expressed by believers who are, in this sense, "pious,"[1] historically conditioned language plays an essential part in it. It is interpreted in the New Testament in terms such as redemption, the kingdom of God, the Son of Man, and so on, in other words, in the language of faith taken over from pre-Christian society and given a Christian meaning in the light of the historical event of Jesus, thus making that revelation a linguistic event. The Christian revelation, then, can only be approached by us as a reality expressed in an historically conditioned language of faith. This language of faith is not simply a mode of expression clothing an event which believers in the past were able to accept as a pure reality. On the contrary, the interpretative linguistic element is an essential aspect of revelation itself. There is no zone which is free from the changes that take place in language. There is a special historical contingency of the language of faith, just as there is a contingency of the historical event of Jesus. The language of the Bible therefore cannot be "translated" into contemporary language as though it were a child's game of changing a doll's clothes. The problem of Christian hermeneutics is far more complicated than that of language and translation with the language of the Bible as the ultimate criterion.

As a man, Jesus of Nazareth was placed in a contingent event of time—that of the history of the Jewish people who interpreted themselves as the people of God, serving and bearing witness to God in the world. In this—interpreted—history, Jesus had his own special task to carry out, but was confronted by many already existing and widely differing interpretations of the concepts "people" and "kingdom" of God. Among the most important were, for example, the apocalyptical, the eschatological, the ethical and the mystical interpretations, as well as the political interpretation of the Zealots. Jesus defined his own, very personal standpoint within this variety of interpretations, although his death made his message and choice of attitude historically ambiguous. Quite apart from the Church's kerygma or creed, this may be seen as a concise expression of the results achieved by careful historical research into the sources.

We must therefore be careful not to lose sight of this historical contingency of Jesus' appearance when we are speaking in the language of faith about Jesus as the Messiah, the Son of Man, the Lord, and so on. We should also not make the biblical expression of Jesus' words and actions in those concrete circumstances unhistorical and absolute by dissociating it from the historically conditioned linguistic categories of the period in which the event of Jesus was expressed. The linguistic event should not, in other words, be raised to the level of "timeless" categories. The multiplicity of christological dogmas and the different definitions of the kingdom of God, redemption, and so on, in the New Testament itself should be sufficient warning against this practice.

These original creeds are historically ambiguous in their language and, because they are so diverse, they are also conditioned by the historical ambiguity of the concrete phenomenon of Jesus and the fact that it is not diaphanous to human reason. The gospel of Mark clearly aims to safeguard this non-diaphanous quality of the historical event of Jesus by making use of the so-called "messianic mystery." The same is done in the canonical version of the Fourth Gospel, in sharp contrast to the source used, the so-called "miracle narratives," which present us with an almost compellingly visible form of Jesus' divinity. The historical ambiguity of the phenomenon of Jesus, which is open to so many interpretations, appears to anyone reading the New Testament writings against the background of the "non-canonical" oral and written pre-history of the New Testament, which was often extended into later "apocryphal" gospels, to be a consensus of all the canonical writings which interpret Jesus, perhaps in many different ways, as the one Jesus in the light of the kerygma of his death and resurrection.

The problem of the language of faith, then, presents us with a conflict between the historical ambiguity of Jesus' life, work and death on the one hand and, on the other, the religious and social expectations, aspirations and ideologies from which what was expressed in Jesus himself was made historically concrete in the New Testament and the history of the Church.[2] Only in the second place is it a question of a translation into our contemporary culture of the authentic reality of Jesus distilled from this conflict. The relationship with the constantly changing history with its distinctive culture is therefore inherent in the Christian creed and in the whole language of Christian faith.

The Christian who takes the confession of faith, "Jesus Christ, the Lord of history," seriously will at once understand that our relationship with our own contemporary historical situation will naturally play a part in what we have to say in the language of faith about Jesus Christ and his Church. To refuse to acknowledge this fact and to make the language of faith of a given period, even that of the New Testament, absolute would be to deny that Jesus is the Lord of all history, including our own. Speaking in the language of faith, then, is essentially an historical and hermeneutical undertaking. Anyone who denies the historicity of the Christian faith and its language and therefore denies the necessity of this hermeneutical undertaking will inevitably—but mistakenly—believe that a crisis in the language of faith is a crisis of faith as such and, by polarization, force a state of crisis in the Church. On the other hand, the Christian who is aware of the different languages of faith and of the many reinterpretations of Jesus even in the New Testament—all of them, however, confessing faith, perhaps from a different vantage point, in the one Jesus of Nazareth—will realize that we are certainly experiencing a crisis in the language of faith today, but will not regard this process of identification as such as the collapse of the Christian faith itself. (The canonization of very differing early Christian writings in the language of faith did not, for instance, imply a crisis of faith in the past.) As a Christian, he will regard this as an attempt on the part of his fellow believers to express in a critical relationship with the present what was revealed in Jesus, in other words, to express that revelation in faithfulness to Jesus and yet in a different language of faith within the framework of a changed experience of man and the world which has become the flesh and blood of contemporary man's life.

In faithfulness, but in twentieth-century language, Christians are trying today to answer the question: "But who do you say that I am?" (Mark 8. 29; Matt. 16. 15; Luke 9. 20) and this involves an element of risk. It is also, however, evidence of considerable vitality.

The Language of Faith—Not a Ghetto Language

1. Like every language, the language of faith is not a "metaphysical factor." On the contrary, it is the expression of both sense and nonsense

in our concrete, human social history. It is not only the possibility of expression, however, but also the possibility of alienation and "ideology," the place where salvation is found and where it is also absent. Like all use of language, speaking in the language of faith may at any time be suspected of "ideology," in other words, it may be speaking in a fragmented relationship with reality, an abusive use of language in the abuse of power.

The language of faith is made of precisely the same stuff as our ordinary human language is made of, language as a "life-form" (Wittgenstein) and as a social reality. There is no special ghetto language of faith. If it exists as a ghetto language, then it is in this case an anachronistic relic of what was once the everyday, universally intelligible language of human society which had become separated and had ceased to develop along with the rest of human language and had thus become the ghetto language of an enclosed "in" group, intelligible only to this group and to experts. But, since the members of this group or community cannot, in Western society at least, live in a totally isolated ghetto, but are bound to participate in the life of society as a whole, their own ghetto language is bound eventually to become a problem to those who use it, in this case, the believers,[3] who are experiencing an acute crisis in the "language of faith," on the basis of social isolation and marginality. Even though it would be wrong to regard this as a religious dismantling of the "in" group, to use this particular language of faith in isolation deprives it of its evangelical force and makes it a threat to real religiosity.

Language, including that of faith, becomes meaningless, in the sense in which linguistic analysts use the term, if it does not contain a recognizable reference to man's experience in the world.[4] There can, for example, be no real and meaningful possibility of people listening to the message of Christ's redemption and of their being open to give their consent to it if that message cannot be experienced and seen, in however fragmentary a way, in our existence here on earth. Christian salvation is not, of course, the same as our concept of pure humanity, but it is manifested as a promise in the historical process of man's freedom, just as Jesus, in going around doing good, gave concrete form to his message of ultimate salvation. The message of redemption is always threatened with the danger of becoming an "ideology" if it cannot be experienced by man as concrete human freedom.

This is why it is always necessary to verify our speaking in the language of faith against a careful analysis of individual and social alienation and against the hermeneutics of human experience. If it is to be a language that we can understand, what is said about Jesus the Christ in the history of the Church must be recognizably related to our experience in society, in which it is impossible to escape in practice the question of sense and nonsense. If this link with human experience is broken, the language of faith becomes unintelligible in its positive aspect of salvation and its negative aspect, the absence of salvation, and many people become indifferent to the decision for or against the Christian message.

Let me give two examples of this unintelligibility due, in the first case, to the absence of any connection between the language of faith and human experience and, in the second, to an uncritical adaptation to already existing data of human experience. In the first example, biblical and traditional speaking about the kingdom of God becomes unintelligible if the point of what that kingdom means to us is not translated or interpreted,[5] for the simple reason that the early "theocratic" view is no longer meaningful or acceptable to us in our present experience. The necessary critical message of this kingdom of God is denied to modern man if it is not translated into his language. As a second example, I would take the term "God is Father," which has become problematical for quite a different reason. The hermeneutics of experience has, through a psychological process of purification, shown the father-relationship to be an anthropological structure.[6] This inevitably means that there will be a crisis in our experience of faith of the term "God is Father," because we live in a "fatherless" society. The solution to *this* problem of crisis in the language of faith cannot, however, be found in doing away with the religious father-concept. On the contrary, the solution is to criticize society and to change its structures, in order to give the language of faith, in this case the term "God is Father," a function in the criticism of society.

All religious movements, including the Church as the "movement around Jesus," are inextricably part of human society. The real question is whether sufficient critical and creative tension is being maintained between our speaking in the language of faith and the social environment in which we do it. The language of faith is not identical with speaking in the world, but its matrix is always a "secular" speaking within a disclosure experience of faith and together with an evocative and critical surplus.

2. This clearly implies a rejection of all linguistic dualism, which is, of course, to be found in many spheres of human activity. This dualism is, however, especially prominent in connection with the Church and above all when a contrast is made between speaking sociologically about the Church and speaking transcendentally about the mystery of the Church. As believers, we must clearly also speak in the language of faith about the Church even when we are speaking about very ordinary aspects of the Church as a community subject to sociological laws, because it is, in its completely human character, also the community

of God. On the other hand, however, it is not only a sterile abstraction, but also very often a dangerous ideology to condemn sociological speaking about the Church as alien and to speak only in the language of faith without discussing the secular structures of the Church at all. This is clearly a "docetic" way of speaking about the Church and thus subject to criticism in the light of the empirical and analyzable aspects of the Church. There is, of course, a difference between speaking in the language of faith and speaking sociologically about the Church, but both ways of speaking refer to the same reality, with the result that there is no safe zone left over for a dualistic and therefore "supernaturalistic" language of faith. Relating to the same reality, both language games are complementary to each other.

The right of the so-called "two-language approach"—the language of faith and secular speaking, that is, sociological, scientific or historical language—is indisputable, but it is most important not to forget that it is the same reality that is approached and interpreted, although from different points of view and with different questions. To forget this would be disastrous for both approaches because of the danger that the language of faith may become an ideology, possibly in order to justify uncritically accepted social processes in which the Church has become involved.

The classic solution to the problem of "faith and science" was found in a rather facile distinction, namely, that the facts were the concern of science and that faith was concerned with the meaning of the facts. This seemed to do justice to both aspects—a special sphere for the sciences, which were thus not hindered by faith, and a special sphere for faith, which thus remained immune to science. The consequence of this distinction, however, was that the sphere of scientific facts became wider and wider, first in the cosmos, then in the biological world, and finally in man himself and his psyche. On the other hand, however, theologians felt that the real ground of facts was being swept from under their feet. Since then, the ideological aspect of this distinction between the sphere of facts and the sphere of meaning has been exposed by sociologists, psychiatrists and others whose sciences were both analytical and hermeneutic. Scientists, then, were active in the sphere of meaning, while theologians had the feeling that their study was vanishing into thin air. In the meantime, the idea had for a long time prevailed that God was alien to the sphere of facts and reason. The basic concept of creation withered away and theology became pure eschatology—a variety of theologies of hope flourished without any foundation of creation. Even theological hermeneutics became more and more alienated from the facts.

The crisis in the language of faith, then, is partly the result of the "two-language approach," in so far as this theory fails to take into account the fact that it is the same reality that is approached and interpreted, although it is viewed from different standpoints. The sphere of facts must have enough pointers for what is said in the "other sphere" in the language of faith to be meaningful and intelligible despite its inexpressible surplus. It is, above all, this surplus, which cannot be approached by reason, that has to be expressed in the language of faith in the form of parables and stories—in other words, the narrative element has to be used for this surplus in the language of faith. These parables and stories prevent us from identifying what has already been achieved in our history and what still remains to be achieved with the consummation at the end which is God's gift and his affirmation of all that is good, holy and beautiful in history. At the same time, they provide us with a set of models by means of which the Christian community can see the character of God's coming which preserves us both in conversion and in responsible activity in our history. This promise is more than a mere criticism or negation of what is available. It orientates activity and stimulates resolute but provisional activity that is averse to all forms of totalitarianism and of premature "unification" in theory or in praxis. All this is intimately connected with the authenticity of the language of faith.

I cannot go into the so-called conflict of the models of interpretation here, because this would take me too far from my intention of simply pointing out a dualism which is accepted by many Christians and which in fact perpetuates the crisis in the language of faith, especially in the various offshoots of Protestant "dialectical theology" and in the Catholic theology that is derived from it. One of the results of this dualism is the emergence of forms of theology which attempt to resolve the conflict by doing away with one of the two poles of the language of faith and using exclusively a secular way of speaking about faith. This, however, brings about a real crisis of *faith.* We may therefore conclude that there can be no living faith without a language of faith.

Not Simply Language but also Praxis

It is common to speak of a disturbance in communication, in connection with the crisis in the language of faith, between the New Testament (the past) and ourselves in the present. This leads to an identification of the hermeneutical problem with this disturbance in communication, which is attributed to the distance either in time or in society.

It is, however, ambiguous to speak of "distance" in this context, because the New Testament is among us, for example, in the Church's proclamation here and now. The language of faith is therefore problematical in a very concrete form—the Church's claim that the Christian truth that is inherited from the past is still valid today. As long as we see the past, however, as a dead sediment, we shall remain at an abstract theoretical level at which we can only analyze formally the structure of our understanding of our historical experience. We also tend to assume *a priori* that there is no disturbance, but that there ought to be communication with the past. We think within a sphere of meaning which allows the present and the past to be seen as a continuous whole within a changing, widening horizon. As for the validity of this scheme of present-past, it is clear that the scheme itself implies an interpretation and a negative evaluation, in other words, the break between the past and the present is interpreted as a disturbance in communication, but no answer has been given to why this should be so. It has been suggested that, for the sake of the present and a better future, the past should be left as past, because—following the reasoning of the Enlightenment—the present is an emancipation from the past. But this, too, is an assumption and as such implies an interpretation. We are bound to conclude that it is not possible to uphold the abstract scheme of present-past, because, both in a negative and in a positive interpretation, the present and the past are mediated.

The consequence of this is that the universal question of communication—with which our special question, the language of faith, is intimately concerned—is always asked within a certain context of interpretation. Broadly speaking, there are three possible approaches. The first is that followed by J. Habermas, who views the past from the vantage point of a critical emancipation from a previous history that is authoritarian and, in that sense, violent. The second way of looking at the past, that of H.-G. Gadamer, is from the point of view of a history which is, in some way, normative for us. The third way is to approach the past in the light of a critical and selective remembrance of human traditions containing not only many irrelevant and even meaningless events, but also what N. Luhmann has called "sediments of meaning," many of which are extremely important for our decisions in the present about the future. This tendency of a critical *memoria praeteriti* is followed by several of the protagonists of the so-called "critical theories" including J. Habermas and also by such thinkers as H. Marcuse, Kolakowski, P. Ricoeur, J. B. Metz and W. Oelmüller. We may therefore conclude that any consideration of the crisis in the language of faith, of communication and of disturbance in communication includes an interpretation, with the result that the hermeneutical problem cannot be separated from the so-called criticism of ideology. Understanding in and through language, including that of faith, is therefore bound to be not only a question of hermeneutics, but also a criticism of ideology.

Let me illustrate this with one example, that of "redemption." An essential aspect of the evangelical concept of redemption is the call to conversion or *metanoia*. But does this call not become an ideology if it is limited merely to an inner conversion and if the conditions under which this can be realized are absent and especially if the subject to be changed, man not simply as a logical being, but also as a social being who acts, is not realistically defined? Within the context of such questions, speaking in the language of faith about redemption is seen to be closely related to man's commitment to a truly human emancipation from many kinds of personal and social alienation. This emancipation motivated by genuine care for our fellow men and carried out, for example, by those who are active in the spheres of mental and spiritual welfare and social or political work can be seen as a sign and an *arrha* of salvation, although they are not identical.

This, of course, poses all kinds of questions, including, for example, the political implications of the message of salvation and the dialectical tension between inner conversion and social or political reform. Both a purely private language of faith and one which never expresses the mystical element cease to be intelligible and forfeit their critical function with regard to the tendencies to make society more and more private on the one hand and increasingly scientific and technocratic on the other. This new historical situation undoubtedly requires us to test once again our speaking in the language of faith about redemption or freedom.[7]

Soteriological language—speaking about redemption—thus includes both the language of freedom and the language of liturgical celebration and consequently points to praxis and action—or is at least a "performative" language, calling for action—and to our liturgical thanking of God for his redemption which through men of goodwill on earth anticipates the signs of this salvation.[8] Religiosity forms an essential part of the language of faith, which is therefore always doxological, that is, praising God on the one hand, and "performative" with regard to social and political commitment on the other. If these two aspects are separated, the language of faith will become an ideology and the critical commitment of the Christian community will become a theological duplication of what is already being done successfully by those who do not belong to the Church.

The Language of Faith and Critical Remembrance of the Past

One of the many aspects of the crisis in the language of faith is a tendency, since Adolf Harnack, among Protestants to regard the history of Christianity since its origin as a decline and a corresponding tendency among Roman Catholics to justify that history as a necessary organic development.[9] If Christianity really had its origin in Jesus of Nazareth and the response of his disciples to his appearance, then this origin must inevitably be a lasting criterion for the language of faith. It has to be admitted, however, that any pre-critical idealism based on this origin is also pernicious, since the New Testament language of faith, the structures of the primitive Christian community were also mediated by the contingent circumstances of the time—the normative revelation is not provided in its pure form by this origin.

Since our relationship with the past is in itself an option for the future and never purely theoretical, the alternative definition suggested by some of those who have considered this question, namely that, in our attempt to find a new language of faith, there is no theoretical mediation between the past and the present, but a mediation in praxis between the present and the future, strikes me as false. Our relationship with the future is, after all, mediated by our relationship with the past, just as our definite remembrance of the past is mediated by a definite plan for the future. This is why we refer, correctly, to critical and definite memories of the past. An option for a concrete memory of the history of man's suffering is therefore subject to the choice of a plan for the future in which a better history is regarded as possible and necessary for those who suffer and die or are poor and without rights. The fact that our relationship with the past is never purely theoretical has certain consequences for our speaking in the language of faith.

Our attempt to find a new language of faith that is humanly relevant and intelligible cannot be justified by a direct appeal to the New Testament, the "origin," (This proved to be the case in the past as well, in connection with the Church's traditional language of faith.) Biblical language has the task of orientating other languages of faith, both traditional and new, and it has a critical function with regard to them, but it cannot justify them. A language of faith can only be based indirectly and historically on the language of the Bible and this is because it can be shown that a relationship with social, political, religious and popular philosophical ideas of the period played an important part in the biblical language of faith. An authentic language of faith can therefore only be justified indirectly by reference to the language of the Bible.

What was regarded as possible and legitimate by the biblical authors for the expression of the New Testament faith in Jesus Christ in different social situations cannot be denied to Christians at a later period in the history of the Church. This is, indirectly, where the biblical basis of a new language of faith is to be found, both in praxis—for example, a more democratic exercise of authority by the Church—and in theory—for

example, redemption as emancipation from all forms of human alienation. Neither the traditional nor the modern language of faith can
therefore be made absolute. The question concerning a new language
of faith which will express what we, under pressure of the reality of
Jesus, mean by that reality now in our search for freedom in a world
worthy of man today arises again and again in different social and
political situations.

The difficulty of this inevitable question can be found in a choice.
Should we project only our contemporary categories, still used in the
criticism of society, on to this Jesus, thereby creating an unnecessary
theological duplication of an already perfectly meaningful praxis? On
the other hand, should we subject ourselves at the same time to criticism by the reality of Jesus in our use, in the criticism of society, of
these contemporary categories in order to express Jesus in them? This
would apply both in so far as the reality of Jesus is the focal point of
a living community of faith which is directed towards God and man
and which confesses him in prayer and in praxis as the Lord of history
and in so far as this reality is increasingly shown by an historical
approach to be seen as "Jesus of Nazareth." The difficulty of this hermeneutical undertaking is to be found in the circle in which it takes place.
It is to be found in the first place in our need to express this reality of
Jesus in categories which are already given to us, but at the same time
in the fact that we can only come to know what this reality means to us
now by using these categories. In the second place, the hermeneutical
difficulty also exists whether or not our option for the future, within
which we put questions to the Bible, is itself subject to the criticism of
the evangelical promise. This is a fundamental hermeneutical conflict
and one which is critical of ideology. Our modern speaking in the language of faith is bound to take place within this conflict.

In conclusion, I would like to point to the inevitably experimental
character of any period of crisis in the language of faith, as at present,
when there can be no purely scientific guarantee of automatic success.
How should Christians react to this hazardous situation? We should,
I think, above all have trust in the faith of our Christian communities
and in the presence of the Holy Spirit in them. Mistakes will inevitably
occur. It is clear that, in the New Testament, pre-canonical oral and
written traditions were corrected by the canon of Scripture, which had
to rely on those traditions in order to achieve a new language of faith
in a changed situation and that the New Testament itself contains a
very large number of different corrections. This knowledge should help
to dispel all anxiety. In addition to this vigilant trust in the guidance
of the Spirit, we should also remain open to evangelical admonition,
especially in cases when the Christian community is experiencing diffi-

culty in recognizing a particular form of theological speaking as the language of faith. There is also a constant need for evangelical encouragement among those whose hazardous task it is to translate the Christian message critically yet faithfully for the modern world. Finally, in exceptional cases, however risky it may be, we must be prepared to pronounce a *non possumus* if the being or non-being of Christianity is at stake.

If Christians react in this way to the present crisis in the language of faith resulting from great social change, they should not experience any real crisis of faith itself. On the contrary, their faith in Jesus of Nazareth as expressed in the language of faith should be purified and strengthened with the critical help of theology. In a world which they often experience, rightly, as with disillusionment and suffering, they are bound to ask: "Lord, to whom shall we go?" (John 6. 68).

Translated by David Smith

NOTES

1. I have developed this idea more fully in the introduction to my article on "The Problem of the Infallibility of Office," *Concilium,* March 1973 (American Edn., vol. 83).

2. See E. Schillebeeckx, "De toegang tot Jezus van Nazaret," *Tijdschrift voor Theologie,* 12 (1972), pp. 28–60, especially pp. 56 ff.

3. See, for example, L. Gilkey, *Naming the Whirlwind* (Indianapolis, 1969).

4. See E. Schillebeeckx, *Gläubensinterpretation. Beiträge zu einer hermeneutischen und kritischen Theologie* (Mainz, 1971), pp. 13–17.

5. See, for example, O. H. Streck, "Prophetische Kritik der Gesellschaft," *Christentum und Gesellschaft* (Göttingen, 1969), pp. 46–62.

6. See especially J.-M. Pohier, *Vers le Père* (Paris, 1972).

7. Successful attempts to speak, in faithfulness to the gospel, in a new language of faith about the "kingdom of God" and "redemption" have been made by R. Pesch, *Von der "Praxis des Himmels"* (Graz, 1971) and H. Kessler, *Erlösung als Befreiung* (Düsseldorf, 1972).

8. See my paper in the report on the congress held at Nijmegen University, 20–23 March 1972.

9. J. Ratzinger, *Das Problem der Dogmengeschichte in der Sicht der katholischen Theologie* (Cologne and Opladen, 1966), pp. 8–15.

7

The "God of Jesus" and the "Jesus of God"

1974

The New Testament contains the testimony of men who found salvation explicitly from God in Jesus of Nazareth and who therefore called Jesus, in the light of their expectations of salvation and confronted with his concrete historical appearance in history, "the Christ, Son of God, our Lord."

The History of Suffering: Man's Expectation of Salvation

Man's ideas and expectations of salvation and of personal and social happiness have always been formulated in the light of his experience of and reflections about the absence of salvation, suffering, misery and alienation. They have, in other words, arisen from an accumulation of negative experiences throughout a history of suffering that has lasted for centuries. This history, however, has always included fragmentary experiences of happiness and the promise of happiness, of salvation and of unfulfilled expectations, mingled with experiences of guilt and evil. This, of course, is the problem of Job in human history.

What has eventually emerged from this experience and man's reflection about it is a view of what is good, happy and true in the state of being man. Man's longing for happiness and salvation, which has always been subjected to criticism, but which has always survived that criticism, has therefore developed into the idea of redemption or liberation *from* and of going *into* a completely new world. This fundamental idea has, of course, been expressed in many different ways, but it is in general true to say that a people's negative experiences of contrast mark out its ideas and expectations of salvation. It is so to speak possible to read the history of a people's suffering in its expectation of salvation even if the precise traces of that suffering cannot be followed in other sources.

Jesus' own period of history was marked by a proliferation, among both the Jews and the Gentiles, of expectations of salvation and these were expressed in a full spectrum of ideas which had accumulated in centuries of historically experienced salvation and of unfulfilled expectations. The Jewish apocalyptic period, from the Maccabees (167 B.C.) through the Jewish war (A.D. 66–70) to Bar Cochba (A.D. 135), was above all a "history of blood and tears,"[1] which gave rise to an increasing longing for a definitive and radical change in the world.

Within this sphere of general expectations, within which many of the ideas of salvation merged together, the conviction grew, in confrontation with Jesus of Nazareth, that there was "salvation in no one else" (Acts 4. 12). The early Christians expressed their experience of salvation from God in Jesus in ideas which already existed for them and which had been derived from many sources, but which they vitally shared. They believed that their expectations had been fulfilled here and now in Jesus of Nazareth and that they were consequently new men.

After a period of Christian life and reflection, these early believers bore witness, in the New Testament, to their recognition of their salvation in Jesus. It is not possible, however, to disentangle the closely interwoven threads of their expectation of salvation and their happy recognition of the fulfillment of that expectation in Jesus of Nazareth that are found in the New Testament. The question about man's true being and the finding of an answer to this question in the historical man Jesus are correlative. They are, moreover, correlative in that it is not the already existing expectations of salvation that determine who Jesus is, but that, in the light of the history of Jesus, those expectations are not only included, but also changed, adapted or corrected. There is, then, both a continuity and a discontinuity between man's question about salvation and the concrete historical answer which is Jesus.

This means that we encounter great difficulties when we read the New Testament for the first time. We do not live in a social and religious environment with a traditional expectation of a Messiah or a mysterious Son of Man or of the approaching end of the world. We are, in other words, confronted in the New Testament with an early religious society, which is very strange to us today, both in its Jewish and in its Hellenistic expressions of these expectations. Such expectations are always conditioned both historically and culturally, even though the "human predicament" may remain the same.

In the modern world, man's expectation of salvation has assumed the form of a movement of "emancipative freedom." The aim of all the branches of this movement is to redeem mankind from his social alienations. At the same time, many different kinds of scientific techniques, such as psychoanalysis, Gestalt therapy, social work, counseling, and so on, are used to liberate individuals from personal alienations and from a loss of personal identity. A conviction which has become more and more widespread nowadays and which is increasingly used as evidence is that, apart from Jesus, there are so many factors in man's life which really bring historical salvation and make man whole. The expression, "there is salvation in no one else" other than Jesus Christ, so often used by Christians, has therefore become to some extent difficult to understand and to believe. The religious concept of salvation has undoubtedly become narrower in the modern world and it has had to give way to other and visibly effective means of bringing salvation. This has brought the question as to what really saves man into a position of central importance.

It is certainly true that it is possible to eliminate all kinds of human alienations by scientific and technical means. At the same time, however, the only alienations that can be removed in this way are those which result from the presence of physical or psychosomatic conditioning or conditioning by social structures, from the absence of conditioning by infrastructures or of liberating conditions or from the presence of conditioning by freedom that can be helped by human commitment. Human freedom is not, after all, a purely inner freedom. It is physically directed outwards and can only become fully conscious of itself when it encounters free people within structures that make freedom possible.

Man himself is only a possibility of freedom and freedom itself is really a vacuum and without content. Society enables freedom to fill that vacuum creatively, although there is no form or degree of society that can completely fill the vacuum. The individual person, society and "nature" are related to each other in a situation of dialectical tension, with the result that the deepest human alienations can never be fully overcome, either personally or socially. There is, for example, that human suffering which cannot be resolved by social or political measures. Man can still be broken by isolation even in the best social structures, since these cannot automatically make man and society good and mature. Nature can be humanized to a very great degree, but it will always remain alien to man (death is an example of this). Finally, man's finite nature may make him trust in God or it may lead to isolation and anxiety. Within human history, then, and in confrontation with nature and these various data, there is no single identifiable subject which can bring about man's total salvation or a state of real "wholeness" in him. Everything is, in fact, subject to the dialectical tension that exists between the person, society and nature.

Is this deeper problem, then, not expressed in a specific way in Jesus of Nazareth (as in all religiosity)? For slaves, salvation is emancipation. For the man who believes that his life is determined by an arbitrary fate or by evil powers, salvation is achieved in the overcoming of that fate or those powers. The material content of the "Good News," the gospel and salvation, for us changes according to our experience of the absence of salvation. It is clear from the history of Christianity since the time of the early Church that the material content of this Good News of salvation experienced in Jesus has been described in constantly changing forms, a process which is continuing for us.

Both our own longing for salvation today and what was expressed in Jesus make an essential contribution to our formulation of an answer that is faithful to Jesus and at the same time applies to us. The offer of salvation from God in Jesus will therefore subject our longing for salvation to criticism. Is it, then, not those alienations which cannot be removed by scientific and technical means used by man that are expressed in our interpretation of life as Christians in Jesus? If this is so, then it means that these human factors are recognized, confirmed and stimulated as such in this religious interpretation of reality, which has the essential task of liberating man from his deeper alienations and of redeeming him and setting him free so that he becomes autonomous in his adherence to the living God who is transcendent and can therefore make him free.

Man's search for the message and the praxis of Jesus of Nazareth is therefore a search for the structures of what appears in Jesus as really "Good News" in the religious and human sense. It is not therefore a search for confirmation of what we, as men, can probably already achieve ourselves in the scientific and technical sense. However meaningful and indeed necessary it may be, this scientific and technical skill is not, for twentieth-century man, "Good News" from God (see Mark 1. 14–15).

The Question about God and the Question about Man

In the light of what has been said above, it should be clear that Jesus cannot give a universal invitation that is justified by the consent that we give to it in faith, so long as it is not meaningfully demonstrated that we are essentially concerned here, in the man Jesus of Nazareth, with the living God as the creator of heaven and earth who makes us free and at the same time gives meaning to our lives. If the living God, the God of Jews, Muslims, Buddhists, and so many others, is not personally involved in the event of Jesus and does not allow his face to be seen in one way or another in Jesus, then our enthusiasm for Jesus as a man who can inspire and give direction to our lives may well be meaningful, at least within the limited tradition within which he appeared, but it will be non-committed and at the most a cipher for man's possibilities. This may still be inspiring, but it cannot be universally valid.

In his historical appearance, Jesus becomes a renewed and deepened question for us only if and because he is the one who has something definite and definitive to say about God and at the same time about man. In other words, he becomes a question if God is expressed in Jesus as a challenge to man. Within this question, what has to be sought in Jesus of Nazareth is the possibility of signs which may be able to direct man's question about salvation towards the Christian offer of an answer in faith which will point to God's special saving activity in Jesus of Nazareth, an activity that can be identified as such by Christians. The answer to the question about the unique and universal significance of Jesus will therefore inevitably be connected with the revelation, on the one hand, of God's true face and, on the other, of man's true face, in which God's own face becomes to some extent evident and visible.

The question regarding the unique and universal significance of Jesus (as postulated by Christianity) can, of course, only be answered in faith. Any such theological statements made in faith must, however, be based on the history of Jesus or they will inevitably have a fragmentary, divided and therefore ideological relationship with reality. "Who has seen me has seen the Father"—something of this must have been evident in history. (If there had been too great a division between these two levels, Christianity would never have stood any chance.) What is ultimately at stake is an affirmation which is made in faith and which claims to give consent to reality, even though that claim may be a claim based on faith.

We may, however, give our consent, in the language of faith, to a reality, in other words, to something that is not postulated as such by me as a believer, but which urges me to give consent and makes that consent an act of faith. In that case, the reality in question, the historical event of Jesus of Nazareth, must provide the basis of what is said about Jesus in the language of faith and at the same time fill it.

Within the context of this question, there are therefore two points in the interpretation of Jesus today which come together in what is often expressed, wrongly, in the form of a dilemma. Is salvation contained in the historical appearance of Jesus, in his challenging message and in his good and critical words and way of life, in which he was faithful to death? Or is salvation contained in Jesus who was crucified and rose from the dead? The two points involved here are, firstly, is the expression

of God essential to the identity of Jesus (the "God of Jesus") and, secondly, if the first question is answered affirmatively, what does it mean
if the message and the praxis of Jesus' life resulted in failure, in other
words, were rejected (the "Jesus of God")?

The "God of Jesus"

We should not approach the "God of Jesus" expressed in Jesus' life
from the vantage-point of a previously existing idea of what God is, as
though we knew better who God is than who Jesus is. The only way in
which we can gain a perspective of the "God of Jesus" is by examining
the message of Jesus and the praxis of his life. This God was also both
the God of Israel and the creator of heaven and earth. Jesus' appearance
cannot, in other words, be isolated from his past, which was Israel.
Moreover, even though he remains the focal point as well as the norm
and criterion of the whole "event of Christ," he cannot be isolated from
his past, his present, during which he went round in Palestine doing
good, acting with and reacting to his contemporaries, and his future,
which was the community of the Church which developed from him.

One of the data of Jesus' life which has a most firmly established
historical basis is his expression of God in and through his message
of the coming kingdom of God. This can be found in the traditions of
the four gospels.[2] The content of this message of the kingdom emerges
clearly from the original parables, in so far as these can be accurately
reconstructed through the early Christian actualizations. The praxis of
the kingdom of God is expressed above all in *metanoia* or conversion
in these original parables and this central message is also filled with
the praxis of Jesus' life, which is itself a parable of the kingdom of God.

"Rule" was a central concept in the ancient world, like "power." We
do not find these concepts attractive, but, in Jesus' preaching and above
all in his cures and his driving out of devils, the concept of "rule" is
opposed, as the power of love and goodness, to the powers of evil both
within man and outside him. A respect for God's supremacy and therefore for his rule is an essential part of Jesus' appearance and his message and he interpreted God's supremacy as an unconditional desire
for man's good. God's rule is, for Jesus, not a function of human salvation—he is the man who experiences joy in God himself. God's rule is
God's state of being God and our recognition of the rule or kingdom of
God brings about our salvation, our state of being human.

This emphasizes a form of "rule" which is not oppressive, but liberating: "You know that the rulers of the Gentiles lord it over them, and
their great men exercise authority over them. It shall not be so among
you" (Matt. 20. 25–26). For Jesus, man's cause was God's cause, just

as God's cause was also man's cause. This is clearly expressed in the Letter to Titus: "the goodness and the loving kindness (the loving mindfulness of man) of God appeared" (Tit. 3. 4).

The God of Jesus is undoubtedly God. He is not a function of humanity or of human liberation, but he is essentially a God who cares for man, with the result that the whole of Jesus' life was a "celebration" of God's rule and at the same time an "orthopraxis," in other words, a praxis in accordance (orthōs) with the kingdom of God. There is therefore an inner connection between the "kingdom" or "rule" of God and "orthopraxis" as a human phenomenon or a consistent translation of God's love of all men to the level of the praxis of human life. In this praxis, Jesus himself recognized the signs of the coming of God's rule, the kingdom of God. In the praxis of Jesus' own life, then, there was a proleptical or anticipatory realization in practice, not simply in theory, of the new world known as the "kingdom of God" and therefore a realization also of the new praxis that has been sought of a humane, good and true life. In Jesus, eschatological hope (the approaching kingdom of God) is linked with a new praxis of *metanoia*, the aspect of which that "shocks" man being expressed in the parables. The message of the approaching kingdom of God—and Jesus' life itself is a striking parable of this—therefore means salvation from God in Jesus manifested in a new praxis of human life, the living example of which is again Jesus himself.

Jesus was conscious that he had been called to invite, from God, the host, all the guests, among whom were explicitly included all those who had hitherto been excluded from all communication and fellowship at table, namely the "tax collectors and sinners" (Mark 2. 15–17). The lost sheep, the man who was isolated from the group, had to be sought (Luke 15. 1–8; 19. 20; Matt. 9. 36; 10. 6). Jesus' striking solidarity with sinners and his association with them in order to open communication between them and God can be regarded as an offer of salvation, the "Good News" from God (Mark 1. 15).

Against the background of the current apocalyptic ideas and the convictions of the Pharisees, Essenes, Zealots and other similar "remnant" communities and movements, it is not easy to situate Jesus' message and his praxis in a religious and historical context. This is precisely why both his message and the praxis of his life cannot be understood without recourse to his own special and original experience of God. The history of suffering and of the absence of salvation within which Jesus' life was led provides no reason or basis for the certainty of salvation which characterizes Jesus' preaching. The hope expressed in his proclamation of the coming salvation of the world of men in the kingdom of God is clearly based on an experience of contrast. On the one hand, he lived in a human history of suffering characterized by the absence of salvation, peace and justice and by the presence of painful slavery. On the other hand, Jesus had the special experience of God as the one who promotes good and refuses to recognize the power of evil. Jesus' conviction and proclamation of the kingdom of God which set men free here and now in history were fashioned by this religious experience of contrast. He experienced God as the one who gives the future to those to whom no future can, from the worldly point of view, be promised.

Man is thus given a hope that cannot be traced back to his history in the world or to his personal or his social and political experience, yet it is none the less a hope that has at the same time to be fulfilled in this world in terms of man's personal and social and political salvation. Jesus was made conscious of the possibility of this hope by the original nature of his experience of God and this experience had been made possible by what had gone before in the religious life of prophetic Judaism. In other words, the best of Israel's experience of God reached an original and personal climax in Jesus—Yahweh as the one who was to come and who for the time being refused to present his credentials ("I shall be who I shall be," Exod. 3. 14). Believing in such a God was placing one's trust in one who took his identity very seriously and at the same time refused to reveal it fully "in advance." Jesus therefore experienced God as the power of good and "anti-evil," in other words, as man's salvation in the history of human suffering. The "God of Jesus" is a God to whom "all things are possible" (Mark 10. 27) and, in his words and his actions, Jesus has called on us to believe in this God. If we deprive Jesus of his relationship with God in his life and preaching, we deny his historical identity and make him into an "unhistorical" being, a "non-Jesus," someone who was in any case not "Jesus of Nazareth."

The "Jesus of God"

The essence of Jesus' identity that emerges from a critical analysis of the four gospels is that he was not himself concerned with his own identity, but wanted to identify himself with God's cause as man's cause and with the salvation, the wholeness, of man as God's cause.

While Jesus was living in history, a history which was contingent and unfinished, the revelation of salvation in God was, for anyone who was able to experience it in Jesus, also unfinished and still in a process of development. "Christology" is essentially a statement, made in faith, about the totality of Jesus' life, which is therefore presupposed in the Christian experience of "disclosure." It is only Jesus' completed life which is God's revelation in Jesus of Nazareth. Our story of Jesus can only really begin with Jesus' death, as the closure of his whole life, even though our story of Jesus or our recognition of Christ must also be a recognition of Jesus of Nazareth and not a myth or gnosis.

In fact, Jesus' message and the praxis of his life were rejected, because of the purely historical failure of his life and work. For this reason, his message and the praxis of his life, however important they may have been, cannot be the last word or the basis of real hope for us. This problem is resolved in the gospels by reference to faith in the resurrection and, while avoiding a full analysis of the emergence of faith in the resurrection, we are bound to consider its significance within the framework of what we have already said.

It is clear from the "missionary sermons" in Acts (10. 34–43; 2. 22–36; 4. 26–27; 3. 12–26; 13. 16–41) that there was a connection between Jesus and the Spirit. In these sermons, Luke throws light for the Greeks on the meaning of "Christ" as the one who was anointed with the Spirit— for example, declaring that God was with him (Acts 2. 22; 3. 14; 10. 38). Paul said similarly that "Christ is God's" (I Cor. 3. 23). Jesus, in other words, was God's "possession"—this is clear from the same texts in Acts, which speak of "thy Holy One," "thy holy servant," "his servant," "his Christ," "my Son," and so on (Acts 2. 27; 3. 14; 4. 27; 13. 35; 3. 13; 3. 26; 4. 30; 3. 18; 13. 33).

Jesus' rejection by men was counterbalanced by Jesus' belonging to God. In these missionary sermons, then, believing in the earthly Jesus meant recognizing him as God's eschatological prophet of and for Israel, the last messenger from God who was to proclaim the kingdom of God as very close and to bring it in his words and his actions. Believing in the risen Jesus, on the other hand, was recognizing him in his universal significance as the saviour of all mankind. These two aspects are, however, defined by Jesus' belonging to God on the one hand and by God's faithfulness to Jesus on the other.

The resurrection—God made Jesus rise again—therefore confirms Jesus' message and the praxis of his life. It also reveals that his person is indissolubly bound to God and to this message. In Jesus' death and resurrection, man's rejection of God's offer of salvation and the constant provision of that salvation in the risen Jesus encounter each other. The risen Jesus is God's overcoming of man's rejection of the provision of definitive salvation from God in Jesus. God goes so far as to break through man's rejection in the resurrection of Jesus, in whom he gives the future to anyone who has no future and who merits no future. He loved us "while we were yet sinners" (Rom. 5. 8). He shows himself in the risen Jesus to be the power of good and "anti-evil," unconditional goodness which refuses to recognize the power of evil and breaks through it. In his supreme need, in his suffering and crucifixion, Jesus gave up his personal secret, the mystery of his person, his inviolable bond with God, while the Father also gave up his personal secret with regard to Jesus, his constant acknowledgment of Jesus. In this way, the Father-Son relationship is revealed in the death and resurrection of Jesus and we are therefore bound to ask the question about the Trinity.

When he sent Jesus to Israel, God fulfilled the promise of the Old Covenant and affirmed this and his creation. When Israel rejected this offer of salvation in Jesus, God brought about a "new creation" in and through the resurrection of Jesus. In the rejected but risen Jesus of Nazareth, then, the Old Testament was fulfilled and the New Testament was begun. There is a clear continuity between our human history and this new creation on the basis of Jesus' resurrection. At the same time, however, on the basis of the rejection of Jesus as the one through whom the covenant and creation itself were fulfilled, there is also a discontinuity which is inwardly connected with the historical continuity. This link is made by God's new saving activity which transcends the historical failure of Jesus, who fulfilled the covenant and creation, but who was rejected and crucified, and installs the rejected Jesus in a position where he can carry out his function of bringing universal salvation. Within our human history, the integration of Jesus' rejection and crucifixion into his offer of salvation, which is the meaning of his whole life, is the historical index of this transcendence. God has, in other words, redeemed us in Jesus Christ (see 2 Cor. 5. 14–18).

Jesus' resurrection is God's confirmation of his message and the praxis of his life precisely because his "belonging to God" was confirmed by God in the resurrection. This at the same time implies that the content of the eschatological liberation which is expressed in the language of faith as "resurrection from the dead" has to be filled in the light of Jesus' historical appearance, that is, of his words and actions which are confirmed by the crucifixion and resurrection. The question as to whether salvation is found in Jesus of Nazareth or in the crucifixion and resurrection is therefore a false dilemma. This is because Jesus of Nazareth is confirmed by God in the crucifixion and resurrection, whereas this confirmed crucifixion and resurrection is filled concretely in Jesus of Nazareth. In other words, a crucified Jesus who rose from the dead remains a myth or a gnostic mystery without Jesus of Nazareth. In spite of the astonishing message and the praxis of Jesus' life, without the resurrection Jesus of Nazareth would have been a failure, like all the failures of innocent men in the history of human suffering. It would have resulted in a brief hope and would have confirmed the suspicion that many people do not accept it, but do experience its utopian character because of the very nature of their history.

There is therefore no rupture between "Jesus of Nazareth" and the crucified Jesus who rose from the dead. Jesus' death confronts us with a fairly fundamental question about God because of Jesus' life which preceded his death. One answer to this question is that God, whose kingdom Jesus proclaimed, was an illusion on the part of Jesus (and also a God in whom Jesus' disciples were disillusioned). A second possible answer is that Jesus' rejection and death compels us to revise our own understanding of God and even to abandon it as invalid, God's real nature appearing as valid only in Jesus' life and death. God, whom Jesus called absolutely reliable, is, in other words, either a tragic farce or else a God to whom we must confess in the preaching and in the historical failure of Jesus. Faith in Jesus can only occur in the form of a confession to God.

The rupture in this Christian faith is therefore not to be found in Jesus' death. He experienced that death as an involvement in his mission to offer salvation and as the historical consequence of his love and care for men. (This is the minimum of essential historical truth that has to be preserved from the tradition of the Last Supper.) The break is rather to be found in the rejection of his message and the praxis of his life, which resulted in a rejection of his very person. God's confirmation in the resurrection therefore concerns the very person of Jesus and, in that person, his message and the praxis of his life. Both the rejection and God's confirmation of and consent to the person of Jesus therefore give validity to the specific aspect of the event of Jesus, in which the person of Jesus and his task in life (his message and his praxis) form an indissoluble unity. This is why the kingdom of God is able to have, in the Christian confession, the appearance of Jesus Christ and why we can speak about the "Lord Jesus Christ" as synonymous with the kingdom of God as proclaimed by Jesus.

In speaking about God's confirmation of Jesus' person, message and praxis, we have to bear in mind that this statement is also an affirmation of faith and not a confrontation or a legitimation in the purely human sense of the word. The resurrection confirms that God was always with Jesus throughout his whole life, even when he was humanly forsaken in his death on the cross, when God himself was silent. A conviction of faith, the resurrection, cannot be a legitimation of another conviction of faith, that of God's saving activity in Jesus of Nazareth. Any authentic legitimation, which is to be evident to all men, must therefore always be completely eschatological. This is why faith in the resurrection is a prophecy and a promise for this world and, as a prophecy, it is defenseless and vulnerable. Christian life is therefore not justified or made right by history. On the other hand, Christians, believing in the resurrection of Jesus, are liberated by their faith from the need to justify themselves and to claim that God has now to protect and ratify those who are faithful to him in public. The servant is, in other words, no better than the master. Like Jesus himself, the Christian dares to entrust himself to God and to trust that God will justify his life and he is ready to receive that justification, as Jesus did, beyond death. Because he has been reconciled to God's manner of acting in this way, he is also reconciled to himself, to others and to history, in which he none the less still tries to achieve emancipation and redemption. For this reason, he is able to be completely committed, without using violence, to make this world a more just and happy place for all men and to eliminate alienation. Like Jesus, however, the Christian cannot justify himself by producing his credentials, apart from his concrete praxis of the kingdom of God.

The Story of Jesus: A Parable of God and a Paradigm of Humanity

The answer which enables Christians to recognize Jesus as the one who offers definite and definitive salvation from God and therefore to confess the "story of God" in the human story of Jesus cannot be distilled by an exegetical process from a deep analysis of New Testament texts, however necessary this may be if we are to know the real story of Jesus. This is because the mediated nearness of God's offer of mercy to man is conveyed in a more concentrated form than elsewhere in the revealing and the concealing mediation of Jesus. Nowhere else has there ever been such a concentration of concealing mediation—Jesus was even sent to his death in the name of orthodox religion. Nowhere else too is God's direct and gratuitous nearness in him so tangibly present for the one who, in *metanoia* (self-criticism), goes forward openly to meet him—in the tradition of the Church, he is even called the "true God." A person cannot be approached precisely as a person in a process of purely theoretical, scientific analysis. The one who is prepared to take a risk, however, can still recognize, in the story of Jesus, the great parable of God himself and at the same time the paradigm of our humanity, a new and unheard of possibility of existence offered because God himself was concerned with humanity. Part of the plot of the story of Jesus, however, is that his shocking freedom is a scandal to the one who takes offence at him (Luke 7. 23) and is at the same time able to act as a liberation to salvation in the case of the one who dares to trust the fascinating mystery of that story.

The question therefore arises as to whether too precise a theoretical definition of who Jesus Christ is is not more harmful than beneficial. A precise theoretical definition of a divine event which overwhelmed

Jesus and which constitutes the heart and soul of his entire life empov-
erishes that event and is therefore likely to be near to distortion, one-
sidedness and heresy. This is all the more likely in this case, since
Jesus' death was violent. On the basis of a critically justified exegesis,
it is essential to affirm Jesus' integration of his violent death into his
surrender of himself to God and his offer of salvation to men. Despite
this, however, it is impossible to deny the negativity of that death, as
a rejection.

It is impossible, theoretically or rationally, to reconcile or mediate
salvation on the one hand and the history of suffering on the other,
especially when the latter is a history of the suffering of an innocent
and just man.[3] On the one hand, salvation history took place in Jesus'
life. This is a fact which cannot be eliminated by his death or suspended
by it. On the other hand, however, Jesus' suffering and death, as a
rejection, are, from the historical point of view, a pure absence of salvation. This negative aspect cannot be denied. It is impossible to achieve
a theoretical, in other words, a rationally diaphonous reconciliation
between these two aspects. For this reason, we are bound to conclude,
with J. B. Metz, that salvation from God can only be expressed in the
"non-identity" of the history of Jesus' suffering and death.[4]

This situates Jesus' suffering outside God and within the secular
framework of the human predicament and human freedom and this
suggests that Jesus continued to identify himself with God's cause
without contaminating God himself by his own suffering precisely
within this non-divine situation of suffering and death. Even with regard
to Jesus, God remained free: "My thoughts are not your thoughts,
neither are your ways my ways" (Isa. 55. 8). God's sovereign freedom
applies to all men, but Jesus identified himself with this incomprehensible freedom of God in complete self-surrender at the approach of death.
It was precisely in the non-divine aspect of his innocent suffering and
death and therefore in the ultimately non-diaphanous aspect that Jesus
persisted in his personal identification with the kingdom of God that
was to come. God's sublime and definitive revelation thus occurred in
his silent but extremely intimate nearness to the suffering and dying
Jesus, who experienced, in his suffering and death, the depths of the
human predicament and at the same time his inseparable belonging
to God. This is what cannot be theoretically included within a rational
system—it can only be the object of a testimony of faith.

We are therefore bound to be more careful in any attempt to define the
soteriological significance of Jesus' suffering and death theoretically,
above all because we are confronted here with salvation that cannot
be expressed but does offer a basis for living. Our reluctance to do this
also has repercussions on any attempt that we may make to define

Jesus' personal identity theoretically. It is clear that Jesus is entirely both on God's and on man's side. His solidarity both with God in his sovereign freedom and with man is certainly the real definition of the kingdom of God who is concerned with man and of that kingdom which was experienced by Jesus himself in the alienation of his innocent, non-divine suffering and death.

This means that the cross is not what J. Moltmann has called an "event between God and God," but rather the index of the anti-divine in human history, which is transcended from within in Jesus, through his belonging to God. This belonging to God in an anti-divine situation has brought us salvation. Jesus rejected all competition between God's honor and sublimity on the one hand and man's happiness and salvation on the other. But how can all this be given a more precise theoretical definition if it is impossible for us to define God himself more precisely and to define the meaning of humanity?

My intention is not to impose silence or to check reflection about this question. What I have in mind is that a mystery of love and solidarity such as this ought to be approached with a certain reverence. What is more, any "theoretical" theology should also be connected[5] both with "stories"[6] and, even more importantly, with orthopraxis. This orthopraxis is the praxis of the kingdom of God, without which any theory or story will cease to be credible, especially in a world which is demanding justice and freedom. When this is done, theory, story and the praxis of the kingdom of God will become an effective invitation to answer in real freedom the question: "But who do you say that I am?" (Mark 8. 29; Matt. 16. 15; Luke 9. 20).

Translated by David Smith

NOTES

1. M. Hengel, *Judentum und Hellenismus* (Tübingen, ²1973), p. 354.

2. Luke 6. 20; Matt. 5. 3; Luke 7. 28; Matt. 11. 11; Luke 10. 9; Matt. 10. 7; Luke 11. 20; Matt. 12. 28, etc. Mark 1. 15; 4. 11; 4. 26; 9. 1, 27; 10. 14; 12. 34; 14. 25, etc. Matt, 3. 2; 4. 17; 5. 19, 20; 19. 24; 21. 31; 21. 43; Luke 4. 43; 9. 2, 11, 60, 62; 14. 15; 16. 16; 17. 20; 19. 11; 22. 16, 18; John 3. 3, 5.

3. E. Schillebeeckx, "Naar een definitieve toekomst: belofte en menselijke bemiddeling," *Toekomst van de religie. Religie van de toekomst* (Bruges and Utrecht, 1972), pp. 37–55, especially pp. 48–51.

4. J. B. Metz, "Erlösung und Emanzipation," *Stimmen der Zeit*, 191 (1973), pp. 171–84.

5. It is, after all, possible to begin telling a story too soon.

6. See J. B. Metz, *op. cit.*, and "A Short Apology of Narrative," *Concilium*, May 1973 (American edn., Vol. 85).

8

Questions on Christian Salvation
of and for Man

1978

In the post-Vatican II era we have noticed a certain polarization within the Christian churches. In the name of the Christian idea of salvation, many Christians have come to regard our socio-political endeavors to establish peace and justice in our history now as a humanistic and even Pelagian enterprise which endangers "salvation by faith alone." Thus in almost all churches a wedge is driven between the so-called orthodox, contemplation-oriented "churches of salvation" and the so-called heterodox, action-oriented "churches of liberation."

That which in former times appeared to interest religious people only has now become a matter of interest to the human sciences, techniques and activities of all kinds: all are striving after the healing, whole-making or salvation of man in society. It cannot be denied that (apart from the distinction between faith and reason) the quest for an integral and livable humanity, as an issue in itself, more than ever has the attention of all mankind. The answer to this problem is becoming all the more urgent in our present time, as we notice, on the one hand, that people fall short, fail and are injured, while, on the other hand, we can already have fragmentary experiences of human healing, whole-making and self-liberation. For the question of how to reach a livable humanity arises from the context of the actual conditions of disintegration, alienation, and human wounds of various kinds. The quest for salvation, *the* theme of all religions, has now more then ever become the stimulating force of modern history, even in those cases where religion is explicitly disavowed. Religions are not the only explicit thematizations of this universaily human theme of salvation. The quest for salvation is the main incentive of current history, not just in the religious and theological sense, but nowadays also as a theme in itself. Man becomes aware of the fact that human history is the place where salvation or whole-making is decided on; and the decision is an explicitly conscious one.

As a result of the world-wide expansion of our technical and scientific civilization, our actions bear consequences for all mankind. That is to say: the effects of the activities of modern man on the levels of science and technology are to be situated in the macro-cosmos of the common interests of all men. For the first time in human history, mankind as such finds itself faced with the task of accepting world-wide responsibility for the consequences of its activities. This need for a joint responsibility calls for an *ethic* of world-wide responsibility.

For the first time in human history, therefore, mankind is at the crossroads of a critical shift, a point where by his actions (both by what he does and by what he fails to do) man can decide on the future of the *world*, and therefore also on its *meaning*. Moreover, the situation calls for human action which no longer depends exclusively on individuals—rather what is required are arrangements on a socio-political basis. The present pressing demand could be formulated as a call for personal-izing and democratic socialization.

However, what is meant by "meaningful humanity," which ought to be the guiding principle for this joint responsibility? One might ask whether there exists a universally, intersubjectively binding, yet non-dogmatic vision in this respect, acceptable to all men. The critical question, therefore, is the following: Taking account of the level of problem-consciousness man has developed up to this present day, while longing for a better future, what do we mean by a true and good, happy and free human being in a righteous society? What is meant by a *livable humanity?*

We have become more modest today in our attempts to state in positive terms what it means to be human. E. Bloch wrote: "Man does not yet know who he is, but, alienated as he may be from himself, he is able to know for certain who he is not, and, therefore, what it is in this situation of alienation that he does not want to remain, or, at least, ought not remain." The definition of human existence is not a preexis-tent datum. For Christians it is not even just a coming reality, but an eschatological reality. Some would pretend to have a blueprint of what it means to be human. They have a completely outlined image of man, a concrete vision of future society, a complete theory of salvation—a dogmatic system that, paradoxically, appears to be more important than man, for whom it is meant. This totalitarian vision inevitably leads to totalitarian action, which is then only a matter of the application of technology and strategy. Moreover, as a matter of course, the ones who neither accept nor use *this* concept of true human existence are regarded as the enemies of true humanity.

Our times have become more modest in this matter. Nature, creative ordinances and Evolution (with a capital E) cannot provide us with criteria to judge what a livable, true, good and happy humanity means. Neither can they therefore tell us which are meaningful, ethically responsible actions that promote true humanity. Nor can a so-called universal human nature, which, being intrinsically pre-defined (such as is the case with plants and animals), would be directed towards an essentially pre-defined goal. For the same reason, neither can the modern version of this latter line of thought, the so-called law of nature. What is more, self-reflection, independent of time and space, cannot arrive at a crystallization of some kind of general "substratum" of reasonableness among all men.

Structuralists have discovered deep structural constants in human societies, but these do not tell us anything about the specific properties of any concrete society. These structures have no direct relation to concrete empirical reality, but only with the models which man has made of this reality. By doing so, structuralism has indeed discovered one aspect of human reality, namely that man is a model-developing being; but (being consistent) it abstains from the question of how these models relate to reality. Structuralism excludes precisely the human individual, the subject, and therefore cannot provide criteria for a society worthy of human beings.

Existentialism, in its turn, has indeed analyzed "existentialia," i.e., basic dispositions of human experience: fear, despair, love, hope, suffering, death, happiness, finiteness and guilt. And these aspects are extremely important in human life; they are related to the *quest for* what is ultimately worthy of a human being, but as such they do not provide an answer to this question: What is a basis of hope for a livable humanity in the midst of finiteness, guilt and suffering? Clearly they only say what it is we must be liberated from and to what purpose: to reach happiness. But how? And what does true happiness for all and everybody mean?

Finally, neither can we accept the positivistic view of values and norms. In this case, through empirical analysis, one indeed arrives at statements establishing which norms and values are operative in a certain group of society. This sociological insight is indeed important and even extremely relevant, e.g., for positive legislation; in order to be viable a law must indeed be supported by a reasonable consensus of all the members of that society. But it is impossible to elevate "factuals," or actually operative norms which score the highest points in statistical research, to a universal norm of ethical and meaningful human behavior. Highly civilized cultures disappeared in the course of time precisely for that reason.

Therefore, the critical consciousness of man should put us on the right track. If reason is a specifically human faculty, then the human capacity of judging the ambiguous phenomena of human history on the basis of norms is the proper critical task of man. Man is a being caught up in history. In his very essence, man is a narrative, a historical event rather than a pre-determined fact. He reveals something of this essence nowhere but in the course of his historical passage: in the very history of humanity. Man is situated and thematic freedom, not a free initiative in a vacuum or in a void. Salvation and humanity being "whole," integrity in a truly human, free way is precisely the *theme* of the whole story of man. Neither an idealistic nor a materialistic reading of this history does justice to this story of man.

Critical consciousness is not just (a) an awareness of the fact that part of the concrete nature of man consists in his being caught up in an environment of phenomena which give us no direct revelation of the true and the good, but which at the same time render these unrecognizable and veil them in such a way that there is a need for a standard to judge by; it is also (b) an awareness of the fact that the critical capacity of human reason is co-dependent on the historical circumstances in which it is situated, so that even the relation between *reason* and the concrete *historical circumstances* must be reflected on; (c) finally, it is also a consciousness that the past as well as the present and the time in between can be misjudged because they themselves take part in the ambiguity of all that is historical. Human reason is critical, rather than being dogmatic or nihilistically skeptical, only to the extent that it takes into account the ambiguity of the phenomena which reveal and simultaneously veil the true and the good, i.e., to the extent that it takes into account the historical conditioning of human thinking and the ambiguity of meaning or plurality of meaning of every period in time—the past, the present *and* the time in between, which are all open to different interpretations. Therefore, human consciousness is critical only to the extent that it does not stop at passing a critical judgment on the given phenomena, but is also capable of self-criticism with regard to critical reason itself (a thing that seems to have been beyond the grasp of eighteenth-century Enlightenment).

Instead of a positivistic attitude, instead also of a philosophically pre-determined definition of "human nature" (e.g., in the Aristotelian-Thomistic or Spinozian and Wolffian sense), instead, finally, of a historically necessary product of history, which would come flowing from the rational depth-course of history (as in a Marxist definition of true and free humanity), the only thing we have at our disposal is *anthropological constants*. These indeed reveal human values to us. On the basis of these human *values* and in a historical, changing process, we must fill in the concrete *norms* in a creative way. In other words, these anthropological constants point in a general way toward lasting human impulses, orientations, and value spheres, but they do not directly provide us with concrete norms or ethical imperatives on the basis of which, here and now, a more human and livable humanity can be called into existence. They do present us, however, with constitutive conditions (from the analysis and interpretation of our own contemporary situation) which, over and over again, must be filled in and colored anew and which are presupposed in all human activity, if man, his culture and society are not to be desecrated, hurt and made unlivable. Taking into account the socio-historical shape of our concrete society, viewed in the light of the value spheres which are acknowledged to be constants within our current problem consciousness, man is indeed able to set up concrete standards (norms) for human activities on a medium-long or even long-term basis.

I propose to analyze seven of these anthropological constants. I view them as a kind of system of coordinates which focus on the human *person-identity* within *social culture.* We are then concerned with profiles of man and his culture, constitutive aspects which man must take into account while creatively developing concrete norms for ever-growing humanity, and therefore for the salvation of man.

The System of Coordinates of Man and His Salvation

Relation to Human Corporeity, Nature and Ecological Environment

The relation of the human person to his own corporeity—man *is* and *has* a body—and via his own corporeity to the greater nature and to his own ecological environment is a constitutive aspect of our humanity. It also relates to human salvation.

If, in our activities, we fail to take into account this aspect of our humanity, we will eventually control nature in such a one-sided way or condition man in such a way as to destroy the basic principles of our own natural environment, and in doing so we will preclude our own humanity be interfering with our natural management or ecological basis. In our relation to nature and to our own corporeity we are faced with boundaries which have to be respected if we wish to live in a human way and even, in extreme cases, to survive *tout court.* Technical possibilities are, therefore, not necessarily also ethical, humanly meaningful and responsible possibilities.

This also holds for the physical and psychical limitations of our human capacities. Even if we are (still) unable to define in an empirically scientific way the precise limits of human changeability, of human conditioning, of the burden man can take, in an extra-scientific way we are convinced that there inevitably must be such limits. This extra-scientific though cognitive certainty reveals itself in a spontaneous manner in individual and collective protests as soon as people experience that they are being overburdened. The elementary needs of man (e.g., food, sex), his passions (e.g. aggressivity) and his corporeity in general cannot be manipulated in an arbitrary way without man experiencing that his humanity is being affected in its soundness and wholeness, happiness and livability (a thing that will manifest itself in spontaneous resistance).

This first anthropological constant opens a vast field of human values that call for humane standards with respect to one's own corporeity and its natural environment. However, these are standards which we ourselves have to derive from the concrete situation in which we now live. This already opens a perspective on the relationship of man towards nature, which is indeed not exclusively dictated by the human value of mastering nature but also by the equally human value of esthetical appreciation and enjoyment of nature. The limits set by nature itself to its technical manipulation by man and for man reveal a dimension of our human existence which is not exhausted by the technical mastering of nature. On the other hand, this same constant warns us of the danger of an anti-technological or anti-industrial culture. Scientists who reflect on their own enterprise emphasize the anthropological relevance of instrumental reason. The philosophy of culture has analyzed man's incapacity to live in a purely natural environment. Man must create himself a human *Umwelt* in nature if he is to survive without the refined instinct and the strength of animals. For that reason, a rational change of nature is necessary. Thus a "meta-cosmos" (F. Dessauer) is created which delivers man from animal limitation and provides an opening towards new possibilities. In times when the "meta-cosmos" hardly differed from nature, only a small part of the population enjoyed the advantages of culture and the masses were forced to work as slaves in order to free the happy few from material care. (One may rightly wonder whether much has changed in our highly industrialized "meta-cosmos." This first, fundamental anthropological constant seems to be insufficient.) The "meta-cosmos" provides man with better housing and a better home than the natural cosmos. Therefore, technology in itself need not be dehumanizing. Rather it may be a help towards attaining a livable humanity; it is an expression of and at the same time a condition for the humanizing of man. After all, it is a historical fact that all reflection on the meaning of life has always presupposed the creation of a "meta-cosmos." Moreover, the humanization of nature is not completed, although looking at our advanced technology one could easily be led to think it is. Man can indeed influence his own ecological situation within nature, but he remains dependent on it, a situation which manifests itself particularly in those cases where he disturbs the conditions of life. The effort to emancipate man from nature on the one hand, without, on the other hand, disturbing his own ecological basis is an eminently human task which cannot be realized without "instrumental reason."

In addition, it appears that the creation of meaning and the development of certain views on the world and on man is co-mediated by the instrumental technical reason and is not only the result of the immanent development of ideas. Ideas concerning marriage, love and sexuality have shifted in our time (e.g., in comparison with biblical ideas) largely for the sole reason that science and technology could provide means which before were not available to man. As soon as technical possibilities become available, interference with nature looks like quite a different thing from times in which any form of interference with nature was experienced as a sly and therefore evil interference with divine creation ordinances. As soon as this happens, man starts running the risk of concluding he is both capable of and allowed to solve all his physical and psychical, social and general human-life problems in a purely technical way, based only on the factual availability of technical possibilities and capacities. But there is a difference between the technocratic interpretation of the ideal of a livable and humane life and the anthropological relevance of science and technology. The dehumanizing character that is often part of this interpretation does not proceed as such from technology but from the concomitant question of meaning which has already been solved in a positivistic sense. Therefore, it is neither science nor technology with their capacity of promoting humanity which are subject to criticism, but very often their implicit presuppositions and assumptions.

Thus, this first anthropological constant reveals a whole scale of sub-constants of all kinds—e.g., that man is not only reason but also heart, not only reason but also imagination, not only freedom but also instinct, not only reason but also love.

If Christian salvation is indeed salvation *of and for man*, it must have an essential relation with this first anthropological constant. To recall one aspect of what was said before: Christian salvation also has relations with ecology, with the conditioning of man and with the burdens which are being imposed on him in his concrete life here and now. Those who call all this alien to Christian salvation might be dreaming of salvation for angels, but not for men.

Human Existence Is Human Co-existence

Human person-identity entails our co-existence with fellow men. This is also an anthropological constant, which reveals a field of human values in which man must search for standards to promote salvation here and now. Togetherness, fellowship, by which we give ourselves to others and in which we are confirmed in our existence and in our person-identity by others, is part of the building-up of person-identity itself: being allowed to be, the confirmation by others and by the community that we exist, that I am allowed to "be there," with my own name, my own identity, as a personal and responsible self. This person-identity is only possible if others allow me to be myself in my own inalienability but also in my essential limitations (*divisum ab alio,* ancient philosophy said). In this limited individuality, a person has an essential relation to the others, the fellow men. Our very faces (nobody ever sees his own face!) indicate that man is oriented towards and is meant for the other and not for himself. The human face is an image of oneself *for others.* Thus, by this concrete appearance, man is predestined for the encounter with fellow men in this world. This entails the assignment to accept the others in inter-subjectivity as they are, in their differences and in their freedom. It is precisely in this reciprocal relation with others that man will overcome the limitations of his own individuality in a free and loving acceptance of the other, and that he acquires person-identity. The fellowship in which we accept one another as persons, i.e., as goals and ends and not as means to an end, is an anthropological constant which requires norms without which, here and now, sound and livable humanity is impossible. This also implies that well-being and being-whole, salvation and sound humanity must be *universal,* must concern all and every man, not just some privileged persons, even if from the preceding it appears that being-whole entails more than interhumanity on a *personal* level. Nobody can enter into a relation of a real encounter with all people. After all, there is not only an "I-you" relation: the presence of a *third* person, of a "he," is the basis of society which cannot be reduced to an "I-you" or "we" relation. It is especially E. Lévinas who observed this very well. This leads us to a third essentially human dimension.

Relation to Social and Institutional Structures

Thirdly, there is the relation of the human person to social and institutional structures. In the course of history we, human beings, indeed call into being these structures. But they become independent and grow into an objective form of society, in which we live and which in turn influences our interiority, our person. The social dimension is not some- thing that is added to our person-identity, it is a dimension of this very identity. As independent entities, the structures and institutions create the impression of being unchangeable laws, though we ourselves can change them, thus destroying their claims of being natural laws. These much-vaunted sociological and economic laws do not exist independently of what men do or independently of human reason and human will to preserve them. They essentially exist under the historical hypothesis of the objectively present social and economic polity; they are contingent, and changeable, and therefore can be changed by man (although underneath all kinds of social changes, even radical ones, sociologists and cultural anthropologists may perhaps detect a deeper, almost unchangeable stratum, and consequently a structural constant). In treating them as laws of nature or metaphysical issues, the empirical sciences, which rightly point out these sociological or socio-psychological laws, nevertheless fail sometimes to recognize their essential subordination to the hypothesis of our current (changeable) objective form of society.

This constant also reveals to us a field of values, namely the value of the institutional and structural elements for a really humane life: another field of values that requires concrete norms. On the one hand, there is no lasting human life without a certain degree of institutionalizing; person-identity calls for social consensus, to be carried by structures and institutions which enable human freedom and the realization of values. On the other hand, factual, historically developed structures and institutions have no general validity. They are changeable. From this the concrete demand arises to change them where, as a result of changed circumstances, they have come to enslave and disfigure man instead of liberating and protecting him.

The Space-Time Structure of Person and Culture

Time and space, the historical and geographical location of persons and cultures, is an anthropological constant from which no man can escape.

Here we are first of all confronted with a dialectic tension between nature and history, which coincide in concrete human culture and which cannot be removed, not even by optimal social structures. It is a dialectic which belongs to the components of our finite human existence and of which death only is the ultimate exponent, a limit situation. This means that, apart from all kinds of suffering which to a great extent can be reme-

died by man, there are sufferings and threats to life which no technical
or social intervention can remedy. The historicity of man, his finiteness
from which he cannot escape in order explicitly to place himself on a level
above time, makes for the fact that human existence is also experienced
as a *hermeneutical* enterprise, i.e., as a task to *understand* one's own
situation and to *critically unmask* the nonsense in history brought about
by man. In this attempt towards self-understanding, in which the question of truth and untruth is also asked, man can receive help from all
kinds of empirically analytical and theological sciences, but in spite of
this man experiences truth as being at the same time both a thing *remembered* and a thing *to be realized*. If understanding is the specifically
human way of experiencing, then understanding is as universal as history itself. It follows that the pretension to take a stand outside the historical action and thought of man is a threat to real humanity.

Many other problems are connected with this constant. I will point
out only a few. There may be historically and geographically co-defined
acquisitions which, at this point, can no longer be regarded as free or
arbitrary, although they did come up in history at a fairly late date and
at certain places and therefore cannot be called *a priori* necessary or *a
priori* universal presuppositions. Certain values may have developed
which call for standards applying, i.e., in the highly industrialized and
highly cultural conditions in which Western man lives, but not necessarily applying in other cultures.

A few examples may suffice. Owing to the high level of his welfare
Western man is called to international solidarity, especially with regard
to poor countries (apart from the historical question of how far the West
itself is responsible for bringing about the poverty of these countries).
To the extent that this same constant reveals the historical and geographical limitations of each culture, it follows that, in view of the
limited potential of people's imagination in a certain culture, the critical
memory of the great traditions of mankind, and also of its great religious
traditions, will act as a necessary stimulus in the search for norms for
actions that, here and now, promote a sound and livable humanity.
This critical memory plays an important role in man's hermeneutical
enterprise to seek for light for future actions.

Finally, this fourth anthropological constant reminds us of the fact
that the explicit discovery of precisely these constitutive constants is
itself part of a historical process; our becoming conscious of it results
from human hermeneutical praxis.

The Relation between Theory and Praxis

The essential relation between theory and praxis is also an anthropological constant. It is a constant precisely insofar as through this rela-

tion human culture, as a hermeneutical enterprise or a grasping of meaning and as an effort to affect a change of meaning and improve the world, attains durability. On the level of the sub-human (e.g., animal) world, durability and the possibility of survival of the species and of the individual are assured by natural instincts, by adaptability to the changed or changing environment, and finally by the evolutionary law of the strongest in the struggle for life. If man wants to avoid making his own history into a kind of spiritual Darwinism, i.e., a history in which it is the will and the thinking of the stronger ones and the victors who pre-dictate what is good and true for our humanity, then on the human level the dialectics of theory and praxis will be the only humanly responsible guarantee for a lasting and ever more humane culture.

Where dealing with the problem of orthodoxy and orthopraxy, theologians often appear to mix up two levels of thought. On the one hand, there is the level of the *fides qua.* This expression means that faith is only authentic to the extent that it leads to action. Believing but failing to act accordingly reveals that one evidently does not really believe. This is what makes a person's faith "incredible" for others. However, this matter has nothing to do with the problem of theory versus praxis. The latter should rather be situated on the level of the *fides quae* (or of the content of faith): a statement of faith does not become true because it is put into practice or untrue because it is not put into practice. Consistent praxis does not determine the truth value of a theory. The eleventh Feuerbach thesis of Marx about the so-called primacy of praxis over theory can cause confusion in this respect. Marx himself offers an interpretative theory of the world, but he offers a theory which should be read as a criticism of certain groups and which is therefore apt to be used for a particular, determined (society-changing) praxis. Even in this case, theory comes before praxis, but it happens to be a theory with a practical critical intention. Theologians often mix up these two levels and then refer to the primacy of the praxis over faith (see e.g., Th. Schneider, "Orthodoxie und Orthopraxie: Überlegungen zur Struktur des christlichen Glaubens," *TThZ* 81 [1972]: 151). What it really comes down to is the primacy of *faith* (a kind of theory or affirmation of truth), which as such, commits itself to action; *theological* reflection can only follow afterwards, as a "second step," providing a control and criticism of all those forms of action that pass as Christian. Thus, theory *not only* has a post-practical function. It also (consciously or implicitly) precedes the praxis. The praxis as such does not provide a basis for the truth value of a theory (e.g., it is possible to hold a Nazi theory and very consistently to act accordingly, but this loyal consistency has no bearing on the truth value of the theory!).

The Religious and "Para-religious" Consciousness of Man

It seems to me that the "utopian" moment of human consciousness is also an anthropological constant, even a fundamental one.

Here it is the future of man which is at stake. What future does he want? By utopian moment I mean all kinds of (conservative or progressive) totality constructs which enable man to give some meaning to or conquer the contingency or finiteness, the precariousness, including the problem of suffering, failure and death. In other words, I mean the way in which a certain society puts the hermeneutical enterprise into concrete forms in everyday life (see the fourth constant) or, protesting against a pre-given meaning, opts for a different social policy and a different future. Totality visions teach us how to live human life, now and in future, as a humanly meaningful, good and happy totality—a vision and praxis which will give meaning and coherence to human existence in this world (even if only in a distant future).

Here we must mention totality visions of a *religious* nature (the religions) as well as of *non-religious* character—visions on life, on society, world-views and general theories of life in which man expresses what finally inspires him, what kind of human existence he finally chooses, what the ultimate goal he lives for is and why he finds life worth living. All these can be called cognitive models of reality which interpret the whole of nature and history in theory and praxis and, now or later, let them be experienced as (to-be-realized) meaningful existence.

In most—but not all—of these "utopias" people can see themselves as the subject of actions that promote the good and the building-up of a good humane world, without being individually and at the same time personally responsible for the reality of history and its final outcome. Some will call this dominating principle destiny or fate, others evolution, still others "mankind," the species Man as a universal subject of the whole of history, or, in more vague terms, "Nature." For religious people this is the living God, the Lord of history. But, in whatever form, such a totality vision is always a *kind of faith*, except when one adheres to nihilism and therefore professes the absurdity of human life, a kind of faith in the sense of being a utopia that is not subject to scientific tests, and can never be fully rationalized. *Without faith nobody fares well.* In that sense faith, the basis of hope, is an anthropological constant of the whole of human history, a constant without which humane and livable human life and action become impossible; man loses his identity and ends up in neurotic conditions, or has irrational recourse to horoscopes and all kinds of *mirabilia.* Moreover, faith and hope are confirmed as necessary human constants by the nihilistic pretension which calls livable humanity an absurdity, and therefore is without faith and hope.

This implies that faith and hope (whatever we take them to mean) are essential to the health and soundness, the livability and wholeness of our being human and humane. For those who believe in God this implies that religion is an anthropological constant without which salvation for man, redemption and real liberation which passes by a *religious* redemption is a bisected liberation and, moreover, to the extent that it is presented as a *total* liberation of man, smashes to pieces a real dimension of being human, thus eventually dislocating man instead of liberating him.

Irreducible Synthesis of These Six Dimensions

To the extent that these six anthropological constants can be brought together in a synthesis, human culture is indeed an irreducible *autonomous reality,* to be reduced neither in an idealistic nor in a materialistic sense. The synthesis constitutes the man-healing reality which brings salvation. (The synthesis itself must therefore be called an anthropological constant.) The six constants gear into each other and condition each other. They design the basic form of human existence and keep each other in balance. To speak about the priority of "spiritual values" may sound nice, even just, but in fact it may destroy the material conditions and implications of the spiritual values precisely at the expense of these. Undervaluation of one of these deeply human constants dislocates the whole, including the spiritual. It wrongs man and his society and throws out of balance the whole of human culture. In doing so one consciously or unconsciously makes an attack on true and good, happy and free human existence.

On the one hand, it may be clear from the preceding remarks that the anthropological constants which open a perspective on fundamental value areas of human existence in no way provide us with *norms* which, here and now, have to operate on our objective social structures and given culture in order to arrive at more humane behavior. These constants design, so to say, only the system of coordinates in which concrete norms will have to be found in mutual consultation. These concrete norms can only be found after the analysis and interpretation of the concrete social structures and the position man, the person, occupies in them. Starting from the level of our problem consciousness reached up to this point as a minimal vantage point (perhaps this is also an important factor in our reflection on what is human), we can then, on the basis of negative experiences or contrastive experiences, as well as on the basis of already lived meaning experiences, and in the light of what we believe to be a valid "utopia," make an analysis of the gap between the ideal and factuality. The gap analysis will reveal the direction to be taken (allowing for alternative directions, however—cf. *infra*)—a direction which we will have to determine in mutuality and fill in with the concrete norms required at this present moment.

I said that we must allow for all kinds of alternative directions, for there may be huge differences in the way people view the utopian moment of our human consciousness as well as their analysis and especially their interpretation of the analytical results (for the very method of analysis already reveals a certain oriented utopian consciousness). The result will be pluralism, even if we apply a scientific analysis (which takes place within a conscious or unconscious interpretive frame)—pluralism also in the presentation of concrete norms—even if people recognize the same fundamental values to which the "anthropological constants" have drawn our attention. The norms to which each individual subscribes must be made the subject of discussion in dialog and on the basis of intrinsic arguments if we wish to challenge other people with them. Even when their fundamental inspiration arises from a religious belief in God, *ethical* norms (i.e., norms which promote humanity) must be rationally justified in an inter-subjectively valid discussion, i.e., a discussion open to all reasonable people. None of the partners in the discussion can hide himself behind a doubtful "I see what you do not see," while at the same time forcing others to accept his own norm. As in many discussions, the beginning situation can indeed be such that one of the partners in the discussion can see something that others cannot see. But in that case this "something" ought to be clarified for others in a free and rational communication process. Nobody can claim a storm-free zone (even though other partners in the discussion do not necessarily have to agree on the basis of the arguments presented). The fact that one has to learn to live with different views of the concrete norms required to attain livable humanity, here and now, belongs to the very predicament of creating modern, livable humanity. Sadness about this pluralism is itself part of our (especially modern) human predicament which we have to come to terms with. This cannot be done by a dictatorial rejection of other views. The art of living also belongs to the true, good and happy human existence within the boundaries of our historicity and finiteness, at least if we wish to avoid turning into "megalomaniacs" who pretend to be able to pass by their human finiteness. On the other hand, people's readiness to bring about salvation must not proceed from so-called political realism, i.e., from a view of politics as the art of the possible, the attainable, that which is within reach. Politics is the rather more difficult art of enabling that which is necessary for human salvation.

Christian Salvation

Christian salvation, liberation, or definitive and eschatological redemption from God in Jesus deals with the whole system of coordinates in which man can really be himself. This salvation or whole-being cannot be found exclusively in one or another of these constants, e.g., exclusively in ecological slogans, exclusively in "being nice to one another," exclusively in overthrowing an economic system (whether capitalist or Marxist), or exclusively in mystical experiences: "Halleluia, He is risen." Moreover, the true synthesis of all this will be a clear "already" *and* "not yet," both mysticism and political liberation.

Christian salvation, in order to be salvational, must be *universal* and *total*. Consequently salvation, in the sense of that which makes whole, should entail as a minimum requirement that no one group be whole at the expense of another one. This does not imply that Christian salvation can be reduced to the making of a universally human just society. It does imply, however, that the making of such a society is a minimum ingredient of Christian salvation.

This implies that whole-making, salvation of and for man, is also an *experiential* concept. The Christian concept of salvation would lose its rational meaning (i.e., rationally speaking it would not be a concept of salvation) if there were no *positive* relationship between the "justification by faith alone" and the construction of a more just, integrated world. Salvation must be at least a partial and fragmentary reflection of that which is experienced by man as whole-making. Salvation that is merely "promised" loses all reasonableness. Therefore, Christian salvation must satisfy minimum requirements if we wish to prevent this term "salvation," and, with it, *Christian* salvation, from dying the death of a thousand qualifications. By introducing salvation as an experiential concept, we are able, on the one hand, to safeguard God's freedom "to be God," i.e., a reality which cannot be pinned down to our human concepts of salvation, while, on the other hand, man receives the freedom "to be human," i.e., a living creature with his own say in the matter whether a certain type of salvation will or will not take place.

The central issue for the faithful is, then, whether they are actually doing the same thing as non-believers about building a new world of justice. In this case, the faithful world gives just another *interpretation* to this common praxis, which, being just an interpretation, would have no consequences of its own for the praxis. Religion has no contribution of its own to make to a praxis which would remain indifferent to a religious or non-religious interpretation. Consequently, the claim of religion to render an irreducible service to the world becomes problematic and distressingly ambiguous to the degree to which this service is understood as proceeding from extra-religious aims. Conversely, the claim of any religion to present its own specific interpretation of man and of the world is equally problematic and ambiguous to the degree that this interpretation lacks relevance for the praxis. Religion is neither an interpretation of the world which can be divorced from the praxis, nor is it a praxis devoid of all relation to a particular interpretation of man and of the world. It is therefore the task of theology to clarify how religion (or Christendom) serves the world in a way which is both *specifically religious* (or Christian, ultimately founded on prayer) and *practically, even politically active* in the world. For when we speak of religious and Christian consciousness (with its own critical and productive, i.e., action-guiding, force), we are really speaking of a certain pattern of human consciousness. The question, then, becomes: What is specifically religious about this consciousness, i.e., which knowledge and which reality determine our awareness in such a way that it can be called "religious" or Christian? At the same time, this means: How is the reality of man and the world to be judged in the light of this religious consciousness?

On the one hand, a non-dualistic definition of God as pure positivity, origin, basis and source of the promotion of all good things and opponent of all evil has a critically productive force of its own. On the other hand, the mystical praxis of Christianity is linked with its social and political praxis through the non-theorizable mediation of the history of human suffering. Salvation is then realized within the conditions of suffering finiteness.

Human suffering has its own critical and productive *epistemic* power. This should not be reduced to the purposive, emancipatory type of knowledge characteristic of the sciences and technology, nor to the various types of contemplative, esthetic and playful, so-called "aimless" knowledge, which keeps turning around its object. The specific epistemic value of the contrastive experience of suffering based on injustice assumes a *critical* attitude *both* towards the contemplative type of knowledge *and* towards the scientific or technological type. It provides the purely contemplative total perception, which already has some experience of universal reconciliation in its contemplation or liturgy, with a critical element. But at the same time it is critical of the dominating knowledge of the sciences and technology which presupposes that man is merely a ruling subject (thus neglecting the question of priority).

The productive epistemic value of suffering is not just critical of both positive types of human knowledge; it can also become the dialectic link between both, i.e., the contemplative epistemic force of the human psyche and its active dominating epistemic force. In fact, much can be

said in favor of the thesis that the contrastive experience of suffering
(with its implicit ethical demand) is the only experience capable of linking these two intrinsically, since it is the only experience which unites
characteristics of both types of knowledge. For just like contemplative
or esthetic experiences, experiences of suffering *overcome* a person,
albeit that the latter are of a contrastive nature whereas the former are
positive. On the other hand, to the extent that the experience of suffering
is a contrastive experience, it opens perspectives for a praxis which
aims at removing both the suffering itself and its causes. It is on the
basis of this inner relationship, a relationship of critical negativity, both
with the contemplative type of knowledge and with the type of knowledge
which seeks to master nature, that the specific "pathetic" (*pati*) epistemic force of suffering is *practically* critical, i.e., it is a critical epistemic
force which promotes a new praxis anticipating a better future and
actively committed to realizing it. All this entails that, in our given
human predicament and within the context of our concrete social culture, contemplation and action—paradoxically but nevertheless truly—
can be brought together intrinsically only by the criticism of the
accumulated history of human suffering and the ethical consciousness
developed in the course of this history of suffering.

For the experience of suffering as a contrast experience can only exist
on the basis of an explicit longing for happiness, and, to the extent that
this is an experience of unjust suffering, it presupposes at least some
vague form of awareness of the positive meaning of human integrity. As
a contrast experience it indirectly implies an awareness of the positive
vocation of and to the *Humanum*. In this sense, all action which seeks
to conquer suffering presupposes at least an implicit and vague anticipation of a possible, future universal meaning. As opposed to the pur-
poseful knowledge of the sciences and technology and to the purposeless
knowledge of contemplation, the specific epistemic value of the contrast
experiences of suffering is that of a knowledge which begs for a future
and even opens one. Thus, next to "purpose" and "purposeless," "future"
(not evolution but eschatological future) becomes a valid concept. For on
the basis of its ambivalent characteristics (having properties in common
both with contemplation and with action) and of its ethical character
of protest, the specific epistemic value of suffering is that of a knowledge
which does not ask for purposefulness or aimlessness, but for a future:
for more humanity and for the coming suppression of the causes of
injustice. For in the negativity of its experience, or even because of this
negativity, it possesses a form of ethical protest against "letting it be,"
it has a critical epistemic force which appeals for a praxis of opening
the future, a praxis, moreover, which refuses to submit to the self-
evident absolute reign of purposive technocracy (for this is one of the

causes of suffering). Therefore, the contrast experience of suffering is the negatively and dialectically awakening consciousness of a longing and a quest for future meaning and future real freedom and happiness. It is also a longing for the conciliatory, "aimless" contemplation, as an anticipation of universal meaning to be linked, because of the contrastive nature of the experience, with a new future-creating praxis which is to conquer evil and its sufferings.

9

The Christian Community and Its Office-Bearers

1980

This problem is sufficiently clearly outlined in the editorial of this number of *Concilium*. We have therefore no need to return to it here, but will confine ourselves, in this concluding article, to a synthesis and to the question of the Christian community and its office-bearers. In it, we shall reflect critically and theologically about the shortage of priests in the light of the community's apostolic right to office-bearers and to the Eucharist.

A clear discrepancy emerges from the various reports on Christian experience especially between contemporary Church order—or canon law—and a variety of practices to do with office in the Church, especially in what are known as basic communities. In the light of the whole tradition of the Church—one of the spheres of our own theological investigation—how ought we to react to these facts and these reports based on Christian experience? In considering this question, we should bear in mind that, on the one hand, statistics in themselves have no normative value and, on the other, that it is impossible to deny the Christian concern from which these alternative practices emerge.

No Church Community without a Leader

Ecclesia non est quae non habet sacerdotes—no Church community without a leader or a team of leaders (with the powers accepted by the Church). When Jerome[1] wrote these words he was obviously expressing the universal view of the early Church. This patristic comment is an anticipatory judgment on the way so many of us take for granted nowadays the shortage of priests in Church communities. If there is, from the sociological point of view, such a shortage of priests, then there must be something wrong with the way in which Christians see their Church and their office-bearers (and with their practice in this respect).

It is not, however, possible to analyse the present shortage of priests—which continues to give rise to secondary phenomena of questionable value with regard to the Church and especially the Eucharist because of its dubious ideological background[2]—purely and simply on sociological and statistical grounds. It must also be considered from the historical, theological and ecclesiological points of view. A basically theological examination of the problem is also able to bring to light the obstructions and the previous decisions which are at the origin of this shortage of priests and which ought not to exist from the ecclesiological point of view.

A great deal, but not everything, is possible in a Church community. I shall first of all look back very generally at the differently orientated conception of office in the Church during the first ten or so centuries and contrast it with the view that has prevailed during the second Christian millennium. This procedure has not been inspired by an untheological romantic longing to return to the origins of Christianity or by what I believe to be a wrong conviction that chronology—a closeness in time to the New Testament—should as such have priority. In themselves, the first ten centuries of Christianity are in no way to be preferred to the second millennium. What is of fundamental importance here is not chronology, but Christian praxis or *sequela Jesu*. Faithfulness to the New Testament and the great Christian tradition, which is now almost two thousand years old; does not in any way imply repetition—of any period, including that of the New Testament. Our contemporary questions, however, cannot in themselves be normative without a critical recollection of the whole of the Church's past, even though they are a part of that history. A truly Christian answer to these questions can only be obtained, I believe, in a critical confrontation between the present and the past.

I am therefore fundamentally concerned with theological criteria and consequently with the theological significance of the Church's practice with regard to office throughout the centuries in certain changing situations that have been determined by history. The critical point in this connection is whether the Church's practice with regard to office was primarily formed on the basis of theological criteria (although in a definitely historical setting), as was the case during the first ten centuries, or whether it has been fashioned mainly on the basis of extra-theological factors, as has happened in the second millennium.

One of the distinguishing marks of the theologican is his practice of confronting the Church and its living praxis with the whole tradition of faith, all its historically changing contexts and the theological or non-theological models that have, consciously or unconsciously, been invested in that tradition. For all its importance, even the Council of Trent was only one of many regulating factors in the correct interpretation of Scripture, with the result that it does not express the many-sided totality of Christian faith. It only expresses one part of that faith and, what is more, expresses that part in a particular situation that was determined by history. That part is, moreover, exclusive to the Western Church. Even though the Council of Trent expressed 'Christian truth,' it was a contextual truth, that is, it was related in a specific way to a definite Western situation.

The result of this is that, as far as their significance for us today is concerned, all the statements made by all the Church's councils and, even more importantly, all other non-conciliar pronouncements made by the Church must be interpreted not only within their own historical context, but also within the whole of the Christian tradition of faith, in the context of the orientation and inspiration that this long tradition has given to the further history of the Church in the light of biblical and apostolic faith. Throughout the further development of the Church, this inspiration has been expressed again and again in the best possible way in constantly changing situations. The Christian churches have sometimes succeeded in this. Sometimes they have succeeded less well and at times their achievements have been disappointing. Modern theologians are universally in agreement about this, although the Church's magisterium tends still to attach too much value to the 'letter' of earlier pronouncements and to underestimate their historical and hermeneutical aspects.

We have, therefore, to consider the facts in the early, the mediaeval and the modern history of the Churches if we are to assess the significance of the contemporary and alternative forms of office which are arising everywhere today and which deviate frequently from the valid order in the Church and discover the possible theological value of these ways of exercising office. It is also clear that authoritative documents—the authority of which is accepted by Catholic theologians, although that authority may be changing—have always been produced by a new praxis from below. This happened in the fifth century and characterized the image of the priest during the first millennium. It also took place in the twelfth and thirteenth centuries and fashioned the feudal image of the priest. This new praxis from below in the sixteenth century also resulted in the Tridentine, modern and therefore recent and traditional image of the priest. Official documents have again and again sanctioned the Church's practice that has come about from below.

We are at the present moment witnessing all around us the emergence from below of further new alternative or parallel conceptions and practices with regard to the Church's office. These have a clear affinity to the biblical and the patristic understanding of office. In the fairly distant future, then, after a probable process of purification, we may expect what may be called the contemporary 'fourth' phase in the Church's practice with regard to office to be ultimately sanctioned canonically. Critical recollections of past history therefore have the power to open up the future for us.

The First Millennium: A Pneumatological and Ecclesial Conception of Office

The Apostolicity of the 'Community of Christ'

On the basis of the New Testament,[3] the early Church was conscious of its apostolicity. What does 'apostolic' mean here? In the first place, it means the Christian communities' consciousness that they are built on the foundation of the 'apostles and prophets' of the earliest Church. According to the New Testament, living community is a community of believers who take over as their own the Jesus thing, that is, the kingdom of God that is to come as a phenomenon that is essentially linked with the whole appearance and ultimately with the person of Jesus and therefore want to preserve the story of and about Jesus in his significance for the future of all men. In this, the emphasis is also, but less on a teaching which has to be kept as pure as possible and more on the 'story' of and about Jesus and on the *sequela Jesu*, that is, a Christian praxis of following Jesus that has to be experienced as radically as possible, according to the orientation and inspiration of the 'kingdom of God and his righteousness' (Matt. 6:33). This is the power of the love of a God who is orientated towards mankind, which is the Christian dream seen as the idea of power making the future: 'Behold, the dwelling of God with men' (Rev. 21:1–4). Basically, what we have here is an assembly of believers, a community in which the vision of 'a new heaven and a new earth' is kept alive with reference to Jesus of Nazareth confessed as 'the Christ, God's only beloved Son, our Lord' and in bearing prophetic witness to conforming to the praxis of this kingdom of God.

This community of God is also a brotherhood in which the power structures dominating the world are broken down (Matt. 20:25–26; Mark 10:42–43; Luke 22:25) and all men are equal, although it might be possible to say that only the least of men, the poor and the oppressed are 'more equal' ('all men are equal, but some are more equal than others'!). All are called, although there are differences in function and, within these functions, even differences of office between the universal commitment of all believers to the community and specifically official ministries, especially that of the leader or the leading team of the community.[4]

Christian churches, then, are, according to the New Testament, apostolic. This includes the apostolic proclamation of Jesus' own message (of the kingdom of God) and Jesus' person, and therefore his death and resurrection cannot be separated from that message: 'The gospel of Jesus Christ, the Son of God' (Mark 1:1) or the 'gospel of God' (Mark 1:14). This apostolicity of the Christian community is placed in a dialectical relationship with the apostolicity of the Church's office (or the so-called *successio apostolica*). The apostolicity of the Christian community after all includes the apostolic mediation of faith and therefore also the lasting importance of the original document in which the 'gospel of Jesus Christ' is kerygmatically narrated, in other words, the New Testament, which is placed over and against the sphere of understanding of what is known as the Old Testament. The apostolicity of the content of the faith of the community is critical from the point of view of the New Testament: 'What you have heard from me before many witnesses entrust to faithful men who will be able to teach others also' (2 Tim. 2:2). It is primarily less a question of an uninterrupted succession or continuity of office and more a question of an uninterrupted continuity in the apostolic tradition or the content of faith.

It is from this that the fundamental self-understanding of the Christian community is obtained. It is the 'community of Jesus,' that is, by gathering as a community around Jesus as salvation in God's name, according to the witness borne by the apostles.

This community has—from the sociological point of view—a right to leaders and, for a community of God, this right is also an apostolic right. As the community of Christ, this community also has, on the basis of Jesus' mandate: 'Do this in memory of me,' an ecclesiological right to the celebration of the eucharist. It was, moreover, on the basis of this apostolic orientation that the New Testament communities and the communities of the early Church lived.

From the very beginning there were many offices and ministries in the Church. It cannot be established on the basis of the New Testament that there is only one office that can be historically divided up in descending order into different fragments. (This is a legitimate view, but it is not the only one and it is certainly abstract, unhistorical and purely theological and nothing more than that.) In the constitutive phase of the early Church, the 'apostolate' of those who founded the community—what is known in Scripture as the 'apostles and prophets'—was undoubtedly to some extent unique, but, as soon as the first generation of apostles and prophets had disappeared, the problem of leadership in the Church arose explicitly for all the churches. This problem, which became acute round-about A.D. 80 to 100, was one which even preoccupied Paul just before his death, which was expected at about that time (see, for example, Phil. 2:19–24). It was also at this time that the Church's office was given concrete, although still very flexible outlines in the different communities and at the same time was subjected to theological reflection as office, even though less interest was taken in the structures of office.

The pace-setters or leaders of the communities had died and the question was: How ought it to go on? On closer inspection, the use of pseudonyms—a fairly universal practice in profane circles in the ancient world—provides us with a positive view of the meaning of this practice. New leaders, who had often previously been collaborators with the apostles or 'spontaneous' leaders, followed in the footsteps of the founders of communities or of those who had maintained the tradition of the Church in certain communities—such men as Paul, Peter, Barnabas, James and a certain John. When these new leaders wrote letters to their communities, these were written in the name of the apostle who had been the tradition-bearer of the community in question. The Pastoral Epistles (Titus and 1 and 2 Timothy) were, for example, written as though they had been written by the Apostle Paul himself (although the latter was by that time already dead). It is precisely because the communities, together with their leaders, thought of themselves as 'Pauline,' for example, that the letters written by their new leaders were originally attributed by the communities themselves to Paul. It is clear from this that these communities consciously wished to think of themselves as 'apostolic' communities—as communities of the Jesus who had been proclaimed by the 'apostles and prophets' as the crucified but risen Jesus. An entire theology of the 'apostolic community' and the 'Church's office' is concealed within this pseudonymity.

The transition from the original Church to the post-apostolic churches (which are still New Testament churches) is clear from Eph. 4:7–10 and 4:11–16. After their death, these apostles and prophets, together with other founders of communities were called the foundation of the Church (Eph. 2:20). The new leaders, who were then, in that Church, called 'evangelists, pastors and teachers' (Eph. 4:11; and see 2:20; 3:6), had to continue to build on the foundation that had already been laid. The post-apostolic community leaders were therefore characterized by two inseparable qualifications. On the one hand, they were, like the apostles (1 Cor. 4:1; Rom. 10:14–15, 17), in the name of Christ in his service. On the other, however, the new situation, in contrast to the first Christian generations, was to be found in the fact that the Church office-bearers knew that they were bound to the apostolic inheritance. The post-apostolic office-bearers had therefore to take care of the original apostolic experience from which the communities had to live. They had, in other words, to safeguard Christian identity and evangelical vitality.

In this, office was clearly embedded in the whole complex of other ministries that were needed for the building up of the community (Eph. 4:11). The specific and distinctive character of the charisma of office within many other ministries is to be found in the fact that those bearing office had their own special responsibility, in solidarity with the whole of the community, for maintaining the apostolic identity and the evangelical vitality of the community. What was, from the New Testament point of view, of primary theological importance here was the demand of apostolicity, not the manner of appointment. The apostolicity of the communities founded by the apostles and prophets is, then, the source and the basis of the apostolicity of the Church's office. No historical guarantees can be discovered in any other view.

Historical Form within the Church

(a) In A.D. 451, after taking different forms for years in the various Christian communities, but in the long run becoming fairly uniform, this New Testament view was given an official canonical sanction. This is to be found in canon 6 of the Council of Chalcedon. This canon reproduces in a juridical form the view of the New Testament and the early Church of office in the Church. This view is moreover vividly confirmed by patristic theology and various liturgical forms used in the early Church. Not only are all forms of 'absolute ordination' condemned in this canon—they are also declared invalid: 'No one, neither priest nor deacon, may be ordained in an absolute manner (*apolelumenos*) . . . if he has not been clearly assigned to a local community, either in the city or in the country, either in a *martyrium* or in a *monasterium.*' This important text continues: 'The sacred Council concludes that their ordination (*cheirotonia*) is null and void . . . and that they may not carry out any functions on any occasion.'[5]

What theological view of the Church's office does this statement contain? It is that it is only someone who is called by a definite community to be its leader and pace-maker who may receive ordination. This *ordinatio* was primarily the accreditation of a believer as office-bearer to a definite community that had itself called this particular fellow-Christian and had designated him as its leader or president or had accepted and confirmed the appearance of one or more of its members in charismatic leadership. An absolute ordination—that is, the designation of someone (*cheirotonia*) or later laying hands on someone (*cheirothesia*)—without that candidate having been asked by a particular community to be its leader (or, if he had successfully appeared, without his having been accepted by the community) is, according to this canon of the Council of Chalcedon, null and void.

This canon, then, reveals the fundamentally ecclesial view of office in the early Church. The concept of *ordinatio* therefore includes not only—and even especially—a bishop's laying on of hands together with *epiclesis* or prayer to the Holy Spirit, but also—and primarily—being called, appointed or accepted (*cheirotonia*) by a definite Christian community.

The community calls and this is the calling or vocation of the priest, but, because the community regards itself as a 'community of Jesus,' the ecclesial appointment is at the same time experienced as a 'gift of the Holy Spirit,' in other words, as a pneumatological event. This dialectical bond, formulated canonically, between 'community' and Holy Spirit or between 'community' and 'office' points to the fact that the distinction between the power of ordination and the power of jurisdiction were at that time not only unknown, but also unthinkable from the point of view of ecclesiology.[6] 'No bishop should be imposed on the people if the people do not want him.'[7] 'The one who must lead all the people must be chosen by all the people.'[8]

According to this view, then, office is essentially ecclesial and therefore pneumatologically determined. It depends in no way on a private and ontological qualification of the individual person bearing office and is also in no way separate from an ecclesial context. What is in the balance here is the essential relationship between the community and office. Paulinus of Nola recorded that he was 'ordained' in an absolute manner in Barcelona. He describes this ordination in a tone of pious irony, in words that can be translated as 'There I was, orphaned, dressed in rags and tatters, alone in front of our Lord, a priest without a community' and declares that he was *in sacerdotium tantum Domini, non etiam in locum Ecclesiae dedicatus.*[9] Isidore of Seville called men who had been ordained in an absolute manner men without heads, 'neither a horse nor a man,'[10] in other words, neither fish, flesh nor fowl.

The bond between the community and office was so strong in the early Church that it was in principle impossible to be transferred to another community (although there were exceptions to this general principle for reasons of mercy and discretion—the so-called principle of *oikonomia*).[11] Another important consequence of this view of the Church's office was that an office-bearer who, for any reason, ceased to be the leader of a community *ipso facto* became a layman again in the full sense of the word.[12]

The view underlying this concept is this: It is not the possessor of the 'power of ordination' who may lead the community and therefore also lead in the celebration of the eucharist, but the leader who, by being accredited by and to a definite community (that is, *ordinatio* or *cheirotonia,* which is not the same as *cheirothesia* or the laying on of hands), receives all the necessary powers for the leadership of a Christian community. Because the community regarded itself, however, as a 'community of God,' the 'Body of the Lord' and the 'temple of the Holy Spirit,' a liturgical framework, in which supplication was made for God's charisma to be given to the leader appointed (in other words, *cheirotonia* became *cheirothesia*), was given at a very early date and almost automatically to this accreditation by and to the community. This was, then, not a sacral action, but a *believing sacramentality*.[13]

We may therefore conclude that a situation in which a community was unable to celebrate the Eucharist because there was no bishop or presbyter present was unthinkable in the early Church. As Jerome commented: 'No Church community without a leader.' On the basis of the right of the community to the Eucharist, the leader of the community also has the right to lead in the Eucharist. The community cannot, moreover, live evangelically without the Eucharist because it is a Eucharistic community, that is, a community that celebrates the Eucharist. If there is no leader, it chooses a suitable candidate from its own ranks. What are involved here are the evangelical identity and the Christian identity of the community.

(b) This understanding of office that prevailed in the early Church and was officially recorded in the document of the Council of Chalcedon is also expressed in the earliest known liturgy of the laying on of hands, the *Traditio Apostolica* of Hippolytus, which dates back to the first half of the third century.[14] According to this 'Apostolic Tradition,' the whole local community, together with its leaders who were already present in the community, chose its own bishop, its own presbyters and its own deacons.[15] We also know from other texts that the community might expect the one who had been called to accept this mission, even against his own will, because the community had a right to leaders by virtue of its necessary apostolicity, its Christian identity and its evangelical vitality.[16] The local Church put the apostolic faith of the candidate to the test and bore witness to that faith. This is a clear indication of the conviction in the early Church that the community itself is primarily apostolic. Because the leader (who was at that time the bishop) was given a specific responsibility for the apostolic community, it was the community that received the leader which first tested the apostolic foundation of his faith.

Although the local church chose its own leader, it did not give itself its office-bearer in an autonomous way. The choice by a 'community of Christ' was, because of its Christian nature, experienced as a gift of the Holy Spirit. This was expressed liturgically and sacramentally by the laying on of hands by bishops of neighbouring local churches. (From the time of the Council of Nicaea onwards, at least three bishops were required.) In this practice, the communion embracing all Christian churches is vividly expressed, in that it shows that no single local church has a monopoly of the gospel or Christian apostolicity, but is subject to the criticism of the other apostolic churches.

Supplication was made in the prayer or *epiclesis* pronounced over the candidate recommended by the community as its leader (who was in fact a bishop) for the gift of the 'power of the *pneuma hugemonikon*,' the spirit of leadership, and the 'power of the *pneuma archieratikon*,' the spirit of high priesthood. Supplication was also made over a member of the episcopal council, the presbyter, for the 'spirit of grace and counsel of the presbyteral college.' Finally, supplication was also made over the deacon, who was at that time completely in the service of the bishop and was able to do anything that he was authorized to by the bishop, having a spiritual charisma 'under the authority of the bishop.'

In this whole procedure, the emphasis is clearly placed, despite certain differences, on the power of the Spirit which proceeds from the Father to the Son and from the Son to the apostles and for which supplication is made by the community which is founded on the apostles together with their leaders over those whom the community has chosen to be its leader (the bishop) and his helpers (the presbyters and deacons). It is interesting to note that Hippolytus has not prescribed any unchangeable formula in any of the three cases (the episcopate, the presbyterate and the diaconate). As he says himself, his 'Apostolic Tradition' was intended to help leaders to improvise, 'so long as the prayer is soundly orthodox.'[17] No liturgical accreditation or *ordinatio* was required in the case of other ministries in the Church such as those of the catechist, the lector or the sub-deacon.[18]

The pneumatological and ecclesial view of office that prevailed in the early Church also emerges clearly from this liturgy. What comes from below is experienced as coming from the Holy Spirit, with the result that there is no dualism between what comes from below and what comes from above. The important aspect is, moreover, the gift of the power of the Spirit, so that no distinction is made between grace and 'sign.' This is stressed by a section in the 'Apostolic Tradition' on the *confessores-martyres*, that is, those Christians who were arrested because of their faith and who suffered for the Christ thing, but were not, for some chance reason, put to death. Such Christians were believed to possess the charisma of the Spirit because they had borne witness to their faith by suffering. If a community wanted to have such a Christian as its leader (its deacon or presbyter), no laying on of hands was required.[19] By virtue of the power of his faith, he already possessed the necessary power of the Spirit.

It is important, however, to note that even these candidates had to be (liturgically) accredited by and to the community (although the laying on of hands was omitted in their case). This, then, is clearly a confirmation of the two aspects of the early idea of *ordinatio*—on the one hand, the ecclesial aspect relating to Church order of an accreditation to the Church and, on the other, the pneumatological and Christological aspect of a charisma of the Spirit. Office in the Church, then, is constituted by being accredited by and to the Church as one bearing office and by being graced with the charisma of the Spirit (whether this takes place institutionally or charismatically). This charisma of the Spirit is different according to the tasks allotted to the candidate by the community.

With regard to the New Testament, the difference in the later Church can be found in the fact that the signs that were originally differentiated in the New Testament were, at the later period, combined in the one episcopate, with the result that the theory emerged that there was only one office—the episcopate—and that all the other offices were only partial tasks, participating in the one episcopate. In my opinion, this is a possible theology which is legitimate, but not necessary. Nonetheless, it is also clear that 'office' in the Church has, from the very beginning, always included collegiality. There has, in other words, always been a united pluralism of Christians provided with different charisms of office.

The First "Sacerdotalization" of the Church's Office

It is clear from the pre-Nicene literature especially that the early Church found it difficult to call its leaders 'priestly.' According to the New Testament, only Christ and the Christian community were priestly. The leaders were in the service of Christ and the priestly people of God, but they were never called priestly themselves. Cyprian was one of the first Christians to show a clear preference for the Old Testament terminology of the sacrificial priesthood and compared this with the Christian Eucharist.

In this way, there was a gradual sacerdotalization of the vocabulary of the Church's office,[20] although this was initially used in the allegorical sense. Cyprian was also the first to say that the *sacerdos*, that is, the bishop as the leader of the community and therefore also in the Eucharist, acted in this capacity *vice Christi*, that is, in the place of Jesus.[21] Augustine, on the other hand, refused to call bishops and presbyters 'priests' in the sense of mediators between Christ and the community.[22]

With his 'Apostolic Tradition,' Hippolytus is obviously at a transitory stage. In his *epiclesis*, he speaks simply of the 'Spirit of the high priesthood' that is attributed to the episcopal leader. On the other hand, however, he says again and again that the bishop is *as* a high priest (*Traditio Apostolica* 3 and 34), which points to continuing influence of the Old Testament and the patristic use of allegory. These comparisons are, however, not made in connection with the presbyters, who are therefore clearly seen as non-priestly, although they were (to varying degrees according to the different local communities) increasingly permitted, as time passed, to replace the bishop in leading in the Eucharist (without needing a new 'ordination' to do this).

It is therefore hardly possible to speak of priests in connection with both bishops and presbyters in the pre-Nicene period of the Church's history. In the early Church, the Old Testament name for Jewish priests—*sacerdos*—was used in an allegorical sense and even then it was initially only employed in connection with the bishop,[23] who was at that time the figure in whom the local community identified itself and found its unity. In the long run, however, presbyters also normally came to lead in the celebration of the Eucharist (because they were in fact the local leaders of smaller communities) and for this reason they too came ultimately to be called *sacerdotes* or 'priests.' They were, however, still known as priests *secundi meriti*, in other words, priests who were subordinate to the episcopal leader.[24] This, then, was the beginning of the process of sacerdotalization at least of the vocabulary used in connection with those holding office in the Church.

Priestly Office-Bearers and the Eucharist

There would at first sight seem to be a connection between the 'priesthood' and the Eucharist in the light of the development outlined in the preceding section. This is, however, not the case, at least as far as the whole truth is concerned. In the early Church there was an essential connection between the community and leader of the community and therefore also between the leader of the community and the community that celebrates the Eucharist. This is an essential nuance in this context.

It is a fact that the 'Church's office' did not develop in the New Testament from and around the Eucharist. It did, however, develop from and around the apostolicity of the community, that is, from the need to proclaim and admonish and to build up and lead the community. In whatever way the word is used, 'office' has to do with leading the community. It was apparently not a separate problem for the New Testament authors as to who had to lead in the Eucharist, since none of them tells us anything about it. Paul does not call the Eucharist an apostolic tradition, but a tradition from the Lord himself (see 1 Cor. 11:23), to which even the apostles were bound.

The Eucharist was, after all, Jesus' parting gift to the whole of his community: 'Do this in memory of me.' As the community of Christ, then, the community has an inalienable right to the celebration of the Eucharist. There is no indication anywhere in the New Testament of an explicit link between the Church's office and presiding at the Eucharist. This does not, however, mean that any believer can lead in the celebration. In the house communities at Corinth, it was the hosts who led in the house celebrations of the Eucharist, but these men were also the leaders of the same house communities. In any case, what can be said with certainty is that a sacral and mystical foundation of the function of the office-bearer in the Eucharist cannot be found anywhere in the New Testament.

This, however, does not mean that the Eucharist is in any way seen in the New Testament as being totally dissociated from the concept of office.[25] There is in fact only one place in which a factual connection is established between 'leaders' and leading in the liturgy and this is a fairly vague reference (Acts 13:1–2). If it is borne in mind that the early Eucharist was modeled on the Jewish table prayer or *bir'kath hammazôn*, the 'blessing of the food,' in which it was certainly not possible for anyone to lead,[26] it should be obvious that the leaders of the community also led in the celebration of the Eucharist by virtue of the fact that they were leaders. This is also clear from texts that appeared at about the same time as the last part of the New Testament. 'Prophets and teachers' were the leaders in the Eucharist according to the earliest level of the Didache and 'presbyters' according to the later level. All of these, moreover, led in an official capacity.[27] In the First Epistle of Clement, the bishop-presbyters led.

We may therefore summarize the general view in this way. Whoever was competent to lead the community was also *ipso facto* the leader in the Eucharist. (In this sense, leading in the Eucharist does not need to be a separate competence or power, apart from being the competence of the leader of the community.) What we have here is clearly the 'presidency of the community' (essentially exercised by an individual or in a team): 'We receive the sacrament of the Eucharist . . . from no one other than the president of the community.'[28]

This aspect was stressed in the Church from the time of Ignatius of Antioch onwards. At that time, the bishop was in fact the leader of the community and for this reason no Eucharist was to be celebrated in opposition to the bishop's will.[29] Both in the case of Ignatius and in that of Cyprian later, the underlying intention here was to preserve the unity of the community. The figure of unity in the community therefore also led in the Eucharist, which Cyprian described as the 'sacrament of Church unity.'[30] Although the problem of office also played a part here, what was primarily at stake was the apostolicity and the unity of the Church: 'No Eucharist outside the community of the Church.'[31] What is stressed in this teaching is above all that a 'heretical' community has no right to the Eucharist. Even in the case of Ignatius, the question of the official leader in the Eucharist is subordinate.[32]

What is more, in the early Church the whole of the believing community concelebrated under the leadership of the leader of the community. According to a later, but still early *Liber Pontificalis,* everyone concelebrated (*tota aetas concelebrat*).[33] Some scholars have inevitably asked whether *concelebrare* had exactly the same meaning then as it has now. Was it used in the early Church in the same technical sense as it had been used in the second Christian millennium? The critical counterquestion that seems most appropriate is: On what grounds can we give theological priority to a narrower technical meaning? This may, after all, equally well be a narrowing of vision. Leading in the Eucharist in the early Church was only the liturgical aspect of a much more diverse official presidency in the Christian community. The one who was recognized as the pace-maker in the community also led in the Eucharist.

In the early Church, moreover, the community itself was the active subject of the *offerimus panem et calicem.*[34] The specific function of the *sacerdos* who leads in the Eucharist should not be defined in the light of later interpolations into liturgical books. (Examples of this practice are: *Accipe potestatem offerre sacrificium* and *sacerdos oportet offerre.* Such interpolations assume a later *potestas sacra* in the priest that is isolated from the community and therefore absolute.)

In the solemn Eucharist (which was initially improvised), that is, the thanks and praise or anaphora spoken by the leader, the latter appeared primarily as the prophetic leader of the community with pastoral responsibility for that community who proclaimed the history of salvation and therefore praised and thanked God and in this way announced the presence of salvation to the assembled community. It was for this reason that the leader took the gifts offered by the whole community which were transformed by the Holy Spirit into the gift of Jesus' body and blood.

It has been pointed out by many theologians, including, for example, Y. Congar, D. Droste, R. Schultze, K. J. Becker and R. Berger, that the integral subject of all liturgical action—and this includes the action of the Eucharist—in the early Church was the *ecclesia* itself, never the 'I' of the leader alone.[35] Concelebration was therefore not limited at that time to a shared celebration of the Eucharist by concelebrating priests. It was an action performed by the whole believing people present.[36] The people celebrated and the priest only led in service. Even when it is clear that concelebrating priests are meant, there was only one leader and the others concelebrated silently. The *recitatio communis* (regarded as necessary for 'concelebration') is not mentioned in the early Church.[37] This is why the Eucharist could always take place in the early Church in the assembly of the community.

Laymen as Leaders?

The question as to whether a lay person may lead in the Eucharist is a modern question. For the early Church, it was a wrong way of posing the problem. In the first place, it was the bishop who, albeit in collegial association with his presbyters, was the leader of the community and it was therefore he who also led in the Eucharist and who was alone in this. He was, as we have seen, the ecclesial figure of unity. Gradually (with the growth of the communities, which were originally cities, into what we would now call 'provinces' of the Church) his non-priestly helpers or presbyters obtained permission to lead in the Eucharist in his absence (although they had not in any sense been ordained to do this). The point of departure in the discussion of this question in the First Epistle of Clement is that the episcopos-presbyter normally led in the Eucharist. The author, however, adds: 'or other eminent persons . . . with the full consent of the whole Church,' since 'everything must take place in accordance with order.'[38]

The acceptance of a leader by the Church was therefore clearly of decisive importance. Ignatius, who called the bishop, as the figure by whom the community identified itself, the real leader in the Eucharist, at the same time also recognized cases in which it was possible and permissible for him to be replaced.[39] He does not mention presbyters or deacons explicitly as potential replacements in this context.

We do, however, have one, and only one explicit testimony in the early Church to the fact that, in emergencies, a layman was permitted to lead in the Eucharist. Tertullian, who nonetheless makes a clear distinction between *ordo* (official accreditation to and by the community) and *plebs*, the believing people or 'laity,' says that it was by definition the leader of the community who led in normal circumstances in the Eucharist and, for Tertullian, this meant the bishop together with his council of presbyters. All the same, he also notes: 'Where there is no college of accredited servants, you, layman, must lead in the Eucharist and baptize. Then you are your own priest, for, where two or three are gathered together, there is the Church, even if all those are lay people.'[40]

In exceptional circumstances, the community therefore chose its own leader *ad hoc*.[41] Although Augustine was opposed to the sacerdotalization of the Church's office-bearers, a process making the bishop or presbyter a mediator between God and the people, he explicitly denies that the layman had any right to lead in the Eucharist, even in emergencies.[42] Tertullian did not make his statement under the influence of Montanism. On the contrary, he criticizes the Montanists for letting laymen lead in the Eucharist although there was no extreme emergency and in this way denied the specific character of the Church's office.[43]

In holding this view, Tertullian was not so isolated in the early Church as it might at first sight seem, even though the unstable terminology clearly played a part in this question. Anyone who was invited in such circumstances by the community to lead in the community (and therefore also in the Eucharist) was, by the very fact that he was accepted by the Church (the early practice of *cheirotonia*), *ipso facto* an office-bearer. He was 'accredited,' in other words, he had power and competence as the leader of the community. It was this that Augustine had in mind, with the result that there was, despite the differences in terminology, a real consensus. The specific character of the Church's office was defended by everyone. What was not defended was a power of sacral ordination or a concrete manner of official accreditation.

We must now consider the view with regard to the Church's office that came to prevail in the second millennium. In contrast to those that we have just discussed, the new and later conception expressed an exclusive concentration on office as such and a greatly reduced emphasis on *ecclesia*. It was also above all a juridical view in which the concepts of sacrament and law were dissociated from each other.

The Second Millennium: A Direct Christological Foundation and a Privatization of Office

Two Latin councils of the Church, the Third Lateran Council (1179) and the Fourth Lateran Council (1215) sanctioned, in principle, a fairly radical re-interpretation of the early Church view of office. Gratian had mentioned canon 6 of the Council of Chalcedon, which forbade all absolute ordinations and declared them to be invalid, in his twelfth century *Decretum*, and even before this, towards the end of the eleventh century, the theologian Hugh of Saint Victor had referred to this same canon.[44] The fact remains, however, that both the Third and the Fourth

Lateran Councils broke away from the view expressed at Chalcedon, not only in principle, but also in fact.

It was, then, the *titulus Ecclesiae* on which a man could, according to the Council of Chalcedon, be ordained (in other words, a man could only be 'ordained' if he had been recommended or accepted as leader by a definite community) that was quite fundamentally re-interpreted in 1179, during the pontificate of Alexander III. According to the new interpretation of this early ecclesiological *titulus Ecclesiae*, no one could be ordained 'if a reasonable livelihood had not been assured.'[45] This was not, at least in principle, a denial of the early ecclesial practice of accreditation to and by the community, but it was a new way of looking at that accreditation—in view of the difficulties encountered in feudal society, accreditation was seen in the light of the priest's ability to support himself or be supported financially.

I conclude that there was no intention of breaking radically with the past at the Third Lateran Council because, 20 years after that Council, Pope Innocent III once again—and for the last time in the history of the Church!—recalled, in 1198, the invalidity of absolute ordinations. (He also added that, on grounds of mercy and in accordance with an old practice of *oikonomia,* priests who had been ordained in an absolute manner might be allowed to continue to exercise their functions on condition that their bishops provided for their upkeep. This is evidence of a compromise between patristic and feudal views.)

In view of the prevailing economic conditions and the number of members of the clergy who led a wandering life (as well as the existence of many 'private' churches founded by worldly lords), the provision of financial support for the clergy was an urgent and painful question at that time. This does not, however, mean that the early *titulus Ecclesiae* was not reduced to a purely feudal matter of a benefice. This change took place on the surface and the early Christian undercurrent was not denied. It was, however, the changed surface that was accepted into the new scholastic theology, with the result that only it was recognized centuries later at the Council of Trent, which sanctioned it in the twenty-third session (1563).[46] To summarize, then, a man has or feels that he has a vocation to the priesthood. He makes an application (this shows that the ecclesial bond had not been completely lost) and is trained for the priesthood and finally ordained. Everything is settled and he only has to wait to know where his bishop will send him. *Ordinatio* continues to be an accreditation of the priest as an office-bearer to a diocesan region, it is true, but the concrete place or community to which he will be sent remains open. What has completely disappeared in this procedure is the call of the community, which was in the early Church the essential element of ordination.

The Third Lateran Council undoubtedly made a clear dividing line between the first and the second Christian millennia in this respect and this change was emphasized by the pronouncement made by the Fourth Lateran Council that the Eucharist could only be celebrated by a 'validly ordained priest.'[47] In itself, of course, this statement is not necessarily in contradiction with the conviction that prevailed in the first Christian millennium, but it is certainly a narrowing down of that conviction. The essential bond that had existed for centuries with the choice made by the community is absent and the ecclesial aspect of the Eucharist is reduced to the 'celebrating priest.'

The full extent of this narrowing down of the vision of the Church's office is clear both from what preceded and from what followed these two councils. It is evident that this fairly radical change did not take place on the basis of theological criteria, but above all for non-theological reasons. It is also certain that the effects of these two councils in this respect at least were not the result of theological intuitions, but rather the consequence of non-theological presuppositions. It is only this which justifies the theological priority of the earlier ecclesial view of the Church's office over the view which is now regarded as valid.

It is certainly possible to ask how this fundamental change in the Church's view of its own office-bearers was able to come about in history. We cannot, of course, analyze the whole phenomenon of feudal society, which is clearly essentially important in this question. Certain historians have blamed the emergence, precisely at the time of the Third and Fourth Lateran Councils, of the theory of a mysterious sacramental character, which formed the basis of the whole theology of the *sacramentum ordinis*.[48] I believe that these scholars are wrong, especially since this very vague theory of the character, dating back to the end of the twelfth century, was nonetheless interpreted in all its medieval modernity by all the leading scholastic theologians—Bonaventure, Albert the Great and especially Thomas Aquinas—in continuity with the early Church.

For these theologians, whose interpretations show certain divergencies, this character points to the visible bond between *ecclesia* and *ministerium*.[49] (A character was, moreover, associated with all ordinations and consecrations, from that of the bishop to that of the acolyte or the sacristan, a factor that can only be explained ontologically with some difficulty.) The word *mancipatio*, in other words, being called and accepted by a Christian community for a definite service or ministry in the Church, was the most sensitive aspect of the character in the Middle Ages and this is essentially in keeping with the view of office in the early Church.

The first official document that refers to a priestly character is a letter from Gregory IX in 1231 to the Archbishop of Paris.[50] The scholastic theologians had, from the beginning of the thirteenth century onwards, stressed the bond between the community of the Church and the sacrament of ordination in their teaching about the character, thus following the conviction that prevailed in the early Church, despite the new armoury of concepts that they used. Seen from the dogmatic point of view, however, the only formulation was that of the existence of the character. What is more, the Council of Trent clearly wanted to leave the field free for further theological explanations, including the view held by certain theologians that the character was only a *relatio rationis,* that is, a logical relationship and a juridical fiction. (This was the opinion of Durandus of Saint-Pourçin among others.)

It is clear, then, that it is not possible to base the ontological view of the priestly character on conciliar pronouncements.[51] This character is a medieval category in which the early Church view of the lasting relationship between the community and the office-bearer on the one hand and between the office-bearer and the gift of the charisma of the Spirit are expressed. In the Middle Ages, a distinction was made in this charisma of office between the power entrusted in this office (expressed in terms of a *sacra potestas*) and the 'sacramental grace' that is appropriate to that power. This grace was personal to the one bearing office and enabled him, it was argued, to exercise that official power in a holy and Christian way. It can be said that the process of ontological sacerdotalization was furthered by this distinction made in the charisma of office,[52] but no more than this was achieved by it.

The scholastic doctrine of the character contained certain factors which gave rise, through the medium of other developments, to an ontological and sometimes even magical sacerdotalization of the priesthood. I would like to point to two main factors that furthered this development. In whatever way the character was interpreted in the Middle Ages, ontologically or juridically or even as a juridical fiction, it was in general seen as a direct participation in the high priesthood of Christ. As Thomas Aquinas declared, along with other medieval theologians of 'modern' outlook: 'The sacramental character is a certain participation in the priesthood of Christ.'[53] This conviction does not in itself need to include an ontologization of the Church's office (especially in view of the divergent interpretations of the character), but it does lead to an obscuring of the Church's mediation and to an emphasis on the priest as a mediator between Christ and men, a view that Augustine regarded as heretical.

The main reason for the change that took place in the Middle Ages in the Christian view of office is, I believe, to be found in the revival of interest in Roman law towards the end of the eleventh and at the beginning of the twelfth centuries. It is not, in my opinion, to be found in the sacramental character as such (as many historians wrongly believe).[54] Because of this revival of interest, the power of leadership (in every sphere of life) was juridically dissociated from the concept of territoriality. In the sphere of Church life, this means a dissociation from the concept of the local church. (In this context, territoriality and the local church community should not be seen in the purely geographical sense, but understood as 'human space.') This situation led at the end of the thirteenth century to the well known statement made by Vincent of Beauvais: *Quodque principi placuit, legis habet vigorem.*[55] The principle in this case is that of the *plenitudo potestatis,* in other words, authority as a value in itself, isolated from the community, both in the secular sphere and in the Church. (This was also connected with the struggle about investiture between the *sacerdotium* and the *imperium.*)

It was, then, non-theological, feudal and juridical factors that made the 'medieval' theological change with regard to the Church's office possible. What is more, the dividing line between the 'Spirit of Christ' and the 'spirit of the world' for the Christian was previously to be found in his baptism, his conviction that he had been accepted into the chosen community of God's *ecclesia,* although (as the Church expanded) this dividing line was to some extent shifted to the 'second' baptism, that of the Christian's monastic profession.

Monks had previously been laymen, not priests. For the Christian community, these religious represented their own ideal. The dividing line was, however, shifted even further by the Carolingian Council of Aachen and especially as a result of the Gregorian reforms. At a time when 'everyone' was baptized, the dividing line between the 'Spirit of Christ' and the 'spirit of the world' was placed close to the clergy, who were then the representatives of the Church *par excellence.* The priesthood came to be seen as a personal status in life rather than as an official ministry in the community. It was, in other words, personalized and privatized.[56] What is more, the new ideas about law (*ius*) and jurisdiction led to a division between the *potestas iurisdictionis* and the *potestas ordinis* and a consequent watering down of the earlier concept of 'sacramental right' (a right based on the *sacramentum*).

This is, in my opinion, the fundamental reason why the second Christian millennium became so different from the first. This difference opened the door to absolute ordinations, in which the earlier concept of *ordinatio* became a sacral ordination. This type of ordination made it possible for all kinds of new ideas and practices, which would have been ecclesiologically unthinkable in the first millennium, to arise— practices such as the private mass.[57] A man could be in himself a priest. Many of these new practices were simply not possible in the early Church.

The most important consequence of all these changes is that the earlier relationship between *ecclesia* and *ministerium*, that is, between the community and the Church's office, was transformed into a relationship between *potestas* and *eucharistia*. (This change was made easier by a parallel alteration in the term *corpus verum Christi*. In the early Church, this term referred to the community of the Church. Later, it became the *corpus mysticum Christi* or Eucharistic body. In the Middle Ages, the meaning was quite the reverse.)[58] In the Middle Ages, the priest, who had previously led in the community and had, in other words, been 'accredited' to and by the community in order to lead it, was 'ordained' in order to be able to celebrate the Eucharist.[59] The medieval view of the *sacra potestas* had played a part in this and ordination came to be seen as the conferring of a special power in order that the person given that power might celebrate the Eucharist. The Fourth Lateran Council reacted with logical consistency to this development and declared that only a validly ordained priest was able to pronounce the words of consecration validly.[60] This, however, was a juridical narrowing down of the original intention in the early Church.

The Modern Image of the Priest

During the period of the *ancien régime* in particular, when men were preoccupied with the idea of absolute monarchy, the changed theological view of leadership in the Church that had at least partly been conditioned by the feudal structure of society and the renewed interest in Roman law resulted in an image of the priest that was clearly formulated for the first time by Josse Clichtove (1472–1543). This image of the priest had a deep influence on the Tridentine teaching about the priesthood and on the whole of priestly spirituality during the sixteenth and seventeenth centuries. It was also further elaborated by Pierre de Bérulle and the French school and formed the background to all the spiritual writing about the priesthood in recent centuries up to the time of the Second Vatican Council.[61]

Biblical, patristic and scholastic ideas were connected in this modern image of the priest with the new situation brought about in modern society. The priest was seen, in a hierarchically structured Christian society governed by a power based on divine law, as a man set apart from the world and lay people (who were responsible for the 'secular' reality). Clichtove saw the Christian priesthood as an extension of the levitical priesthood in a theocratic society.

The basis of this modern spirituality of the priesthood is the sacramental grace of the priest. The priesthood came to be seen as sacrificial and to be experienced in society in the priestly state, which gradually assumed more and more monastic characteristics. Priestly celibacy was no longer seen (as it had been, for example, by Thomas Aquinas) as a purely disciplinary measure in the Church,[62] but was almost attributed to divine law and, as far as its spirituality was concerned, was regarded as forming an essential part of the state of the priesthood as set apart from that of the laity.

The modern image of the priest, then, is completely clerical and hierarchical. Luther and Erasmus had fulminated against the decline of priestly morals and, in reaction against this decline, the Catholic reformer of priestly spirituality, Josse Clichtove, correctly defended the spirituality, of the priest, but he did this by pouring it into a juridical mold. The priesthood thus came, in his teaching, to be placed in the light of an absolute value given to law. Only part of the foundation for this development had been laid in the Middle Ages with its image of the priest. What we have had in the second Christian millennium, then, from the sixteenth century onwards especially, has been a distinctively modern and juridical tightening up of the medieval image of the priest. In the twentieth century, an important contribution has been made by Pius X, Piux XI and Pius XII, making this modern image of the priest more popular.[63]

Despite a certain continuity, it is possible, then, to distinguish three images of the priest (which are also socially conditioned) in the history of the Church. These are the patristic, the medieval and the modern images of the priest. On the basis of a renewed sensitivity to man, society and the Church, contemporary critics of the priesthood are above all preoccupied with the modern image of the priest.

Continuity and Divergence between the First and the Second Millennia

The Pneuma-Christological Basis of Office in the Early Church and the Non-Ecclesial Christological Basis of Office in the Modern Church

Despite the peculiarly Latin and Western aspect of the theology of office that has developed in the Roman Catholic Church since the twelfth century, there are two underground lines of continuity running through the entire two thousand years of tradition in the Christian experience of office in the Church. On the one hand, there is the continuous opposition, which can be clearly distinguished in the early, the medieval and the modern Church, to the celebration of the Eucharist in which the idea of the universal *communio ecclesialis* is rejected or denied. On the other hand, there is both the early and the modern conviction that no Christian community can ultimately and autonomously itself be the final source of its own office-bearers.

In the first Christian millennium and during the pre-Nicene period especially, Christians expressed their view of office above all in an ecclesial and pneumatological way, in other words, in terms of what might be called a Pneuma-Christology. During the second millennium, however, the Church's office has been given a directly Christological basis and both the ecclesial mediation and the part played by the Holy Spirit have been thrust into the background. What has arisen in the second millennium has been a theology of office without an ecclesiology. This movement began in the Middle Ages, when a Christology that lacked a fully elaborated independent ecclesiology that mediated that Christology was followed by the so-called treatise on the sacraments. Although Thomas, for example, always spoke of *sacramenta Ecclesiae*, the sacrament was later defined, in a technically abstract way, as a *signum efficax gratiae*, in which the ecclesial aspect was suppressed and the sacramental power was directly based on the *sacra potestas* that the priest personally possessed. In the way, the ecclesial and charismatic significance of office and its pneumatological meaning became obscured and it became at the same time increasingly enclosed within a juridical framework and dissociated from the sacrament of the Church.

Although in many respects Vatican II returned to the theological insights of the early Church, the view of the Council regarding office in the Church and especially the terminology employed in the relevant conciliar documents express an unmistakable compromise between these two great blocs of tradition in the Church.[64] The ecclesial aspect of office is once again stressed in *Lumen Gentium* and words such as *ministeria* and *munera* are used in preference to *potestas*. The term *potestas sacra* occurs several times, but the classical terms—*potestas ordinis* and *potestas iurisdictionis*—cannot be found anywhere in the document. There is, on the contrary, a clear break with these two parallel terms, in the sense that the power of jurisdiction is essentially already given with ordination. At least fundamentally, then, the early view of the *titulus Ecclesiae* of office has been restored to a place of honor and at least a beginning has been made to breaking the juridical stranglehold on the Church's office.

'Priest' and 'Lay'

Quite soon after the New Testament period, following the Jewish model, in which a distinction was made between high priests and the people,[65] a similar distinction was also made, for example, in the First Epistle of Clement, between *klerikos* and *laikos*.[66] These two terms do not, however, point to a distinction of status between 'priest' and 'lay.' A man was *klerikos* if he occupied an office or *kleros*.[67] What we have here is a functional distinction, not in official functions, but in charismatic functions of a specific kind within the Church.[68]

In the light of the whole tradition of the Church, the distinction between priest and lay must be interpreted as an affirmation of a specifically and sacramentally ecclesial function, not as a separate status in the Church. Even in the Middle Ages, theologians refused to regard the relationship between priests and lay people as a relationship between *praelatio* and *subiectio*.[69] The Church is a brotherhood and the dilemma between an ontological and sacerdotalistic view of office on the one hand and a purely functionalistic view on the other must therefore be overcome in and through the theological concept of office in the Church as the gift of the Spirit of an ecclesial charisma of office and as the ministry of leadership in the community and everything that this implies in a community of Christ.

Sacramental Office

It is clear from this that there has always been a non-sacral, but nonetheless sacramental meaning of office which was therefore correctly associated, even in the early Church, with a liturgical accreditation.[70] From the ecumenical point of view, the question of the technical meaning of the word 'sacrament' must at present remain open, but we are bound to recognize that, from the point of view of content, all the Christian churches that acknowledge the principle and practice of office are agreed about the essential elements constituting what the early Church called *ordinatio*. These are, as we have already said, the candidate's being called or accepted by the community (this is the ecclesial aspect) and the charisma of the Spirit (the Pneuma-Christological aspect). In normal circumstance, these elements are, as we have seen, linked by an official laying on of hands accompanied by an *epiclesis*. In this way, both the ecclesial and the pneumatic aspects of office are given concrete liturgical form in the shared celebration of the community.[71] The Greek Orthodox theologian J. D. Zizioulas has expressed the increasing consensus of opinion among theologians of different confessions. We may summarize what he has said in the following way:[72] The sacramental office is the act through which the community realizes itself. Without provoking any contrast between 'charisma' on the one hand and 'office' (or 'accreditation') on the other, the charisma of office is essentially an accreditation or *ordinatio* which is ecclesial by being related to the community, pneumatological and sacramentally juridical. The so-called validity or ecclesial character of ordination is not strictly speaking connected to an isolated sacramental action on the part of the Church (although it normally is in practice and, what is more, connected to the liturgical action of laying on of hands). It is rather connected to the action of the Church community as a whole, that is, as an apostolic community in communion with all other local churches. From the point of view of the Bible and the teaching of the early Church, we are therefore, in the light of this view, justified in giving a positive ecclesiological evaluation to the extraordinary ministry of office, that is, a ministry carried out in exceptional circumstances.

The Christian Community Is a Community That Celebrates the Eucharist

For both the early Church and the modern Church (especially since the Second Vatican Council), it is not possible to think of a Christian community without the celebration of the Eucharist. There is an essential connection between the local *ecclesia* and the Eucharist. Following the Jewish model, at least 12 fathers of families (and therefore 12 families) gathered together in the pre-Nicene Church had a right to a leader and therefore to someone who would lead the community in the celebration of the Eucharist.[73] In the case of smaller communities outside the cities, the original leader (who was a bishop) was soon replaced by a presbyter or 'pastor.'

What we may in any case conclude from this is that the early Church regarded a shortage of priests as impossible, even though, of course, the problem was never expressed in this way. The contemporary shortage of priests can therefore be subjected to the criticism of the view of office held in the early Church, because this modern shortage has origins that lie outside the sphere of the Church's office itself. At present there are clearly more than a sufficient number of Christians, both men and women, who possess this charisma in the ecclesiological sense. These include, for example, the many catechists working in Africa and the many pastoral workers of both sexes in Europe and elsewhere. These Christians do in fact lead in their communities and are pace-setters and figures by whom the communities can identify themselves. They are, however, at the same time prevented in fact from being 'accredited' liturgically for reasons that are extrinsic to the essential character of the Church's office. They cannot therefore lead in the Eucharist and the service of reconciliation. From the ecclesiological point of view, this is a very wrong situation.

Office and the Universal Church

We must finally consider the relationship between office in a local church and office in the universal Church. In the ancient world, the universal Church was not regarded as a reality that was superior to the local churches. In the beginning, there was no supraregional organization, although patriarchates and metropolitan churches soon developed and local churches were included within them in a unity that went beyond the city framework. During the first five centuries, the 'primacy of the union of love' of the patriarchal *Sedes Romana* or the Chair of Peter in Rome became increasingly recognized.[74]

The early idea of the universal Church was taken up again by the Second Vatican Council. According to the conciliar Constitution on the Church, it was 'in and from such individual churches' that 'there comes into being the one and only Catholic Church.'[75] The universal Church is made present in the local church and the Christian belongs to the universal Church because he belongs to a local church, not vice versa. It is precisely for this reason that no single church is able to have a monopoly of God's Spirit.[76] It is also possible for Christian communities to criticize each other in the spirit of the gospel. Christian solidarity with other Christian communities is also an essential aspect of even the smallest basic communities in the Church. This kind of ecclesial concern cannot be referred to higher authorities.

This is also the reason why the presence of spokesmen and leaders from neighboring local communities has always, since the earliest Christian times, been required at the liturgical accreditation of particular Christians as office-bearers to and by a particular community. Within this structure, local office-bearers also have the task of governing the universal Church, the union of love, as critical spokesmen and leaders of their own communities. According to the Catholic view, they are also in solidarity with that leader of the local community who, as the ultimately binding factor, has the Petrine function in the Church.

A Critical Theological Evaluation of Contemporary Alternative Forms of Office

It should be clear from this historical and theological outline that the constant factor in the Church's office can be found only in concrete and historically changing forms. My point of departure in this evaluation is an insight that all Christians may be assumed to share, namely that Church order, however much it may change, is a very great good for Christian communities. In one form or another, Church order forms part of the concrete and essential appearance of the 'communities of God,' the Church. This Church order, however, is not there simply for its own sake. Like the Church's office, it is also at the service of the apostolic communities. It cannot be an aim in itself, nor can it be given an absolute value. This is all the more important because it is clear that Church order has at all times in the Church been firmly rooted in history. Certain forms of Church order that have been brought about by particular situations in the Church and society in the past (and therefore certain criteria for the admission of office-bearers in the Church as well) reach, at a certain moment in time, their ultimate limits—there is clear sociological evidence of this in man's concrete experience of the shortcomings of Church order of a particular kind in changed circumstances.

Changes in the dominant image of man and the world, social and economic upheavals and new socio-cultural attitudes and emotions can all lead to a situation in which the Church order that has developed in history contradicts or even prevents what it sought to safeguard in the past, namely the building up of a Christian community. From such an experience of contrast, experiments in new possibilities of Christian and Church life can spontaneously arise (as indeed they did in New Testament times). Experiences of what is defective in any given system have a regulatory value. It is, of course, obvious that even a fairly unanimous experience of what has in fact gone wrong in a valid Church order that has developed in the course of history does not in any sense imply that there will necessarily be complete agreement about how that order should be put right. That can only emerge from the experience of putting a number of new models to the test. These may fail—they are, after all, experiments. Failure is in no way reprehensible—it is simply one phase in the search for a new Christian discovery. What is gradually revealed in all these attempts is the obligatory character of the new possibilities of life for the Church that are required but have not yet been given a concrete form.

It is also an indisputable sociological fact that, in changed times, there is always a danger of ideological fixation with regard to the existing Church order because there is always a great deal of inertia in the case of an established system which is frequently orientated towards self-preservation. This applies, of course, to every system in human society, but it is particularly true of the institutional Church which rightly regards itself as the community of God, but often wrongly displays a tendency to identify old, even venerable traditions with unchangeable divine dispensations. Even the Second Vatican Council displays much more caution in this respect than many of us believed to be the case at the time of the Council itself. One example of this in our present context is that there is a suggestion in the Tridentine document on the 'sacrament of order' that the threefold division in 'holy orders'—the episcopate, the presbyterate and the diaconate—goes back to divine law.[77] The Second Vatican Council replaced this *divina ordinatione* ('by divine dispensation') of the Tridentine canon by the words 'from antiquity.'[78]

Against the background of the existing Church order, then, new and sometimes urgently required alternative possibilities are often only to be seen through the medium of what is bound to be regarded as at least temporarily illegal. This is not a new phenomenon in the Church—it has always been the case. In the early and high Middle Ages, when scholasticism was still very free (in contrast to later scholasticism, which had nothing to say about this fact), this temporary illegality was even raised to the status of a theological principle in the theory of the *non acceptatio legis* or the rejection of the law from above by opposition at the base. Whatever the value of the law may be, it is rejected in certain cases by the majority and thus becomes in fact irrelevant. It is clear from this that there is, in the history of the Church, a way along which Christians can, working from below or from the base, develop a praxis in the Church that may be temporarily in competition with the praxis that is officially valid in the Church at that particular time. This new praxis from below may, however, in its Christian opposition, ultimately even become the dominant praxis of the whole Church and in the long run be sanctioned by the official Church. (And, as history never ceases, the whole process may then begin all over again.)

The various accounts in this issue of *Concilium* of praxis deviating from the official Church order have, I believe, in the first place a threefold effect—of diagnosis, criticism of the existing ideology and dynamism—and, in the second place, a normative value. This normative value is not based on its purely factual nature. It functions as a justified Christian reflection in which a Utopian orientation towards the future is anticipated on the one hand and, on the other, a Christian apostolic conviction that has been tested against the whole history of Christian experience is expressed.

This normative power of factual experience reigns supreme in modern secular society, but none of us would be bold enough to assert that pure facts or statistics in themselves have any normative value. To assert this would be a great blunder, since to do so would be *a fortiori* to attribute an even more massive authority to the much more massive factual dimension of the existing Church order. The official Church order has, however, to justify itself with regard to varying experiences of Christians in respect of that Church order in history. In the same way, the new alternative and critical forms of praxis in the Church and the Church's office also have to justify themselves with regard to our historical experiences. A simple alternative—something that is new for its own sake—is meaningless. A particular praxis in the Christian community, whether it is new or old, is only authoritative if it contains the Christian *logos*, that is, the apostolicity of the Christian community. As Paul said, everything is permitted, but not everything leads to salvation.

Accounts of new alternative forms of praxis in the Church are historically always connected to memories and experiences of what has failed, sometimes absurdly, in the valid system and of the obstacles raised by that system. It is quite legitimate to take as one's point of departure when judging the authority of an alternative praxis in the Church such factors as our present-day experience of our own existence, the demands made by contemporary man and human rights. This is also the obvious way to proceed. I would personally prefer, in view of my experience of the toughness of any system, to take another and strategically more advantageous starting-point. I would therefore begin with what is accepted and defended by both parties in the Church from the point of view of the building up of the Christian community. By both parties here, I mean those who defend the official prevailing Church order and those who advocate an alternative critical praxis.

My point of departure, then, is the right of the Christian community to be able to do everything that is necessary to become a true community of Jesus and to extend that community. This right, both parties would agree, has to be exercised in union with and subject to the criticism of all the other Christian communities. This is a situation which can impose certain restrictions, as Vatican II pointed out. A variant of this starting-point would be the right of the Christian community to the Eucharist as the heart of the community. (The Second Vatican Council also stressed this aspect of the life of the community.) Another variant is the apostolic right of the community to leaders, a leader or a 'significant other person' who will clarify or give dynamic power to the fundamental values of the group or criticize the community.

The official Church also accepts these apostolic affirmations, but at the same time takes as its point of departure decisions that have already been made in the history of the Church (concerning, for example, the criteria for admission to the Church's office). These may in fact be an obstacle to this original right of the community to a leader when the world and the Church are placed in different circumstances. The present shortage of priests (which can be explained, at least partly, in the light of previously made decisions in the history of the Church) has led, for example, to all kinds of substitutes for the ministries of the Church. In addition to an authentic multiplicity of differentiated ministries (necessary in the situation in which Christian communities are placed

today), an inauthentic multiplicity has also arisen, only because ordination or sacramental accreditation to and by the community has been
withheld.

The difficulty confronting the image of the priest today can easily be
seen if it is approached in this way, in the light of what is accepted by
those who defend the existing Church order and by those who propose
an alternative praxis. It should be quite clear to everyone that, in present
circumstances, the celebration of the Eucharist is threatened, reduced
to a banal level or even impeded. It is also evident from a great number
of accounts of negative experiences of the 'service' priest's functioning
within a sacral view of the Church's office that this image of the priest
makes the Christian meaning of the community and the Eucharist in
contemporary society ridiculous.

This is happening, moreover, at a time when there are, in many
countries, very many men and women giving themselves wholeheartedly
and sometimes for many years to pastoral work in their Christian community. It is only too obvious from the negative experiences that have
been recorded that the existing Church order has become ossified as
an ideology and is an obstacle to what it originally intended to achieve.
The only reason for this almost insuperable difficulty in an unchanging
Church order is the absence of celibate male priests. (And celibacy and
male sex are not theological concepts.)

Very many Christians are unable to accept this situation and for them
these negative experiences are an incentive to initiate an alternative
praxis, without waiting for the existing system to change. This is also
the reason why the phenomenon of alternative praxis, which occurs
almost everywhere at present, has a diagnostic significance with regard
to the symptoms of serious sickness in the existing system and can
function as a criticism of the ideology underlying the traditional practices. Christians instinctively recognize that the New Testament datum
of the priority of the community over office (and *a fortiori* over criteria
for admission to that office which are not in themselves necessary) is
clearly expressed in this kind of alternative praxis. It is also a sociological fact that existing laws in any society (including that of the Church)
are seldom contested if they are inwardly convincing. In the case of the
Church, such dispensations are disputed by no one as long as their
(Christian) *logos* or rationality is not doubted.

At present, however, we are witnessing within the Church throughout
the world a wave of alternative praxis and this in itself is a clear indication that the existing order in the Church has lost its credibility and is
in urgent need of revision. That order no longer has the power to con-
vince many Christians and the result is a spontaneous and widespread
appearance of the socio-psychological mechanism of the *non acceptatio*

legis. If the Church intends, despite these signs, to maintain the existing order, it will only be able to do this now by authoritarian means (because there is a complete lack of conviction in the case of many of the Church's 'subjects'). To follow this course would only make the situation more precarious, because an authoritarian way of imposing Church order would go against the grain in modern man's experience of his own existence.

The third effect of this alternative praxis is that of dynamism, because many Christians are gradually coming to recognize that this praxis provides a new credibility structure and that they can identify themselves with it. This dynamism is not to be found in the pure fact of alternative praxis. The dynamic force comes from the fact that Christians see in this new praxis a modern form of apostolicity because of the presence in it of the Christian *logos*. Since the new praxis strikes them as convincing, it eventually acquires authority and the power to recruit others. What we cannot claim, however, is that this conviction, which is based on experience and inspires and determines the lives of many Christian communities and their office-bearers, does not possess an inherent Christian apostolicity even before it is recognized publicly by the official Church and that it will only acquire that apostolicity when it has been sanctioned by the Church. On the contrary, recognition is granted later, after it has become clear that the Christian *logos* is already present in it as a meaningful Christian possibility here and now.

As a theologian, I am bound to say that the alternative praxis of critical Christian communities that are inspired by Jesus as the Christ is, in the first place, both dogmatically and apostolically possible (although I cannot go into all the details here). It is, in my opinion, a legitimate Christian and apostolic possibility which is demanded by our present needs. To call communities 'heretical' and to say that they are already outside the Church (because of their alternative praxis) is, I believe, meaningless from the point of view of the Church. In the second place, given the existing canonical order of the Church, this alternative praxis is not even *contra* or against the order, but *praeter ordinem*, that is, it is not in accordance with the letter of the Church's order (it is *contra* that letter), but it is in accordance with what (in earlier situations) that Church order really wanted to safeguard.

It is obvious that a situation of this kind can never be pleasant for the representatives of the prevailing Church order, but they should listen to the accounts given by Christians of their negative experiences with the present order and be alert to the damage that they do to Christian communities, the Eucharist and the Church's office. If they do not, they may be seen as defending an established system rather than the Christian community and its Eucharistic heart. At a time when men have become very sensitive to the power structure underlying many systems, to cling persistently to the prevailing system when all kinds of experiments (some of them, of course, no doubt lacking in substance) are flourishing would cause pain to those who still love the Church.

Since alternative praxis of the kind described here is not *contra* or directly opposed to Church order, but only *praeter ordinem*, it can also be defended from the ethical point of view when the Church is placed in difficult circumstances. (We cannot, of course, pass any judgement here on subjective intentions.) When certain spokesmen of the official Church speak in this context of 'people who have placed themselves outside the Church,' they are not only expressing themselves peevishly and in a way that is alien to the Church—they are also speaking in a way that is very redolent of what the Church has always called 'heresy.' Even the Second Vatican Council had trouble in defining the frontiers of membership of the Church. There are, of course, such frontiers. That is undeniable. But who would presume to define them? What is more, to speak in this way is posthumously to call earlier centuries of authentic Christian experience heretical and to condemn the New Testament search for the best pastoral possibilities.

I would at the same time like to say in this context that it would be equally out of keeping with the apostolic spirit to pursue alternative praxis in a triumphalistic way. It must always be a temporarily abnormal situation in the life of the churches. Personally—and I stress that this is no more than a very personal conviction—I believe that there ought to be some kind of strategy or 'economy' of conflicts. Where, for example, there is clearly no urgent need for an alternative praxis based on the pastoral requirements of the Christian community or communities, there is also no need to put everything that is 'apostolically' or dogmatically possible into practice. If this is done, there is always a danger that, in critical communities, the community is subordinated to the problem of office and adapted on the basis of the office-bearers' own problems concerned with the crisis of identity.

We should also not make the alternative forms of praxis into a mystery. Our attitude should be governed by realism and sobriety. Renewal in the Church usually begins with illegal deviations and it rarely happens that attempts at renewal come from above. When this does happen, the attempts are sometimes dangerous. Vatican II is an example of both movements. In its Constitution on the Liturgy, the Council sanctioned, to a very great extent at least, the illegal liturgical practice that had arisen before the Council in France, Belgium and Germany. On the other hand, when the conciliar attempts at liturgical renewal were given a concrete form and expression after the Council—and were thus imposed from above—this renewal found many Christians quite unprepared, with the result that it met with resistance in many Church communities.

The objection is often raised that changes or alternative praxis are not justified in the Christian sense or from the point of view of the Church by the fact that they are different or new. This is basically correct, but it is incorrect in its implicit assumption, since the same can be said of the established Church order in changed circumstances. That order is not legitimated simply on the basis of the inertia of its own factual existence. It can also be suspected of being in decline and therefore of being in fact an obstacle to the authentic life of Christians in the Church at a time when the image of man and the world is changing. What is venerable and old cannot take precedence over what is new simply because it is venerable and old.

It is possible that I shall be criticized for seeing the Church in an exclusively horizontal dimension, in other words, in accordance with the model of a social reality, and not as a charismatic datum from above. My reply to this criticism is to reject this dualism in the Church on the basis of the New Testament. Of course we should not speak exclusively in descriptive, empirical language about the Church. We must also speak in the language of faith about the Church as, for example, the 'community of Jesus,' the 'body of the Lord' or the 'temple of the Holy Spirit.' In both kinds of language, however, we are speaking about the same reality.

The gnostics showed a strong tendency to divide the Church into a 'heavenly' part (that would nowadays be regarded as beyond the reach of sociologists) and an 'earthly' part (capable of every kind of evil). This same tendency is displayed in the criticism outlined in the preceding paragraph. The Second Vatican Council reacted strongly against the division of the Church into two parts; the Church, as a human 'society' and as the 'body of Christ,' should not, it insisted, 'be considered as two realities,' as 'the earthly Church' and the separate 'Church enriched with heavenly things' (*Lumen Gentium* I, 8).

The obstacle to the renewal of the Church's official ministries is based above all on this dualistic conception of the Church (a view that is often expressed in apparently Christian terms such as 'hierarchical'). The consequence of this is that (because of the shortage of priests) Christian lay people are allowed to be as actively employed as possible in the pastoral sphere, but are prevented from being sacramentally accredited to the Church's office. We are, however, bound to ask whether this development in the direction of non-office-bearing or non-sacramentally confirmed pastoral workers (a development that can only be understood in the light of the historical impediments that have been imposed on the Church's office) is theologically sound. All that we can say with certainty is that it preserves the superseded sacral image of the priest.

Finally, I should point out that it would, in my opinion, be wrong to place all the blame for this on Rome. Leadership or authority can only be exercised meaningfully and appear in changed forms if both the people and their office-bearers (including the bishops) have reached a sufficient level of consciousness. It is not possible to ask the highest authority in a world Church to change the order prevailing in that Church if that change does not meet with the approval of the majority of Christian communities. To do this would probably mark the beginning of a massive schism, requiring an equally massive ecumenical operation twenty years later. We have been made wiser, let us hope, by our knowledge of previous divisions in the history of the Church.

For this reason, I regard the critical alternative communities as ferment in a universal process which Christian consciousness is being formed and therefore as a necessarily exceptional position within the one great union of the apostolic churches. They occupy a marginal position, continuously stimulating Christian consciousness, so that the great Church will be made ready to receive another Church order which is more suitable for the modern world and its pastoral needs and which will give a contemporary form in our own times to the apostolic character of the Christian community.

Translated by David Smith

NOTES

1. Jerome *Dialogus contra Luciferianos* c. 21; *PL* 23, 175.

2. Some have been discussed elsewhere in this issue. See also F. Klostermann, ed. *Der Priestermangel und seine Konsequenzen* (Düsseldorf 1977).

3. I have not attempted to analyze the different structures of office in the New Testament here. For this the reader should consult the relevant exegetical works. All that I have done is to outline the spirit in which office in the Church is viewed in the New Testament.

4. 1 Cor. 12:28, where official ministries are mentioned together with all kinds of other, non-official ministries.

5. *PG* 104, 558; see also 104, 975–1218; 137, 406–410. See also P. Joannou–*Discipline Générale Antique* I-1 (Grottaferrata 1962) pp. 74–75; V. Fuchs *Die Ordinationstitel. Von seiner Entstehung bis auf Innozenz III* (Bonn 1930); C. Vogel 'Vacua manus impositi' in *Mélanges liturgiques* (B. Botte) (Louvain 1972) 511–524; J. Martin *Die Genese des Amtspriestertum in der frühen Kirche* (Freiburg 1972).

6. For the Jewish background to the Christian idea of *cheirotonia* as *cheirothesia* (laying on of hands), see K. Hruby 'La Notion d'ordination dans

la tradition juive' *La Maison-Dieu* 102 (Paris 1970) 52–72; E. Lohse *Die Ordination im Spätjudentum und im Neuen Testament* (Göttingen 1951); A. Ehrhardt 'Jewish and Christian Ordination' *Journal of Ecclesiastical History* 5 (1954) 125–138.

7. Cyprian *Epist.* 4, 5; *PL* 50, 434. See also F. Nikolasch *Bischofswahl durch alle konkrete Vorschläge* (Grass and Cologne 1973); K. Ganzer *Papsttum und Bistumbesetzungen in der Zeit von Gregor IX bis Bonifaz VIII* (Cologne 1968), which describes the historical development leading to the break with the earlier Church order.

8. Leo the Great *Ad Anast. PL* 54, 634. See also L. Mortari *Consecrazione episcopale e collegialità* (Florence 1969); H. Dombois *Das Recht der Gnade* (Witten 1961); R. Kottje 'The Selection of Church Officials' *Concilium* 63 (1971) 117–126; H. M. Legrand 'Theology and the Election of Bishops in the Early Church' *Concilium* 77 (1972) 31–42.

9. Paulinus *Epist. I ad Severum* c. 10: *CSEL* 29, 9.

10. Isidore *De ecclesiasticis officiis* II, 3: *PL* 83, 779.

11. There has been some discussion of the so-called *chorepiscopi* or bishops of country districts, but this situation confirms the principle of the early *titulus Ecclesiae*; see A. Bergère *Etudes historiques sur les chorévêques* (Paris 1925); T. Gottlob *Der abendländische Chorepiskopat* (Amsterdam 1963).

12. C. Vogel 'Laica communione contentus.' Le retour du presbytre au rang des laics' *Recherches de Science Religieuse* 47 (1973) 56–122.

13. There are traces of the transition from *cheirotonia* (accreditation or ordinatio by means of an official acceptance on the part of the community) to a liturgical *cheirothesia* (or imposition of hands) in 1 Tim. 5:22; 2 Tim. 1:6; see also 1 Tim. 4:14.

14. B. Botte *La Tradition apostolique de saint Hippolyte, Sources chrétiennes* 11 bis (Paris 1963) (= *Liturgiewissenschaftliche Quellen und Forschungen* 39 ed. B. Botte [Münster 1963]); B. Botte 'L' Ordination de l'evêque' *La Maison-Dieu* 98 (Paris 1969) 113–126, and *Etudes sur le sacrement de l'ordre* (Paris 1957) 13–35; A. Rose 'La Prière de consécration par l'ordination épiscopale' *La Maison-Dieu* 98 (Paris 1969) 127–142; C. Vogel 'L'Imposition des mains dans les rites d'ordination en Orient et en Occident' *La Maison-Dieu* 102 (Paris 1970) 57–72; *ibid. Le Ministére charismatique de l'eucharistie, Studia Anselmiana* 61 (Rome 1973) 181–209; J. Lecuyer 'Episcopat et presbytérat dans les écrits d'Hippolyte de Rome' *Recherches de Science Religieuse* 41 (1953) 30–50; H. J. Schulz 'Das liturgisch sakramental übertragene Hirtenamt in seiner eucharistischen Selbstverwirklichung nach dem Zeugnis der liturgischen Überlieferung' in P. Bläser et al. *Amt und Eucharistie* (Paderborn 1973) pp. 208–255; *ibid.* 'Die Grundstruktur des kirchlichen Amtes im Spiegel der Eucharistiefeier und der Ordinationsliturgie des römischen und des Byzantinischen Ritus' *Catholica* 29 (1975) 325–340; H.-M. Legrand 'Theology and the Election of Bishops,' cited in note 8; J. H. Janssens 'Les Oraisons sacramentelles des ordinations orientales' *Orient. Christ. Periodica* 18 (1952) 297–318; V. Brockhaus *Charisma und Amt* (Wuppertal 1962) pp. 674–676; V. Fuchs *Der Ordinationstitel*, cited in note 5.

15. Hippolytus *Traditio Apostolica* 2, 7 and 8.

16. Y. Congar 'Ordinations *invitus, coactus,* de l'Eglise antique au canon 214' *Revue des Sciences Philosophiques et Théologiques* 50 (1966) 169–197.

17. Hippolytus *Traditio,* 9.

18. *ibid.* 11 and 13; see also 15 and 19. In the *Constitutiones Apostolorum* 8. 21, 2 and 8. 22, 2, which are dependent on the *Traditio Apostolica* and appeared at the end of the fourth century A.D., hands are also laid on sub-deacons and lectors, in other words, the process of clericalization was continued.

19. B. Botte *La Tradition apostolique,* cited in note 14, pp. 28–29. Botte denies that the confession made by suffering or *martyrium* replaced ordination. See also C. Vogel 'L' Imposition des mains,' in the article cited in note 14. These scholars are right in that those who bore witness to faith were not automatically 'leaders' (even though they already possessed the charisma of the Spirit). A *receptio Ecclesiae* (and therefore *cheirotonia,* but without *cheirothesia*) continued to be required. See M. Lods *Confesseurs et martyrs, successeurs des prophètes dans l'Eglise des trois premiers siècles* (Paris and Neuchâtel 1950); D. van Damme 'Martus, Christianos' *Freiburger Zeitschrift für Philosophie und Theologie* 23 (1976) 186–303.

20. See V. Saxer *Vie liturgique et quotidienne à Carthage vers le milieu du IIe siècle* (Rome 1969) pp. 194–202; A. Jansen *Kultur und Sprache. Zur Geschichte der alten Kirche im Spiegel der Sprachentwicklung von Tertullian bis Cyprian* (Nijmegen 1938).

21. *Sacerdos vice Christi vere fungitur* (Cyprian *Litt.* 63: PL 4, 386). See B. D. Marliangeas *Clés pour une théologie du ministère* (Paris 1979) p. 47.

22. Augustine *Contra Ep. Parmeniani* II, 8, 15 and 16: CESL 51, 1908 (*PL* 43, 49–50).

23. See P. M. Gy 'La Théologie des prières anciennes pour l'ordination des évêques et des prêtres' *Revue des Sciences philosophiques et thèologiques* 58 (1974) 599–617.

24. B. Botte 'Secundi meriti munus' *Questions liturgiques et paroissiales* 21 (1936) 84–88.

25. This is what J. Blank claims in *Das Recht der Gemeinde auf Eucharistie. Die bedrohte Einheit von Wort und Sakrament* (Trier 1978) pp. 8–29. This view has to be given a little more light and shade (see further).

26. See K. Hruby 'La "Birkat ha-mazon' " *Mélanges Liturgiques* (Louvain 1972) 205–222; L. Finkenstein 'The Birkat ha-mazon' *Jewish Quarterly Review* 19 (1928–1929) 211–262; T. Talley 'De la "Berakah" à l'Eucharistie' *La Maison-Dieu* 125 (1974) 199–219.

27. See J. Audet *La Didachè* (Paris 1958).

28. Tertullian *De Corona* 3. See also Justin 1 *Apol.* 65, 3 and 67, 5. See also A. Quacquarelli 'L'epiteto sacerdofe (hieres) ai crestiani in Giustino Martire, Dial. 116, 3' *Vetera Christianorum* 7 (1971); C. Vogel 'Le Ministère charismatique de l'eucharistie' *Ministères et célébration de l'Eucharistie* pp. 198–204; M. Bévenot 'Tertullian's Thoughts about the Christian Priesthood' *Corona Gratiarum,* Part 1 (Bruges 1975).

29. See Ignatius of Antioch *Ad Smyrn.,* 8, 1–2. See also M. Jourgon 'La Présidence de l'eucharistie chez Ignace d'Antioche *Lumière et Vie* 16 (1967)

26–32; R. Padberg 'Das Amtsverständnis der Ignatiusbriefe' *Theologie und Glaube* 62 (1972) 47–54; H.-M. Legrand 'La Présidence de l'eucharistie selon la tradition ancienne' *Spiritus* 18 (1977) 409–431.

30. Cyprian *Epist.* 45.

31. Cyprian *Litt.* 69, 9, 3; 72, 2, 1; *De unitate Ecclesiae* 17.

32. This is a tradition that was valid both in the East and in the West. See, for example, Jerome *Epist.* 15, 2; Innocent I *Epist.* 24, 3; Leo the Great *Epist.* 80, 2; Pelagius 1 *Epist.* 24, 14; Aphraetes *Dem.* 12 *de Paschate* 9; *Decret. Gratiani* II, c. 1, q. 1, c. 73 and 78; Peter Lombard *Sententiae* IV, d. 13.

33. This can be found in *Vita Zephyrini* 2 (ed. L. Duchesne I, pp. 139–40).

34. See D. Droste *'Celebrare' in der römischen Liturgiesprache* (Munich 1963), especially pp. 73–80; R. Schultze *Die Messe als Opfer der Kirche* (Münster 1959); R. Raes 'La Concélébration eucharistique dans les rites orientaux' *La Maison-Dieu* 35 (1953) 24–47; R. Berger *Die Wendung 'offerre pro' in der römischen Liturgie* (Münster 1965); Y. Congar 'L'Ecclesia ou communauté chrétienne sujet intégral de l'action liturgique' *La liturgie d'après Vatican II* (Paris 1967) pp. 241–282; E. Dekkers 'La Concélébration, tradition ou nouveauté?' *Mélanges Liturgiques* (Louvain 1972) 99–120; B. Botte 'Note historique sur la concélébration dans l'Eglise ancienne' *La Maison-Dieu* 35 (1953) 9–23.

35. See, for an apparent exception in the Gelasian Sacramentary, Droste, in the work cited in note 34 at p. 80.

36. At the end of the eleventh century, Guerricus of Igny wrote: 'The priest does not consecrate alone and he does not sacrifice alone. The whole assembly of believers consecrates and offers together with him' (*Sermo* 5: *PL* 185, 57).

37. See especially E. Dekkers in the article cited in note 34, 110–112; R. Berger, in the article cited in the same note, 246; R. Schultze in the article cited in the same note, 188.

38. I Clem. 44, 4–6. See also M. Jourgon 'Remarques sur le vocabulaire sacerdotal de la Prima Clementis' *Epektasis* (In honour of Card. Daniélou) (Paris 1972) p. 109; J. Blond *L'Eucharistie des premiers chrétiens* (Paris 1948) pp. 38–39.

39. See note 29 above.

40. Tertullian *De Exhort. Cast.*, 7, 3; see also *De praescriptione* 41, 5–8; see also G. Otranto 'Nonne et laici sacerdotes sumus? (Exhort. Cast. 7, 3)' *Vetera Christianorum* 8 (1971) 24–47.

41. See G. Otranto 'Il sacerdozio comune dei fideli nei reflessi della 1 Petr. 3, 9' *Vetera Christianorum* 7 (1970) 225–246. See also J. Delorme 'Sacerdoce du Christ et ministère (á propos de Jean 17)' *Recherches de Science Religieuse* 62 (1974) 199–219; J. H. Elliot *The Elect and the Holy. An Exegetical Examination of 1 Peter 2, 4–10* (Leiden 1966). It should be noted that the term 'priestly people of God' does not have a cultic significance. It points to the election of the Christian community.

42. Augustine *Litt.* 3, 8: *CSEL* 34, 655.

43. See note 40 above.

44. *Decretum Gratiani* I, d. 70, c.1: ed. Friedberg, I p. 254; see also Hugh of Saint Victor *De Sacramentis*, II, p. 3, c. 2: *PL* 176, 421.

45. Mansi XXII, 220; see also R. Foreville *Latran I, II, III et Latran IV* (Paris 1965).

46. DS 1764 and 1776.

47. Fourth Lateran Council, Denzinger and Schönmetzer 802.

48. See DS 825. See also, among others, E. Dassmann *Charakter indelebilis. Anpassung oder Verlegenheit* (Cologne 1973); H.-M. Legrand 'The "Indelible" Character and the Theology of Ministry' *Concilium* 74 (1972) 54–62; P. Fransen 'Wording en strekking van de canon over het merkteken in Trente' *Bijdragen* 32 (1972) 2–34. See also note 49 below.

49. E. Schillebeeckx *Sacramentele heilseconomie* (Antwerp and Bilthoven 1952) pp. 501–536.

50. Denzinger and Schönmetzer 781 and 825.

51. See P. Fransen, in the article cited in note 48, and E. Schillebeeckx, in the work cited in note 49.

52. This ontologization of the character in the modern era and especially in the spirituality of the priesthood can be seen, for example, in the theory suggested by J. Galot, who made the character the foundation of priestly celibacy; see his 'Sacerdoce et célibat' *Nouvelle Revue Théologique* 86 (1964) 119–124.

53. *Summa Theologiae* 3a. q. 63, a. 5. This also applied to the characters of baptism and confirmation, each in its own specific way.

54. R. J. Cox *A Study of the Juridic Status of Laymen in the Writings of the Medieval Canonists* (Washington 1959); L. Hödl *Die Geschichte der scholastischen Literatur und der Theologie der Schlüsselgewalt* (Münster 1960); W. Plöchl *Geschichte des Kirchenrechtes* (Vienna, 2nd. edn. 1960) I p. 224ff; K. J. Becker *Wesen und Vollmachten des Priestertums nach dem Lehramt* (Freiburg 1970) pp. 113–121; M. van de Kerckhove 'La Notion de jurisdiction dans la doctrine des Décrétistes et des premiers Décrétalistes, de Gratian (1140) à Bernard de Bottone' *Etudes Franciscaines* 49 (1937) 420–455; P. Krämer *Dienst und Vollmacht in der Kirche. Eine rechtstheologische Untersuchung zur Sacra Potestas-Lehre des II. Vatikanischen Konzils* (Trier 1973); Y. Congar *Sainte Eglise* (Paris 1963) pp. 203–238; *ibid.* 'R. Sohm nous interroge encore' *Revue des Sciences Philosophiques et Théologiques* 57 (1973) 263–294; J. Ratzinger 'Opfer, Sakrament und Priestertum in der Entwicklung der Kirche' *Catholica* 26 (1972) 108–125; *ibid. Das neue Volk Gottes* (Düsseldorf 2nd. edn. 1970) pp. 75–245.

55. *Speculum Doctrinale* VIII, 34. See G. de Lagarde *La Naissance de l'esprit laique au déclin du Moyen-Age* I (Louvain and Paris 1956).

56. From the Carolingian period onwards, this tendency towards privatization is noticeable and the earlier idea of *tota aetas concelebrat* became a mere *in voto* by the whole people; see, for example, Innocent III *De sacro altaris mysterio* III, 6: *PL* 217, 845.

57. See, for example, O. Nussbaum *Kloster, Priestermönch und Privatmesse* (Bonn 1961); A. Häussling *Mönchkonvent und Eucharistiefeier* (Münster 1973).

58. H. de Lubac *Corpus Mysticum. L'eucharistie et l'Eglise au Moyen-âge* (Paris 2nd. edn., 1949); Y. Congar *L'Eglise de saint Augustin à l'époque moderne* (Paris 1970) pp. 167–173 (= *Handbuch der Dogmengeschichte*, III-3c [Freiburg 1971] pp. 105–108).

59. Expressing the view of all medieval theologians, Thomas said: *Sacramentum ordinis ordinatur ad eucharistiae consecrationem* (*Summa Theologia* 3a q. 65, a. 3).

60. DS 802. A more precise formula was suggested in 1957 in a *Responsum Sancti Officii:* 'Ex institutione Christi ille solus valide celebrat qui verba consecratoria pronunciat,' (*Acta Apostolicae Sedis* 49 (1957) 370).

61. See J. P. Massaut *Josse Clichtove. L'humanisme et la réforme du clergé* 2 volumes (Paris 1969); also the critical discussion by G. Chantraine 'J. Clichtove: témoin théologique de l'humanisme parisien' *Revue d'Histoire Ecclésiastique* 66 (1971) 507–528. See also H. Jedin 'Das Leitbild des Priesters nach dem Tridentinum und dem Vatikanum II' *Theologie und Glaube* 60 (1970) 102–124.

62. *Summa Theologiae*, 2a, 2ae, q. 88, a. 11.

63. See A. Rohrbasser, ed. *Sacerdotis imago. Päpstliche Dokumente über das Priestertum von Pius X bis Johannes XXIII* (Freiburg 1962). For a historical survey of these tendencies, see E. Schillebeeckx, 'Creatieve terugblik als inspiratie voor het ambt in de toekomst,' *Tijdschrift voor Theologie* 3 (1979) 266–293.

64. A. Acerbi *Due ecclesiologie. Ecclesiologia giuridice ed ecclesiologie di communione nella 'Lumen Gentium'* (*Bologna 1975); P. J. Cordes Sendung und Dienst* (Frankfurt 1972); P. Krämer *Dienst und Vollmacht in der Kirche* (Trier 1973); Y. Congar 'Préface' in B. D. Marliangeas *Clés pour une théologie du ministère* (Paris 1978) pp. 5–14. See also note 54 above.

65. Isa. 24. 2; Hos. 4. 9.

66. 1 Clem. 40. 4–5.

67. *Traditio Apostolica* 3; Hippolytus here insists that the bishop has the task of coordinating the *klerio*, in other words, the different ministries.

68. An interpolation, taken from one of Pius XII's encyclical letters, will be found in *Lumen Gentium,* 10. According to this insertion, the priesthood of all believers differs essentially from the official priesthood (*essentia et non tantum gradu differunt*). In the light of the whole Church's tradition, this must be interpreted as an affirmation of the specific nature of this Church office, not an insistence on a difference in status.

69. See, for example, Bonaventure *In IV Sent.,* d. 24, p. 1, a. 2, q. 2; Thomas Aquinas *In IV Sent.,* d. 24, q. 1, a. 1, ad 1.

70. For the origin of the term *ordo*, see P. van Beneden *Aux Origines d'une terminologie sacramentelle: ordo, ordinare, ordinatio dans la littérature latine avant 313* (Louvain 1974); B. Kübler 'Ordo' in Pauly and Wissowa *Realenzyklopädie* XVIII-1 (Stuttgart 1939) pp. 930–934; T. Klauser *Der Ursprung der bischölichen Insignien und Ehrenrechte* 2nd. edn. (Krefeld 1953).

71. B. D. Dupuy 'Theologie der kirchlichen Ämter' in J. Feiner and M. Löhrer, eds. *Das Heilsgeschehen in der Gemeinde, Mysterium Salutis* IV-s (Einsiedeln 1973) pp. 488–525, especially p. 495.

72. J. D. Zizioulas 'Ordination et communion,' *Istina* 16 (1971) 5–12, and H. Vorgrimler, ed. *Amt und Ordination in ökumenischen Sicht* (Freiburg 1973) pp. 72–113.

73. This information is given in *De vita S. Gregorii Thaumaturgi: PG* 46, 909.

74. L. Hertling 'Communio und Primat' *Una Sancta* 17 (1962) 91–95; W. de Vries *Rom und die Patriarchate des Ostens* (Freiburg and Munich 1963);

N. Afanassieff *et al. La primauté de Pierre dans l'Eglise Orthodoxe* (Neuchâtel 1960); A. Brandenburg and H. J. Urban, eds. *Petrus und Papst* (Münster 1977); H. J. Mund, ed. *Das Petrusamt in der gegenwärtigen theologischen Diskussion* (Paderborn 1976); K. J. Ohlig *Braucht die Kirche einen Papst?* (Mainz and Düsseldorf 1973); J. Ratzinger, ed. *Zum Wesen und Auftrag des Petrusamtes* (Düsseldorf 1978).

75. *Lumen Gentium* 23 and 26; *Christus Dominus* 11; *Sacrosanctum Concilium passim.* See also H. Marot 'Note sur l'espression "episcopus catholicae Ecclesiae" ' *Irenikon* 37 (1964) 221–226.

76. H.-M. Legrand *Unam Sanctam* 74 pp. 105–121 and 'The Revaluation of Local Churches: Some Theological Implications' *Concilium* 71 (1972) 53–64; L. Ott *Le sacrement de l'ordre* (Paris 1971), especially pp. 42–44.

77. DS, 1776.

78. *Lumen Gentium* 28.

10

Secular Criticism of Christian Obedience and the Christian Reaction to That Criticism

1980

It is always a valuable exercise to recall great traditions both in the religious and the non-religious spheres of collective human experience with the aim of creating a better and more human future for mankind. Such traditions may throw a critical light on certain blind spots when we consider them with our present-day, but nonetheless correct and new, attitude towards so many things and relationships. Provided that our vision is always critical, these early traditions can be both liberating and productive, thus making growth in man's true humanity possible.

Among these great human traditions, there have always been, on the one hand, 'pagan witnesses.' These were known as 'this world' in the Johannine writings and 'the people' in Mark. Present-day Christians usually call them 'the modern world.' They have always been critical of Christian obedience and of Christian humility, which is closely linked to this. It is always good for Christians to listen to this 'pagan' criticism, even when it is no longer completely correct from the historical point of view.

On the other hand, there are the 'Christian witnesses.' These are those whose experience of authentic Christian obedience has inspired them to criticize the secular self-sufficiency of man who does not appear to be aware of his loneliness and his non-solidarity.

I have been asked by the directors of the November issue of *Concilium* (on Spirituality) to provide, in broad outline, a survey of both sides of this mutual criticism. This would, of course, be quite a considerable historical task and to do justice to it would require a lengthy article. Here I can do no more than analyze a few fundamental phenomena drawn from history. These will be taken, on the one hand, from Graeco-Roman criticism of Christian obedience in antiquity and, on the other, from the resumption of that criticism in the modern world, within the new situation that has existed since the Enlightenment. This modern criticism has, after all, been to a great extent inspired by the Middle Stoa.

The 'World's' Criticism of Christian Obedience

The Greek Idea of Human Grandeur

Going back to a much longer Greek tradition, Aristotle expresses a supreme disdain for every form of servile subjection.[1] It should not be forgotten that this was, at that time, a social reality on a massive scale and that the élite owed its privileged position to slavery, something that was not necessarily borne in mind in the Greeks' theories of human grandeur. Man's grandeur was contrasted by that élite with servile subjection and this was expressed in the typically Greek view, which was later also taken over by the Romans, of man's 'greatness of soul' or magnanimity (*megalopsychia;* translated by Cicero as *magnanimitas*). This can also be rendered as great or fine humanity or, as we have rendered it here, as human grandeur. It was regarded by the Greeks as being based on an ethically good attitude to life (*kalokagathia*).

Although the basic attitude was seen as the same, the Greeks distinguished between two different aspects of this one human grandeur. On the one hand, there was the idea of an active and political grandeur, which characterized those who were manly enough to form grandiose plans and were able to carry them out. Such men were able to 'hold the world in contempt' if their cause was great enough and rise above it by their own human greatness and by the veneration of others. On the other hand, there was also contemplative and ethical grandeur, in which human greatness consisted basically of ethical excellence and of which Socrates was regarded by the Greeks as the prototype.[2] Because of his inner self-respect and self-image, this wise Greek man was able to transcend all the external vicissitudes of human life. What is more, this wise, contemplative man regarded the man who was politically great as a dangerous fool who had to be kept down. The external world could, it was thought, only be transcended by man's inner, ethical value.[3]

This ideal was given various forms in Greek philosophy. The Greek could, like Plato, scornfully transcend this shadowy world and look forward to the divine world of ideas as a model for the correct organization of the terrestrial world-order that had been reduced to chaos by short-sighted politicians. On the other hand, he could also follow Aristotle and reject any order transcending this world, place God outside human life[4] and expect all salvation of and for men to come only from and through men and, what is more, only within life on this earth. The notion that it is better to give than to receive has a distinctively Greek background.[5] The ethical, active subject is dominantly virile and superior to whatever or whomever is the 'receptive subject,' that is, the subordinate, dominated element or the 'female principle' of the receptive subject.[6] Because this magnanimous, typically male man has virtue in himself, he is able to transcend the terrestrial world outside himself, even in default of the latter, because he knows that he has, on the basis of his own inner virtue, a right both to be honored by all other men and to all terrestrial goods. The Aristotelian man of grandeur keeps to the golden mean between vanity or boastfulness and 'smallness of soul' or pusillanimity (*mikropsychia* or *pusillanimitas;* sometimes called *humilitas* or modesty). Both these attitudes are vices, because they imply a mistaken knowledge of oneself, except in the case of the really small man, for whom such humility is suitable. The man who, however, has a sense of grandeur does what is good, not because it is offered by someone else, even a god, but because he regards this as good and beautiful in itself.[7] Such a man is 'autarkic.' He can do without everyone and everything and has no need of anything, not even God. In contrast with small and servile men, he will, laughing scornfully and condescendingly, ironically conceal his own grandeur[8] and he knows in particular that he is superior to those who have political power in this world and that he is above all superior in ethical wisdom. His only need is for friends of like mind and he is satisfied with intercourse with them.[9] He is autonomous and free and at the service of the one great cause, regarding his own external life as nothing.[10] This humanly great man would normally be the king of the country.[11] He is conscious that he should have that status, but he is able, autarkically, to renounce the honor that others apparently begrudge him. This, then, is a brief summary of Aristotle's teaching.

Greek thought about this question, however, went even further than this. The Stoics were even more radical than the radically minded Aristotle, at the same time adapting his ideas so that they were more accommodating to men's religious needs. They denied, for example, the Aristotelian principle that man had some need of external goods before his acquisition of virtue. From the very beginning, it was sufficient for the wise Stoic simply to have a subjective ethical intention, on the basis of which he condemned not so much the outside world of sense-perception, as that world in so far as it lay outside man's free will and appeared as fate in contrast with man's freedom. The harmony of the world-order, that is, the will of God, could call on man to sacrifice his own individual aspirations, with the result that he would have to defer, as far as his own will was concerned, to the law of the universal divine Logos, which was Reason in all things.

Stoic condemnation of the world, then, is purely ethical. In contrast to Platonic and Aristotelian human grandeur, the greatness of the wise Stoic was accessible to all men—both the slave (Epictetus) and the emperor (Marcus Aurelius). This was the period of Graeco-Roman cosmopolitanism, the so-called brotherhood of all men: 'Homo, res sacra homini' (Seneca).

Unlike the original Stoics, the Middle Stoa, a little later, was aware of the illusory and utopian nature of man's direct knowledge of the will of God. Perfect harmony between human reason and universal divine reason was seen as a chimera. The new element that these Middle Stoics introduced into wisdom was that there had to be intermediaries between God's will and human will. In this way, we are able to know the will of God, at least with a probable knowledge, and carry it out, through the private natural tendencies of the individual things by means of which universal order is achieved. By obeying our private and individual natural aspirations, we translate the universal law in a probable and correct way. In other words, we obey God in this way. This Stoic view became extremely important historically in the whole of the western world, both Christian and non-Christian.

In this version of Greek philosophy, the dominant norm of human grandeur is man's subjection to the will of God. Despite this, however, this Greek attitude towards life (an attitude that was also adopted by the Romans, since this Greek ideal was universally disseminated by Rome in the later 'imperial' Stoa) was characterized by an exclusive trust in man's powers in his attempt to obey God's will. For the man of grandeur, praying to God was only a prayer of thanksgiving and never a prayer of petition or a supplication for help. (See Cleanthes' famous hymn to Zeus.) The Greeks did not, in other words, kneel in front of God and implore him for help. To do that would have been contrary to man's dignity and autarky. Seneca's saying: Deo parere, libertas est,[12] that is, man's freedom consists in obeying God, expresses a Stoic conviction that man owes his existence to God, but that, precisely for this reason, he no longer has any need of God and is able only to rely on his own powers.[13] According to this pantheistic view, trust in God is only possible in the mode of human trust in oneself. The climax of the 'pagan spirituality' of Greece and Rome was reached perhaps in the teachings of Marcus Aurelius, in which it is possible to detect signs of what Christians would call a humble obedience in faith. An example of this is the saying: 'Why should God not help us even in those matters that are within our power?'[14] Here, as elsewhere, this great humanist shows that he has some need of God, but at the same time even this humble confession is an expression of the Stoic's self-sufficient autonomy. We can therefore say that, in default of a correct concept of God and his creation, those qualities known as Christian obedience or humility could not thrive in 'pagan' soil. At the same time, however, the pride with which the Greek was human is also a criticism of Christian humility.

This Greek spirit (which was elaborated in various ways, including neo-Platonism later) came about as the result of a tragic experience of life. Looking at himself and his own human powers, the Greek could be optimistic and he was able to cope with life. He was, however, pessimistic when he looked outside, that is, at the 'world' or at society, believing that man was smashed to pieces by the vicissitudes of blind fate. Man's inner dignity and happiness could only be disturbed by things outside him. Salvation or human redemption had to be sought in some technique by which man was able to transcend the world on the basis of his own unthreatened and self-sufficient grandeur. Freedom, then, was, for the Stoics, a privatized and inner independence and it could in fact be accompanied by an absence of social and political freedom. But, even though they were religious, these philosophers never sought refuge with a god or implored him to send them a favorable fate. His own autonomous conscience bore witness to the fact that the magnanimous man did not, as a 'good man,' deserve adversity and that, in adversity, not he, but fate was wrong. This *contemptus mundi* or scorn of the world was therefore the other side of the coin of man's autarkical grandeur and had nothing at all to do with a *contemptus sui* or a denial of oneself.

As soon as this Graeco-Roman attitude came in contact with the humble obedience of Christianity, it found itself in conflict with it. The Greek saw Christian obedience as a direct attack against man's grandeur.

'Pagan' Human Grandeur as a Criticism of Christian Obedience and the Reaction of Christians

Christian Humility as Servile Cowardice

Pagan philosophers only condemned the Christian witness of martyrdom, an action described by the *Acta Martyrum* as the most powerful that a Christian could perform. Why, then, was this rejected by pagan philosophers, when the pagan *magnanimus* or man of great soul was ready to lay down his life for a great cause? It is, moreover, a historical fact that many Stoic philosophers were martyrs and either murdered or at least banished from Italy because of their ideals, which included criticism of society. Despite this, however, it is undeniable that high-minded pagan thinkers such as Epictetus, Marcus Aurelius and Celsus[15] regarded the obedience of Christian martyrdom as weak and cowardly pusillanimity and even as a perverse disgust for human life. They certainly did not think of it as human grandeur or *magnanimitas*. Their criticism of Christians was that they crept up to a god to implore him tearfully to help them and, in martyrdom especially, did not trust in their own autonomous powers.

Humility as the Only True Human Grandeur

The Fathers of the Church almost always began their arguments by making a distinction between genuine humility and its many spurious forms—after all, they were also Greeks! After this, they tended to respond to the pagan arguments with counter-arguments, insisting that only humility was true human greatness. In so doing, they frequently provided an analysis of the pagan attitude towards this concept. It is also remarkable that, with the exception of Augustine, both the Greek and the Latin Fathers accepted as their point of departure that the pagans also had a clear notion of humility. (This conviction persisted until the middle ages.)

Christians were aware, on the other hand, that the pagan author Celsus had said, in his anti-Christian polemic,[16] that Christian humility was a plagiarism taken from the writings of Plato and that, in doing that, the Christians had misinterpreted Plato. The Platonic *tapeinos* or humble man always bore witness to a 'well regulated' form of humility and, according to Celsus, that reasonable order was not present in Christian humility.[17] Christians, after all, permitted thieves and prostitutes to enter what they called the kingdom of God[18] and this was abhorrent even for the permissive Greeks.

Augustine, however, was firmly convinced that humility was an original Christian quality that was unknown among the pagans, who were in fact completely unaware of it.[19] The Greek Christian Origen dealt most fully with Celsus' criticisms. He too pointed to various possible caricatures of Christian humility. He believed that authentic humility was a virtue that was practiced only by great Christians, just as magnanimity was the privilege of great pagans. In other words, according to Origen, only saints were humble and only that form of humility could be called really human grandeur. Humility did not confront man with the world—it confronted him with God and the only suitable attitude for man in that situation was one of humble obedience. To humiliate oneself, then, was a patristic virtue which meant seeing oneself in relationship to God, who was, Origen taught, alone great, while every man, confronted with him, was small.[20]

Augustine expressed this patristic conviction very clearly: *Tu homo, cognosce quia homo es. Tota humilitas tua, ut cognoscas te.*[21] In other words, true humility consists in knowing that you are man, because true humanity is firstly being God's creature and secondly being bruised by sin. Knowing oneself in the light of God therefore brings about a humble obedience in faith and, by means of a radical change of the pagan concept, this obedience is called magnanimity or human grandeur.

Over and against pagan humanism, then, the Fathers of the Church stressed God's greatness and human misery. The patristic and, later, the medieval theologians (up to the time of Thomas Aquinas) were therefore able to identify authentic humility with magnanimity, thus mystically transforming the pagan concept. In patristic theology, the emphasis was on the grandeur of God who had mercy on man in his smallness. This emphasis led to a radical change in the typically pagan concept of the *contemptus mundi* or scorn of the world. In pagan philosophy, *spernere (despicere) mundum* or looking down on the world was the other side of the coin of man's autarkical self-assertion over the fortunes and misfortunes of fate that came upon man from outside. Scorn of the world was, in other words, an expression of human grandeur. On the basis of Christian faith in God's creation, however, this Greek *contemptus mundi* or scorn of the *world* was extended in patristic teaching to a *contemptus sui* or denial of *oneself*. *Spernere mundum* or looking down on the *world* became *spernere seipsum* or despising *oneself*. In other words, Christians regarded the human grandeur of the pagans confronted with the cosmic and social outside world as nothing, especially in the presence of God. In this way, a real confrontation with pagan thought was avoided and a purely Christian solution was found for the problem. There was, however, no question of a synthesis between pagan grandeur and Christian humility. A legitimate pagan criticism was not elaborated in a Christian sense. It was simply refuted. The relationship between man's liberation of himself and salvation in God's name was not solved, although this was the real pagan contribution that Greek philosophy could make to Christianity as a criticism.

Human Grandeur from God

Christians became more conscious of this problem in the twelfth century, although the non-religious version of pagan philosophy (that is, Aristotle's view of human grandeur) was unknown at the time. The ideas that were in fact known then were in the main those of the Middle

Stoa. In the Augustinian tradition of the middle ages, Bernard made a distinction that remained predominant throughout the whole period. Briefly summarized, it is this: man can be seen from two different points of view. In the first place, he can be seen in himself, that is, in what he is in himself and would be without God, in which case he is nothing, mere dirt and shadow. He was, after all, created 'from nothing.' In the second place, he can be seen in his relationship to God the creator, through whom he is positively what he is and to whom he owes all his human greatness. His human greatness is therefore God's greatness in him.[22] Even a Stoic philosopher would probably say something of the same kind, although his spirituality would still be fundamentally different from the Christian's here.

This is very clearly revealed in Bernard's more precise definition of this distinction (which was strenuously opposed by Thomas Aquinas). According to Bernard, our human share in our humanity is sin and evil, injustice and disaster, whereas God's share in our humanity is goodness and salvation, justice and happiness.[23] The negative element is therefore our contribution, whereas the positive is God's, with the result that 'humility' points to man's contribution and magnanimity to God's. It would never, of course, have been possible for a Greek to express himself in this way! Even Bernard, however, was to some extent reserved in his belittlement of man, making a distinction between *humiliatio*, which is a humiliation forced on man from outside, and *humilitas*, which is spontaneously and happily accepted in a personal manner. In his own words, *humilitas iustificat, non humiliatio*,[24] that is, man is justified not by being humiliated from outside, but by a humility that he has chosen himself. Finally, we can only be humiliated by ourselves—a conviction which really reveals something of the attitude of the Middle Stoa. *Humiliari*, keeping oneself lowly, therefore has nothing to do, either in patristic teaching or in the Christian middle ages, with *se humiliare*, humiliating oneself. It is clear, then, that Bernard regarded the humble man as authentically autarkic and autonomous and, what is more, *causa sui*. Although his teaching is obviously in the patristic tradition, it also reveals something of the Greek idea of autonomy.[25]

We may therefore conclude by saying that pagan humanism stressed human grandeur as coming from and through man himself, even though, in the imperial Stoic tradition, it is also a gift from God. At the same time, this grandeur is entirely lacking in humility. Human grandeur is also accompanied, in this Graeco-Roman teaching, by an ignorance of God's true divinity. The Church Fathers and the medieval theologians, on the other hand, recognized the true grandeur of God, but failed to understand man's secular grandeur and to give it a proper place in creation. This failure colored and frequently discolored the concept of Christian obedience. It is therefore possible to say that both the pagan philosophers and the Christian theologians of that period failed to combine human grandeur with humility and, in the teaching of both, one of the two aspects was undervalued. This meant that each side failed to criticize the other legitimately.

Thomas Aquinas' Synthesis

An attempt to form a synthesis was made by Thomas Aquinas in the thirteenth century, when Christians came into contact with pagan and fundamentally Aristotelian conception of human grandeur. The fierce discussions that arose between 1250 and 1277 were the direct result of the shock that this contact gave to medieval Christians. Several theologians, notably Albert the Great, had prepared the way for Thomas's work of synthesis by pointing out the particular direction in which he should proceed. The fact remains, however, that it was Thomas alone who, after a long period of hesitation, formulated that synthesis into which the pagan criticism of Christian humility and obedience was assimilated and in which the pagan view was at the same time criticized. It cannot be denied that Thomas to some extent explains Aristotle's ideas away and christianizes him in his synthesis, but, despite this, he displays a fine sense for his distinctively pagan impulse and in the long run does justice to this.

After some hesitation, then, Thomas made this synthesis, which is to be found especially in his *Summa Theologiae* 2a-2ae. qq. 161 and 129. It dates back to 1271. He does not deny that the Church Fathers mystically transformed the pagan idea of magnanimity, but, on the contrary, admits for the first time that it was in many ways a right idea and thus criticizes the traditional Christian view of man as a miserable creature on whom God has mercy.[26]

In Thomas's opinion, humility has nothing to do with the outside world or with man's fellow-men. It is only concerned with man's relationship with God. Whereas the Aristotelian virtue of magnanimity regulates man's passion for grandeur (as a mean between recklessness and despair) in the service of man himself and therefore also in the service of man's humanity, Christian humility regulates that same human passion in relation to God. Humility is therefore an essentially religious virtue. In the light of his faith in God's creation from nothing, Thomas is able to repeat the traditional distinction that man, seen purely from the point of view of man himself, has nothing of his own (that is, in contrast with God; all that man has of himself is sin), but that, seen in his relationship to God, everything that is positively present in him is a pure gift from God.[27]

This statement is, however, only apparently the same as Bernard had said in the previous century. Thomas, after all, makes an addition (which is fundamentally Greek), namely that man has a value of his own which is not exclusively derived from God: 'an inalienable human value that is peculiar to him.'[28] In other words, according to Thomas, man has a grandeur of his own and that grandeur cannot be made to vanish by a form of medieval mysticism. Man is a subject, even with regard to God, and is therefore responsible both for his good actions and for his evil deeds. No one else, not even God, is responsible for that man's actions.[29] He is magnanimous and is therefore able to know his own strength. He knows the extent of his capabilities and is not afraid to accept his grandeur. But, because he is also humble, he knows that his power is a gift from God. This knowledge does not, however, impede his human movement. It is clear, then, that Thomas was not concerned with the drama of God's grandeur as contrasted with the smallness of man, but rather with the drama within man himself, that is, the tension in man between human grandeur and human misery. Magnanimity is a virtue of human hope and is expressed through man's own power. It is also directed towards increasing man's humanity.

In this way, Thomas succeeds in rehabilitating man's trust in himself, which is a quality that is in no sense in opposition to the humility that presupposes man's magnanimity and at the same time includes it in faith in God the creator who brings salvation. 'Pagan' humanistic trust in oneself is therefore included in God's grace, which on the one hand heals bruised man and, on the other, enables him to share in community with God. Thomas is therefore clearly opposed to the patristic and medieval belittlement of man and restores his human trust in himself, stressing that his grandeur comes from himself and his own powers, although those powers are a gift from God and man often damages them. Christian hope, then, is included within the one perspective of salvation, which transcends all human power and to which man can only react with hope, and at the same time also includes man's human trust in himself *sub Deo*.[30] Only the man who obeys God absolutely in faith and expects all salvation to come from him alone is able to trust in his own strength to save that part of humanity in man and society that is both confirmed and transcended by God.

Thomas therefore provided the foundations for our own distinctively modern mode of life, which is not based on the monastic model of the middle ages, but has developed in accordance with more autonomous, profane structures. Despite the fact that, at the level of mysticism, he often makes pronouncements that are almost identical with those made by the Church Fathers and the medieval theologians, he cannot be regarded as working within the Augustinian tradition of the middle ages. Even at this mystical level, however, it is possible to distinguish a substructure in which man's autonomous human value is emphasized. Towards the end of the thirteenth century, the distinctively profane structures of the 'modern' world were beginning to develop[31] and the foundations for a non-monastic, Christian spirituality had been laid by Thomas. His restoration of humanism at the individual level in the sphere of Christian spirituality became the basis of his doctrine of social justice at the level of society.

The drama of the modern era that followed the period in which Thomas Aquinas was active took two forms. On the one hand, a few years after Thomas's death, Siger of Brabant's theory, which gave a very one-sided emphasis to pagan magnanimity, thus upsetting the balance in Thomas's synthesis, was condemned by the Church, mainly on the ground that Siger refused to call humility a virtue. On the other, there was, much later, in the sixteenth and seventeenth centuries (despite the emergence of neo-Stoicism), a strong tendency on the part of Christian spirituality to revert to an earlier Augustinianism, with the result that it became ineffectual in the modern world. By that time, Thomas's statement, emphasizing both the Christian and the humanistic dimensions: 'A minimization of the perfection of God's creatures is a minimization of the perfection of God's creative power,'[32] had been totally forgotten, with the result that the modern world looked outside Christianity for the man that it really needed.

As we have seen, Thomas laid the foundations for a structure which would have given form, within Christian obedience in faith, to man's pathos for large-scale undertakings to promote human development. He also provided the foundations for a complete trust in man as well as in his scientific and technical skill in solving the problems of the world. Despite this, however, it cannot be disputed that this human pathos, as first expressed in synthesis by Thomas, has become effective, for the most part, outside the Christian churches (and therefore, of course, often without the perspective that those churches might have offered). This tendency began with the Enlightenment, which can therefore be seen as an inevitable reaction against sixteenth and seventeenth century Augustinianism.

Modern Man and Christian Obedience

Modern Man's Criticism of Humility

Humility was criticized in a new way by Descartes, who stressed man's assertion of himself in magnanimity, which Descartes called *générosité.*[33] He was fundamentally concerned with the inalienable ego as the subject of free will. That ego is opposed to any form of servile humility. A new protest based on man's will to power and directed against Christian submissiveness is expressed in Descartes' criticism. Man is seen as in control of himself and the superiority complex of his 'generous' consciousness, inspired by the rediscovery of human grandeur, takes the place of 'Thy will, not mine, be done.'

Spinoza was less inhibited by Christian traditions than Descartes and regarded man's proud assertion of himself as the basis of all virtue. Humility and arrogance he saw as twins; both of them the daughters of an illusory imagination or of dreams.[34] Man, Spinoza taught, had to find his true place and his greatness in the identity of the universe with himself.

Kant was violently opposed to *humilitas spuria* or cringing humility.[35] Although 'phenomenal' man was, for Kant, only an exchangeable value, 'noumenal' man, the person, was an end in itself. Man is rightly conscious of his smallness and real humility when confronted with the law, but he is himself the one who makes and supports that law, with the result that the only proper attitude for him is not one of servile submissiveness, but an assertion of his ethical dignity. He is, after all, autonomous and does not need grace and forgiveness or any form of privilege. He is no one's servant. As the subject of the law he has no need to humiliate himself 'even in the presence of a seraph.' Kant mocked the piety of the psalmist, who declared. 'I am a worm and no man,' claiming that 'anyone who makes himself into a worm should not complain if he is trodden on.' Kant was, however, not so naïve as Descartes or Spinoza, neither of whom seemed to be conscious of man's evil intentions. He saw through man's deceitfulness and the injury that it did to man's dignity as an end in itself. He discovered a new form of ethical pride in man's negative experiences of humiliation.

It should not be forgotten in this context that the Enlightenment was preceded by religious wars in Europe. In the light of the deep division in Christianity, both Catholics and Protestants became aware that the political unity of the State could no longer be guaranteed by religion as the basis and expression of social life. If it was to survive as a State, it had to be emancipated from religion, which had acquired a socially disintegrating function. The integrating principle was, from this time onwards, to be enlightened reason, which was in fact a bourgeois or middle-class reason, concerned with what could be calculated and had an exchangeable value in the public sense, with the result that everything else was relegated to the purely private sphere of personal convictions.

According to Kant, the Enlightenment was 'man's exodus from the state in which he has not yet come of age and which is caused by his own guilt,' in other words, from his inability to make full use of his own reason without the guidance of others. Authority has to be justified. It has to be capable of being discussed in public. It cannot exist simply on the basis of its 'being there' historically. If it does, it simply produces servants and slaves. If it loses its social plausibility structures, it becomes inhuman coercion. The Enlightenment therefore regarded authority as a relic that had survived from feudalism and the new society as based on a 'contract,' which presupposed the equality of all men and their freedom to enter into a contract. The only form of authority that the Enlightenment regarded as valid was the authority of autonomous knowledge or cognitive competence.

Analyzes made by B. Groethuysen and others[36] have shown that the history of freedom in the Enlightenment was in fact a very curtailed history of freedom. The specifically class characteristics of the middle-class 'citizen' (that is, not as a *citoyen,* but as a member of a particular economic class) were defined as universally human characteristics (something that had already been done by most of the élitist Greek thinkers in classical antiquity). In other words, specifically middle-class norms were regarded as universally human norms.

This new vision was not so much the result of a new way of looking at life. On the contrary, a new praxis, dominated by the economic principle of exchange, gave rise to the new vision. Life, in other words, took priority over ideas. Even God was made a middle-class citizen in this process, rewarding the good and punishing the bad and thus acting as the guarantor of middle-class society. This also led to a break both with nature and with universal order, which was, of course, not a Stoic action. Nature, the Enlightenment thinkers believed, was dominated by God's natural laws, but man was all-powerful in the human sphere.

God was obliged only to give man his due—in accordance with a kind of contract. Modern man requires guarantees which enable him to know that his efforts do not go unrewarded—the spirit of trade clearly had an effect on religion in the Enlightenment! God's power as it were stopped where human freedom began and God and man were in competition with each other. God became simply the ultimate judge, the 'executive power of middle-class consciousness in the hereafter.'[37] Virtue and ethics were therefore divorced from their relationship with God and truthfulness, honesty and good manners became the foundation of the enlightened way of life. Religion was reduced to ethics and deprived of its mystical and its political potential. The separation of religion from politics, from redemption and liberation, from mysticism and politics is a fundamental characteristic of this individualistic and 'middle-class' religiosity.

Religion also became a separate and private sphere of emotion and sentiment. Man, in his subjectivity, became the measure of all things. This subject, however, was a purely individual self-assertion and not in any way an affirmation of one's fellow-man's freedom in solidarity with him. This middle-class religion therefore eventually became a means by which the people could be made to accept misery in society and injustice caused by other men. The man who was not a middle-class citizen was the victim of this situation and became servile man.

Finally, at a later stage, Nietzsche[38] condemned humility as the product of Judaism and Christianity and a complex of deep resentment. The good news that Jesus proclaimed to slaves became bad news for the powerful. Nietzsche regarded Christian humility as a servile and vindictive distortion of a plebeian consciousness that denies itself in the expectation of eschatological revenge. Magnanimity—in Nietzsche's view, the attitude of the superman—was once again the privilege of a ruling class that created its own values and then made them into universally human norms.

The Christian Criticism of the Privatized Autonomy of Enlightened Reason

Christians are nowadays much more conscious of the fact that God's will can only be known through the mediation of history. They also know that there are dangerous ways of speaking about God's will! If it can only be made known through the medium of man's experiences in the world—a process in which the Christian community and its leaders have to play an interpretative role—then it is true to say that man can never be confronted 'unambiguously' with the will of God.

We may go further and say that ethics are different, as a language game, from religion, which is not simply ethics and cannot be reduced to ethics, despite that fact that there is undeniably an inner connection between religion and the ethical life. An understanding of God and his will must logically be preceded by an understanding of the difference between good and evil. This also means that we should not in the first place define our moral obligations in terms of God's will, but in terms of what is directed towards the dignity of human life. On the other hand, however, the man who believes in God will inevitably and correctly interpret what he regards here and now as worthy of man as an expression of God's will, without sacrificing any of the serious purpose of that will or reducing God himself in a middle-class way to the level of a merely eschatological judge of man's use of his autonomy.

These historical ways of mediating God's will, followed, among others, by those in authority in the Church, add a dialectical dimension to Christian obedience. 'Illegality' can, in certain cases, be interpreted, in a Christian sense, as a higher form of trust in God's Spirit, since there is also a way of trusting God which cannot be traced back to obedience to the authority of the Church. Christians' eyes may have been opened to this by the Enlightenment!

On the other hand, however, the Christian attitude towards authority and obedience may be no more than a protest against the purely cognitive competence of all authority as interpreted by enlightened reason. Authority also has a liberating function with regard to man's true humanity precisely because his critical memory of certain liberating but still unassimilated traditions is an inner, constitutive aspect of his critical reason.[39] Man's state as a subject in solidarity with his fellow-men, which enables him to recognize his fellow-man's freedom and state as a subject, also forms part, in a fully human and theological sense, of the social constitution of the subject.[40] The autonomous middle-class subject is fundamentally criticized from this vantage-point because of his individualistic, utilitarian and non-biblical view of 'autonomous freedom,' which acts to others' disadvantage. The principle of exchange, which is reflected in the Enlightenment view of freedom and autonomy, is here revealed, in the light of the Christian tradition, as a diminished form of freedom which in fact makes others (and indeed even the major part of the world's population) victims of a concept of freedom. We are, however, bound to consider, in the difficulties that Christians have with the feudal and patriarchal way of exercising authority (a practice that was justifiably criticized by the Enlightenment), whether the discomfort that some modern Christians experience with regard to religious authority is not connected with a liberal, middle-class view of human freedom and autonomy. All of us who have been brought up in the West are, after all, products of that middle-class culture! In this case, our memory of evangelical freedom has not fully assimilated the latter's criticism of the autarky of the Enlightenment, with the result that we often identify middle-class freedom with evangelical freedom.

Christians should not reject the advances made by the Enlightenment in the process of man's liberation, but they should certainly transcend the diminished freedom of the Enlightenment and, what is more, do this dialectically, by following the direction that J.-B. Metz called that of solidarity of their fellow-man's freedom.[41] It is only if they succeed in doing this that Thomas Aquinas' original view of human grandeur and magnanimity will once again be incorporated into Christian spirituality. If the Enlightenment view of freedom is not dialectically transcended, however, there is a grave danger that a misunderstanding of Thomas's teaching will lead to an increasingly optimistic belief in human progress and a great advance in the ideology of development, thus strengthening and furthering the enslavement of two-thirds of the world's population.

Finally, Christian obedience is above all listening and watching out for the *kairos*, the opportune moment and especially listening obediently to the cry of two-thirds of the world's population for liberation and redemption and then acting in a concrete way in accordance with the voice of God. This is one fundamental form of Christian obedience and one that is derived from the authority of suffering man.

Translated by David Smith

NOTES

1. *Nicomachean Ethics* 1124b, 20–1125a.

2. See, for example, A. J. Festugière *La Sainteté* (Paris 1942); ibid. *Contemplation et vie contemplative selon Platon* (Paris 1936); M. Pohlenz *Griechische Freiheit* (Heidelberg 1955).

3. The final version of Aristotle's doctrine on magnanimity is contained in his *Nicomachean Ethics* 1123a, 34–1124b, 6.

4. *op. cit.*, 1099b, 11–14.

5. *op cit.*, 1167b, 16–1168a, 34; also 1224b, 10–23.

6. *op. cit.*, 1167b, 30–1168a, 34; 1124b, 5–12.

7. *op. cit.*, 1116a, 17–29.

8. *op. cit.*, 1124b, 18–23 and b, 30–31.

9. *op. cit.*, 1169b, 23–28.

10. *op. cit.*, 1169a, 18–20.

11. *Politics* III, 13: 1284a, 3ff.

12. Seneca *De Clementia* 15, 7; see M. Pohlenz *Die Stoa*, 2 vols. (Göttingen 1959).

13. Seneca *Litterae* 4, 1; Epictetus *Dissertationes* II, 16, 11–15.

14. Marcus Aurelius *Meditations (Ta eis heauton)* IX, 40.

15. Epictetus *Dissertationes* IV, 7, 6; Marcus Aurelius *Meditations* XI, 3; Celsus, in Origen *Contra Celsum* VII, 53; VI, 75.

16. P. de Labriolle *La Réaction païenne. Etude sur la polémique antichrétienne du premier au sixième siècle* 2nd ed. (Paris 1942), W. Nestle 'Die Haupteinwände des antiken Denkens gegen das Christentum' *Archiv für Religionswissenschaft* 37 (1941) 51–100; E. Dekkers ' "Humilitas." Een bijdrage tot de geschiedenis van het begrip "humilitas" ' *Horae Monasticae* (Tielt 1947) 67–80; N.-I. Herescu 'Homo-Humus-Humanitas' *Bulletin de l'Association G. Budé* (Paris June 1948) 68ff.

17. Origen *Contra Celsum* VI, 15.

18. *op. cit.*, III, 61.

19. Augustine *Enarr. in Ps.* 31, 18 (*PL* 36, 270); *Tract. in Joh.* 25, c. 16 and 19 (*PL* 35, 1604).

20. Origen *Contra Celsum* VI, 15; III, 62.

21. Augustine *Tract. in Joh.* 25, 16 (*PL* 35, 1604).

22. Bernard *Sermo* V (*PL* 183, 530–532 and 534).

23. *idem. De Consideratione* II, 11 (*PL* 182, 754).

24. *idem. Sermones in Cantica* 34; *Sermones de diversis* 20; *Sermo de conversione ad clericos* 7 (especially *PL* 182, 841).

25. This aspect is neglected in R. Bultot's studies *La Doctrine du mépris du monde* Vols IV-1 and IV-2: *Le XIe siècle* (Louvain and Paris 1963).

26. R. A. Gauthier *Magnanimité. L'idéal de la grandeur dans la philosophie païenne et la théologie chrétienne* (Paris 1951).

27. 'Omnis creatura est tenebra vel falsa vel nihil, *in se* considerata; (hoc dictum) non est intellegendum quod essentia sua sit tenebra vel falsitas, sed quia non habet nec esse nec lucem nec veritatem *nisi ab Alio*,' *De Veritate* q. 8, a. 7 ad 2; 1a–2ae. q. 109, a. 2 ad 2.

28. According to Augustine, 'ominia sunt bona bonitate divina' (*PL* 40, 30); this was corrected by Thomas as follows: 'Unumquodque dicitur bonum bonitate divina, sicut primo principio exemplari, effectivo et finali totius bonitatis. *Nihilominus* tamen unumquodque dicitur bonum similitudine divinae *sibi inhaerente*, quae est formaliter *sua* bonitas denominans ipsum,' 1a, q. 6, a. 4.

29. See a very acute text in Thomas's commentary on Job, in which man is seen as the ultimate subject. In it, Thomas defends Job's questioning of God: 'It seemed as though a discussion between man and God was improper because God, in his eminence, transcends man. It is important, however, to remember here that truth does not differ according to the person who speaks it; that is why no one speaking the truth can be said to be wrong, whoever his partner in the conversation may be,' *Expositio in Job* c. 13, lect. 2.

30. 'Spes, qua quis de Deo confidit, ponitur virtus theologica; . . . sed per fiduciam, quae nunc ponitur pars fortitudinis, homo *habet spem in seipso*, tamen *sub Deo*,' 2a–2ae. Q. 128, art. unic., ad 2.

31. See, for example, G. de Lagarde *La Naissance de l'esprit laïque au déclin du moyen âge*, 4 Vols (Paris 1956–1962).

32. *Summa Contra Gentiles* III, 69.

33. Descartes *Traité des passions* III, art. 155–160.

34. Spinoza *Ethica* III, 26, 55; IV, 52, 53, 55, 57.

35. Kant *Die Metaphysik der Sitten. Ethische Elementarlehre* I, Suhrkamp Taschenbuch VIII, ed. W. Weischedel 2nd ed. (Frankfurt 1978) pp. 553–584, especially pp. 568–571.

36. B. Groethuysen *Origines de l'esprit bourgeois en France* (Paris 1927) and, with a more complete critical apparatus, *Die Entstehung der bürgerlichen Welt- and Lebensanschauung in Frankreich*, 2 Vols (Hildesheim and New York 1927 and 1973). Partly dependent on him are, for example, L. Goldmann *Der christliche Bürger und die Aufklärung* (Neuwied 1968) and

D. Schellong *Bürgertum und christliche Religion* (Munich 1975). See also *Christianity and the Bourgeoisie, Concilium* 125 (1979) p. 74ff; T. Lemaire *Over de waarde van kulturen* (Baarn 1976).

37. See Groethuysen *Origines* cited in note 36, at p. 123.

38. Nietzsche *Jenseits von Gut und Böse* 260, 261, 267, Kritische Gesamtausgabe, ed. G. Colli and M. Montinari (Berlin 1968) pp. 218–224 and 230–231.

39. J.-B. Metz *Faith in History and Society* (London and New York 1980) *passim.*

40. E. Schillebeeckx *Christ. The Christian Experience in the Modern World* (London and New York 1980) pp. 736–738.

41. J.-B. Metz 'Produktive Ungleichzeitigkeit' *Stichworte zur 'Geistigen Situation der Zeit,'* ed. J. Habermas, 2 Vols (Frankfurt 1979) Vol 2 pp. 529–538; see also *ibid.* 'Wenn die Betreuten sich ändern' *Publik-Forum* 13 (27 June 1980) 19–21.

11

Christian Identity and Human Integrity

1982

A great deal of what is offered with a decorative description as 'humanism' has a barely hidden ideological character. This is quite clear from slogans that can easily be found in books and articles. On the one hand, for example, it is possible to read: 'What is Christian is human and what is human is Christian.' On the other, I have recently read this statement: 'What is communist is human and what is human is communist.' It would not be difficult to find other examples of similar statements. A misuse of ideological language of this kind should not, however, cause us to overlook the real question of the relationship between 'humanity' and what is proposed by religion and philosophy as their most profound convictions concerning human life. We should rather accept it as a warning against prematurely making syntheses and identifications.

Whatever wealth it may contain, Christian faith is undoubtedly concerned with 'humanity' and certainly with men and women who believe in God. No one, however, possesses exclusive rights over true humanity, which is something that concerns all men. In any case, 'humanity' is an abstract term. It exists only in very diverse cultural forms, although this may be on the basis of a fundamentally identical biogenetical substratum. Any hegemony of a definite culture is therefore pernicious, because it is tainted with 'regionalism' and imperialism.

The Danger of Being Theologically Squint-Eyed

One encounters more pseudo-problems in theology in the case of pairs of concepts such as 'humanity and Christianity,' 'human freedom and grace,' 'evolution and creation' and even 'self-liberation and justification by grace alone' than in almost any other area. Quite frequently opposing concepts which in fact point to something in reality are projected *as such* into that reality so that they become two opposing or parallel realities which have to be dialectically reconciled with each other. This is, of course, a hopeless task, a good example of which is the struggle about grace that took place in the past in the Catholic Church. This and other struggles were about problems that could not be solved.

At the level of concepts and their linguistic expression, 'humanity' and 'Christianity' (or approaching the kingdom of God) are certainly placed alongside each other. They are frequently equated with each other and then included within the same proposition, as though they were two distinct realities—for example, 'grace and freedom.' The question, however, is whether they can be taken cumulatively. A good human action, performed in freedom, is grace in the concrete, although it at the same time transcends that freedom. A Christian can in this way experience a case of acquired 'humanity' as 'Christian.'

In such statements, the language of faith and empirical and analytical language point to the same reality, but, in both language games, the pertinence of each and its formal approach have to be respected and should not be confused. If they are confused, it is as if the ace of hearts were thrown down on the chess board—meaningless and absurd gesture. (The image is Wittgenstein's.) The theologian who simply studies the causes, the legal aspects and the inner structures of 'human' actions is not concerning himself formally with theology; he is rather reconnoitering the approaches to the territory which he intends to explore and about which he proposes to say something 'Christian.' His exploration of that territory or the 'material object,' even if he is, as a theologian, dependent on other sciences, is for him a theological task in the sense that, without that reconnoitering, the formally theological task is meaningless and something that is done in a vacuum. It is therefore important that he should not forget that the first reconnoitering of the approaches should include other and not purely theological authorities. The theologian who is in fact concerned with these approaches to the territory in which the struggle for salvation or its opposite takes place must first listen very carefully to human experiences and especially to experiences of contrast and also to what other human sciences may be able to tell him. As Thomas Aquinas pointed out, 'multa praecognoscere (theologus) oportet'[1]—before the theologian can act as a theologian, he has a great deal of reconnoitering to do. At that level, it is very important indeed to listen to men and women to what they want to achieve as humanity. In other words, interdisciplinarity is necessary.

The theologian, however, only enters the formally and distinctively theological territory, in which his own distinctive authority can be brought into play, when he includes the territory that he has already reconnoitered within a different language game, asks different questions and looks at it from a different point of view. The language that he has to use here is that of faith, which is one that speaks about salvation coming from God in Jesus the Christ. It is, in other words, not a question of speaking about a different reality, but of speaking about the same reality which has already been reconnoitered in a 'human' way. Interdisciplinarity no longer helps in this case and indeed, it is no longer appropriate. If we tried to bring it into play, we should inevitably be looking asquint at what appears on the one hand as 'human' and on the other as 'Christian.' Two divergent language games are involved, because the reality itself has many dimensions which cannot all be expressed at the same time in a single language game. The material that has first been analyzed by a theologian is then decoded by him in the light of faith. He treats that material as a text that has to be interpreted according to the grammar of Christian hope and faith in God, who is the source of universal, all-embracing and definitive salvation. The question that then confronts the theologian is whether a coming or an approach of the kingdom of God can be detected in this particular human action performed to achieve greater humanity. (He does not look for *the* coming, but for *a* coming of the kingdom in it.)

The Absolute Character of Commitment to Faith and Its Distinctive Form

Speaking about God as the one who saves men and sets them free has to be done in a 'second language game.' It is in fact a speaking about something that has already been discussed in a 'first discourse.' What has first been seen as a 'human reality' is discussed by Christians in the light of its 'Christian content' or the opposite, its value as the absence of salvation. It does not, however, in any way follow from the character of faith as a 'second discourse' that faith and theology are always too late. This belatedness is not the fault of faith and theology as such. It can be attributed to the fact that believers and theologians often arrive too late when the phenomena, which have to be made ready to be discussed theologically in a second discourse, in fact take place. Christians may well have the searchlight of faith at their disposal, but they do not always recognize that a new object is appearing in our human experience and that this requires a theological interpretation. Anyone who arrives too late when the phenomenon takes place is also, of course, too late to throw light on it with the purpose of enabling Christians to practice more effectively.

Theology is speaking about what is absolute but occurs within the relative, in other words, within human praxis in history. This relative matter is, of course, often a matter of life and death. Theology expresses the ultimate and transcendent commitment of men in historical praxis, since, for the believer, human activity in the concrete, including political activity, is always either positively or negatively, but never neutrally, related to the coming of the kingdom of God. Although that kingdom must be realized in and through definite acts performed by men, it can never be reduced to a particular praxis. This does not mean that the absolute and total character of commitment to faith cannot be expressed in a definite or very particular human praxis within a particular historical situation and that it cannot be expressed in this way again and again in particular contexts. We are ultimately judged on the basis of whether we have given food to the hungry and drink to the thirsty (Matt. 25:40).

Christianity is therefore essentially concerned with human integrity, that is, with being whole or with salvation. This does not point to a reduction of 'Christianity' simply to 'humanity,' but it does constitute the concrete historical state within which Christianity can be given form. The absolute character of Christian faith in God is therefore revealed in what is particular, historical and relative, in other words, in historical humanity, even though humanity and Christianity are not identical. Anyone who wants to experience what is absolute in a pure state or as 'available unwrapped' will therefore never be confronted with it—or he will only be confronted with idols. We can only reach 'God's Word' within the confines of our cultural and material possibilities and our own historical sphere of life. The absolute is only made manifest in the greater and smaller phenomena of every day. In everyday life, it is made clear that what concerns man also concerns God and also that God's affair can also concern us in the greater and the smaller context of the life of society and the individual. It is precisely this that the theologian aims to decode—that is why he is a theologian.

We can therefore conclude our preliminary considerations by saying that the transcendence of Christian salvation and faith in God cannot be used as a pretext for an attitude that is neutral with regard to furthering humanity or that is politically neutral. Whatever its content may be, what is Christian and universally human can never be realized outside a definite and particular human context. Since the eighteenth century, we have learnt from the abstract humanity of the Enlightenment how ideological the bourgeois idea of the 'universally human' reality was.

For the Christian, it is certainly a question of the relationship between God and man, in which the world and human history are as it were inserted by God between us and himself as a translation of his inner address, as the medium in and through which man's attention is explicitly drawn to this inner speaking and finally as the space within which man can respond, in his life, to this invitation.

Christians are right to interpret certain actions, including political and social actions, as Christians, that is, as soteriological, even if humanists call the same praxis humanist, in the non-Christian sense. A definite socio-political praxis cannot, after all, be regarded as exempt from its own particular rationality, substance and specific aims; in that sense, there is no action in the world that the Christian is able to claim entirely for himself. The dream, vision or promise of a better society, a fuller life for humanity and an environment 'with a human face,' however, forms an essential part of the essential Christian Gospel, which is the message of the kingdom of a God who is concerned with humanity and who wants men who are similarly concerned with humanity. Christian faith is therefore intimately connected with an ethos of humanity. The criteria for social and political action in the concrete cannot, it is true, be derived from the 'utopia' of the kingdom of God, but this ethical action, which has to be judged according to its own criteria, includes the believer in the theological virtues of faith, hope and charity. A political praxis that is directed towards a more human environment is therefore for Christians as well the socio-political content of Christian hope in terms of historical praxis. For the believer, then, what is political and social cannot be reduced to merely political and social components, since there is more at stake than simply those parts. And it is with this 'more' that is at stake that the theologian is concerned.

Speaking about God in the Context of the Human Search for Liberation

The Religious Question of Salvation

Our ideas and our expectations of salvation, liberation and human happiness are always the result of our concrete experience and our reflection about the reality itself of misery, alienation and the absence of salvation. They are the result of an accumulation of negative experiences in a history of suffering that has lasted for centuries but that is also shot through with flashes of meaningful experience, happiness, partial experiences of salvation, meaning and salvation, even though that history has for the most part been one of unfulfilled expectations, evil and guilt. In the long run, what emerges from this pattern, which is culturally and even geographically diverse, is a vision of what is regarded as a true, happy and good human state for society and the individual. The constant human longing for happiness, salvation and justice, which is again and again subjected to the criticism of facts, but which is constantly and paradoxically reborn from the felt sense of non-sense, therefore inevitably acquires in many different forms, the emphasis of 'redemption from' or 'liberation from' suffering and alienation and at the same time of 'entering a new world.'

What is particularly striking in this human process of experience of the absence of salvation and partial experience of salvation in humanity is that a particular people's own ideas of salvation are not only an attempt to fathom the depths of human suffering, but also an effort to interpret the causes, origins and consequences of that suffering. In the ancient world, this experience of the absence of salvation always has, on the basis of the human depths of the history of suffering that in theory cannot be fathomed and in praxis cannot ever be completely eliminated, a *religious* dimension. This is also the case not only in ancient society, but in the spontaneous experience of all peoples. In the spontaneous view of men, the absence of salvation and alienation cannot be, either theoretically or practically, measured on a human scale. For this reason, men's expectations of salvation acquire a *religious name*. Humanity came, in the past, to expect salvation 'from God.' Despite all experiences of the contrary, mankind has learnt to expect gentleness and mercy in the deepest heart of reality.

The Non-Religious Question of Salvation

What, however, do we encounter in our contemporary, so-called 'secularized' society? What in the past seemed to concern religious people almost exclusively has now come to preoccupy all those who specialize in or are influenced by the human sciences—everyone is looking for healing or human salvation and liberation from enslaved societies. It is hardly possible to deny that, apart from any distinction between faith and reason, the question of a sound and liveable humanity is, as a question, more central than ever before for the whole of mankind and that the reply to that question is given all the more urgently and persistently the more aware we become of our own human failings, the more we recognize that we are treated inadequately and the more sensitive we become to our experience of fragments of human healing and self-liberation. This question of salvation and liberation and of a truly liveable humanity is, however, always asked within actual conditions of disintegration, alienation and hurtful human encounters. The question of salvation and liberation is, of course, the fundamental question posed by all religions. It has, however, now become the great stimulus in the whole of contemporary human existence and, what is more, it is asked outside the sphere of all human religions. It is no longer religions that explicitly systematize the theme of human salvation. The question of salvation is no longer simply a religious and theological theme of redemption and liberation. On the contrary, it is now the driving force of our contemporary history and that, of course, includes our 'profane' history. It is clearer than it has ever been before that human history is the place where decisions and, what is more, explicitly conscious decisions are made about man's healing and liberation.

We may therefore draw a third conclusion in the course of this story. It is this. Anyone who wishes to speak meaningfully about God and Christian redemption must do this within the context of the contemporary theme of salvation and liberation. It is ultimately a question as to whether we can show that there is, in the liberation and the emancipation of men who are seeking a better humanity, something that is absolute or the absolute reality itself, in other words, whether we can show that what concerns man also concerns God. It is only then that we shall be able to show that God's affair can also concern us. If this is true, this religious dimension of our human life also calls for an expression or an articulation and a liturgical celebration of thanksgiving. It also requires a tangibly human expression to be given, in various circumstances, to this mystery in a praxis of the kingdom of God that everyone is able to recognize.

God Is Promise

The Christian faith in creation has a critical and productive power with regard to both pessimistic and optimistic views of human salvation which can be realized in human history and society. (These views are, of course, ultimately unrealistic.) As I have already said above, what in the past only concerned religions is now a shared task confronting all men, even those who are not religious. The conclusion that has from time to time been drawn from this datum is this. If we accept that we owe the introduction of many human values to the Christian tradition, it has at the same time to be admitted that those values have now come to be shared by all men. We are consequently able now, while thanking Christianity for the service that it has rendered to humanity in the past, to let Christian faith itself go. I, however, believe that this would be a very minimal way of viewing the inexhaustible potential for expectation and inspiration that is contained within the Christian faith in creation and the activity of the Spirit of God. It is historically verifiable that inspirations that were originally religious gradually become universal in humanity as a whole, in other words, that they enter the secular sphere. As a demand and an argument for totality, however, this is a disastrous impasse, above all because of our own finite nature, which may be regarded as a definition of 'secularity.' For the Christian, this finite nature can never be separated from the absolute creative presence of God and for this reason it can never be secularized and it can never cease to exist. This creative, saving presence of God is an inexhaustible source of expectation and future hope which transcends the potential for action of the finite.

In the Christian tradition of experience, God is regarded, not as the 'power of life and death,' but rather as 'pure positivity.' He is, in other words, 'a God of the living' who wants all men to be saved and set free. The absolute dividing line between God and ourselves is not God's, but our dividing line. God's free Being is therefore an inexhaustible Promise for man. His name is 'Promise.' The Christian faith in creation includes the fact that God loves us without limits or conditions. His love for us is unmerited, unconditional and unlimited. Creation is an act of God, who in this way on the one hand places us unconditionally in our finite, non-divine distinctive nature which is destined to true humanity and, on the other, places himself in disinterested love as our God, our happiness and salvation and the highest content of true humanity. God creates man freely for the happiness and salvation of men themselves, but even within this act he wants, in sovereign freedom, to be, in the deepest sense, the happiness and salvation of human life. He is a God of people, our God. This, in a nutshell, is the Christian faith in creation. But how does it work out?

How it works out is clear from the history that is made, for good or evil, by men themselves. Faith in creation means that God's Being is revealed. This in turn means that who God is, that is, the distinctive mode of being of God's state of being God, is determined or conditioned by nothing, but is revealed in and through the whole of our history. Christians therefore call God the Lord of that history. The risky venture of creatively giving life to men and women is, seen from God's point of view, an act of trust in man and his history that sets up no conditions or guarantees on man's side. Creation is therefore a blank check for which only God himself acts as surety. It is an act of trust which gives the man who believes in God the courage to believe in word and deed that the kingdom of God, that is human happiness and salvation, is, despite many experiences of the absence of salvation, *de facto* in course of preparation for man, in the power of God's creative action which moves men to realize it.

This is why God, who is the reliable one, is, in his freedom, constantly surprising man. According to the book of Revelation, he is the one 'who is and who was and who is to come' (Rev. 1:8; 4:8). God's Being is unchanging. It is not that of a creature. It is therefore, on the basis of his eternal and absolute freedom, permanently new for finite man. Because his act of creation is an act of his eternal and absolutely free Being, his absolute nature or non-relative nature is at the same time relational, that is, it is related in absolute freedom that is determined or conditioned by nothing to his creature, man in the world. In creating, God takes sides with everything that is created, that is, with everything that is vulnerable because it is contingent. In that way, what concerns man also concerns God, although this does not in any sense diminish man's responsibility for his own history.

It is clearly very difficult for men to believe in a divine Being who in complete freedom determines what, who and how 'he'—or 'it' or she' (human words fail here)—that is, God, really is. Yet this is certainly faith in God. It is only in a very limited way that is restricted by all kinds of conditions that we human beings can freely determine what, who and how we ourselves want to be in accordance with our own plan or view of life. Even there, we often fail to a very great extent. God's Being, on the other hand, is precisely as God wishes it to be, without any elusive or independent remainder. He freely determines what he, as God, wants to be for himself and for us. He does not do this arbitrarily, but in unconditional love. This is the essence of the Christian confession of faith.

God's Being was revealed to us in Jesus. God the creator, who is the reliable one, is the love that sets man free in a way that both fulfils and transcends all human, personal, social and political expectations. God's Being is Promise for man.

That is why our human history can never replace the inexhaustible potential of our faith in creation for expectation and inspiration. It releases reserves of hope and energy in the believer which cannot simply be reduced to purely human expectations. In this sense, man can only realize the promise of his own being as grace. As Ignatius of Antioch rightly said: 'Only when I am come hither shall I be truly a man.'[2] Ultimately, humanity is an eschatological gift of the Spirit, the fruit of God's liberating love in Jesus Christ—a fruit which God allows to ripen in and through the historical praxis of men, while he himself always transcends this in a sovereign manner.

The indefinable nature of definitive salvation and eschatological freedom, that is, of the *humanum* that is sought and found only fragmentarily and yet always threatened, can therefore only be expressed in the symbolic language of metaphorical speech that goes further than all conceptuality. There are three great 'metaphors,' expressed in many different sounds, in the New Testament which suggest the complete *humanum.* The first of these is the definitive salvation or radical liberation of all men into a brotherly and sisterly community or society where the master-slave relationship no longer exists. This is known in the New Testament as the 'kingdom of God.' The second is known in the New Testament as *sarx* or 'flesh.' It is the perfect salvation and happiness of the individual person within the perfect society, known in the Christian tradition as 'resurrection of the flesh,' that is, the resurrection of the human person into his corporeality. The third 'metaphor' is the fulfilment of the 'ecological environment' that is so necessary for human life that is suggested in the biblical idea of the 'new heaven and new earth.'

These three metaphors of visions orientate the activity of Christians in this world in a direction that is in no way vague and undefined, but is very clear and definite. (It is indicated by the dynamism of the symbols themselves.) This is so, even though they cannot, without being mediated in a human context, ever provide a direct blueprint for personal and socio-political action here and now.

The Way of Suffering through and for Others

It should be clear from what I have already said that all religious and Christian speaking about God is at the same time a critical and productive speaking about man and that religious and Christian speaking about man is also a speaking about God. It is precisely because God's Being is 'love of man' that these two aspects cannot be separated. This inevitably means that what is specifically religious and Christian is essentially concerned with what is specifically human. Christianity cannot be Christian if it does not take 'humanity' seriously—humanity is precisely the place where God is sought and encountered. This insight into Christian faith is provided by creation and Christology as realities of Christian experience (and only secondarily as 'theological themes'). Our existence in time is given shape as today, yesterday and tomorrow, that is, as trust, memory and expectation, by this 'hermeneutical circle' of protology and eschatology, that is, of memory and expectation.

When Ignatius of Antioch wrote his well-known words: 'Only when I am come hither shall I be truly a man,' he did that on the eve of his approaching death as a martyr. True humanity is also concerned with the way of suffering through and for others. This is clearly the fundamental theme of the gospel of Mark, the first letter of Peter and the epistle to the Hebrews. It can even be seen as the basic theme of the whole of the New Testament. In this sense, what is 'Christian' assumes a 'human' form in its heights and depths, but at the same time this is a humanity that is able to trust in God's absolute saving presence both in suffering and impotence and in prosperity and adversity. The active search, which always takes place within a cultural, social and even geographical context, for the incomprehensible mystery of the ultimate *Humanum* in fact merges into the mystery of the 'suffering righteous man,' who has been entrusted to us in the living example of the eschatological 'suffering prophet' Jesus, the 'Holy and Righteous one' (Acts 3:14) who was rightly called the 'Son of God.' It is here that the 'power'— the biblical *dunamis*—of defenseless and disarming love is revealed. The suffering of our fellow-men is experienced in Jesus' appearance as a task. His death is the result of the irresistible power of goodness. We can either accept this goodness or we can oppose it, but only by torturing and disposing of a man like Jesus, in an act which bears witness, indirectly but in a very real way, to our own impotence.

This, then, is the essence of the Jewish and Christian testimony that is evident in the Old Testament and confirmed in the New. Suffering through and for others, to which our faith bears witness, can therefore be seen as an expression of the unconditional validity of a praxis of doing good and of resistance to evil and innocent suffering. The man who does not limit his commitment to the suffering of others in any way is bound, even now, to pay for it sooner or later with his own death. It is precisely with this that Jesus 'reconciled himself.' He was consistent in his own commitment to man as God's concern. In 'this world,' standing up for 'what concerns man' means in fact suffering for goodness. The self-realization of humanism, which does not take this datum sufficiently into account, is not realistic and ultimately not even 'humanist.'

It is difficult to deny that the Christian creed places great emphasis on Jesus' death and resurrection and says nothing about his message and the praxis of his life, although we know that, in view of the power of 'this world,' Jesus' death can only be understood in the light of his life and message. His death and resurrection are in fact the summary of his prophetic life and message. We are able to see why this is so as soon as we begin seriously to consider his life and message in the light of the New Testament. What we see there is that Jesus does not speak of what is human in the abstract (in ancient, feudal or bourgeois society or in any other form). He speaks of the rich and the poor, the oppressed and the oppressors and others in the concrete and he takes sides. The gospels were written in reaction against 'mythological' and in fact ideological tendencies which later traced the whole Christian creed back to the death and resurrection of Jesus, while suppressing his life and message. Such tendencies always run the risk of making Jesus' message of the kingdom of God, which is so concerned with men, the object of criticism. Political dictatorships led by so-called Christians, who see themselves as 'defenders of Western Christianity' and who celebrate the death and resurrection of Jesus Christ on Sundays, would be impossible if those dictators were really conscious of the fact that Jesus' death and resurrection are based on the life and message of a God who is concerned with humanity and with man, as Jesus shows him to us in human history. 'Orthodoxy' becomes a mere mockery of the Gospel and the Christian tradition in such cases.

In fact, many men have, because of their irrational impulses, which are often expressed politically, the most grotesque expectations of God. One such expectation is that, if you give yourself entirely to God and are exclusively preoccupied with God's affair as something that concerns man, nothing other than God exists for you—God the great bird who swallows up the smaller birds—with the result that you are bound to ignore yourself and the world that God created and loves. But the fact that God's affair is above all a concern for man, that God makes the affair of man his own affair and that this is precisely what is meant by what is known in the Gospels as the 'kingdom of God' is something that goes far beyond all men's expectations. If men think in a purely human way about God, this can result in bizarre and humanly degrading theories and practices. Men have often enough made human sacrifices in their attempts to honor God. This occurred frequently in the past, but is it any different now? Does not the absence of salvation and the presence of so much suffering reveal itself again and again in the contemporary world under the banner of God and religion? Has not at least one Christology made Jesus into a God who does not show mercy to men until the blood of the one who is greatly loved flows? Jesus, however, said: 'If you are conscious of God's approach, do not be afraid' (see Mark 4:35, etc.). God is above all a God of people. He is a God who thinks of human sacrifice as an 'abomination' (see Lev. 18:21-30; 20:1-5). God is a fire, certainly, but he is a fire that burnt the bush without consuming it (Exod. 3:2).

God's choice for 'humanism' would appear to be directed towards a 'humanism of the rejected': 'Blessed are the poor, . . . those who hunger, . . . those who mourn' (Matt. 5:3-12), precisely because they do not oppress or reject anyone, but are themselves rejected. He showed his love for us 'while we were yet sinners' (Rom. 5:8).

Translated by David Smith

NOTES

1. Thomas Aquinas *Summa Contra Gentiles* I, 4.
2. Ignatius of Antioch *Ad Romanos* VI, 2; see *Early Christian Writings. The Apostolic Fathers*, translated by Maxwell Staniforth (Harmondsworth 1968) p. 105.

12

Eager to Spread the Gospel of Peace

1983

How can Christians, together with the leaders of their churches, render a true account of the Gospel in a situation in which the nuclear armaments race can, because of its own inner logic, no longer be controlled and within the framework of a still prevalent ideology, which on the one hand requires an equilibrium of deterrents and the armaments spiral that is so closely connected with it and, on the other, encompasses continuing attempts to control armaments, but on the presupposition of this very equilibrium of deterrents?

This is the situation in which Christians are in fact living today. The churches are 'eager to spread the gospel of peace' (Eph. 6:15), but can they, with the prospect of a nuclear holocaust, influence States in any way in their political ideology of safety? Can they exert an influence both by political activity that is in accordance with that 'Gospel of peace' and by officially speaking as churches?

The Christian theologian who is sustained and inspired by the Gospel of peace cannot formulate any universal laws that will be valid at all times and in all places. He can, however, help in rendering an account of the hope that the Gospel of peace offers to us even in our present, apparently desperate historical situation. The really threatening aspect of the situation in which Christians are living today comes down essentially to this: Every party involved is trying to prevent war by threatening war and, what is more, by increasingly more destructive means. The old saying: *Si vis pacem, para bellum* holds good in our current situation—peace is only ensured by threatening war! In this article, I propose to limit my discussion of this ideology to the implications of this situation for Christians living in the atomic age.

An Outline of the Problem

I shall not try to provide a comprehensive survey of the attitude found in the Old and New Testaments and in the Christian tradition that has resulted from this towards the reality of war. All that I can do here is to attempt to summarize in a few words the contents and conclusions of a number of historical studies of the question.[1]

A Brief Survey

In the light of Jesus' own praxis of peace, New Testament Christianity was radically pacifist. Christians continued to be pacifists in their praxis until about the beginning of the fourth century. In AD 295, for example, the North-African martyr Maximilian said: 'I cannot be a soldier; I am a Christian.' Long before this, Tertullian has already observed that Christians were present in barracks and, although he himself was the son of a centurion, he made an analogy between Christian baptism and the military standard oath and came to the conclusion that they were mutually exclusive. Soldiers who became Christians were eventually permitted to remain in the army, so long as they only carried out peaceful duties (that was possible at that time) and did not shed blood. The latter continued to be forbidden for Christian soldiers.

After the Constantinian and especially the Theodosian change, when the Christian Church took over the function of the Roman *religio* and became a State religion, Christians began to look for criteria by which they might distinguish between a 'just' and an 'unjust' war; they were only permitted to fight in a just war—and time and time again they presupposed that the wars which they actually waged were justified on this count.

It was precisely on this ideology that the theory of the 'just war' foundered. Although he probably did not intend to, Erasmus demonstrated that this theory was untenable in his well-known treatise, *Complaint of Peace*.[2] He may have been the first to do so and chose to seek refuge in the kingdom of inner peace, although even in his own heart he found discord. His ultimate conclusion was that peace could only be found in Jesus. In fact, his theory amounts to an important appeal to man's good will—impotent because it was precisely at this time that Machiavelli was writing his book about war, in which he claimed that war was necessary in order to preserve the power of the State, which lay outside the realm of ethics.

In more recent times, man's good will has become even more tightly enclosed within civil structures, which have in turn been shaped by a clearly defined economic structure. The ethos of peace that philosophers and theologians have attempted to elaborate has therefore come to an impasse formed by the inner logic of power structures.[3]

Since the Second World War, a teleological ethos of responsibility has been developed, above all in papal encyclicals, in which a theory has been evolved along the lines of earlier scholasticism. According to this theory, an action is judged to be good or bad on the basis of its inner relationship with the good or bad effect that is achieved by it. An action with an equally good and bad result is, in the light of this theory given ethical approval, whereas an action which brings about a good result only *in* and *through* achieving a bad effect is ethically rejected without further ado.

On the basis of this theory, Popes John XXIII, Paul VI and John Paul II have declared all the aspects of the nuclear armaments race to be ethically impermissible, each pope stressing this more emphatically than his predecessor.[4] In the present pope's texts, it is not difficult to see that the language game of ethics has to some extent been abandoned now in favor of the language used in bearing witness to the Gospel, a language which transcends that of a purely ethical or juridical approach to the question. In my opinion, with this new evangelical approach we can, as Christians at least, really take up an evangelical position. Purely ethical and rational arguments can, after all, always be made impotent by hostile reasoning, man's unredeemed free will and the logic and ideology of the secular policy of power.

Right and Wrong Questions

But bearing witness evangelically can also be made impotent. This bearing witness may, for example, be too abstract, the evangelical 'peace of Jesus' being simply contrasted with the peace that men are hoping to obtain by means of a strategy of deterrence. There is, after all, a kind of evangelical pacifism which simply leaves the ideological policy of safety followed by sovereign States as it is and does no more than politics that they will also be thrown in great numbers on the scrap-heap and eventually completely disappear and that the way to military détente is therefore bound to be through political détente.

Political détente can, however, only be brought about when political, material and spiritual values are no longer concentrated in a few places, but are more justly distributed among the whole of mankind. The slogan: 'Get rid of nuclear weapons from the world' would seem, now that those nuclear weapons are already with us, to be within reach of becoming a reality in the political sense only when relationships are more just throughout the whole of the world and especially when a just economic system, one that does not make the rich richer by making the poor poorer, is established worldwide. Political pressure and protest of all kinds by Christians as well (and especially by Christians) must therefore first and foremost be directed at the prevailing unjust political economy and the present concentration of power that is the result of it.

It is not possible to dissociate the autonomous rationality of the armaments race from this political and economic complex. We are therefore bound to ask whether the Christian ought, in the 'meantime,' to be resigned to the fact that there is a spiral of nuclear armament? Can he or she do no more than directly proclaim the message of the Gospel in a loud voice? What is certain from the evangelical point of view is that he or she cannot collaborate in this arms race, which in itself costs, both in the East and in the West, millions of human lives already in the starving Third World (even if the weapons themselves are never used). The politicians who favour a policy of safety, both those in the East and those in the West, have only two words to say to this: Too bad! This is because on both sides the ideology prevails that 'the other side is to blame; we are not to blame—we only want justice and true freedom,' each side colored according to its own understanding of justice.

Is this, then, the correct way of expressing the question: We have nuclear weapons with us already; what, then, is the best strategy, given this situation? In my view, this is only half of the truth. The fundamental truth of the situation is to be found in the possession itself of these weapons. In view of the fact that the strategy of deterrence ('on both sides') is meaningless and ineffectual without a readiness also to use these weapons if need be, this deterrence is itself, on the basis of the will to use the weapons, a threat to mankind, inhuman and ethically unjustifiable. Christians may not be naïve, but they may also not conclude a pact with 'this world.'

This concrete situation, however, results in one urgent question that Christians are bound to ask: Can we passively look on while these nuclear weapons are possessed and positioned? Even in the case of nuclear *self*-defense, what will be left of that 'self'? And what are the values that are to be defended in accordance with truth?[5]

In the course of the debate about steps to be taken on the way to unilateral disarmament, Harrie Kuitert has said: 'Ethics without politics are as dangerous as politics without ethics' and others have echoed him in the Netherlands. I am completely in agreement with this statement. Kuitert has also added to this: 'unless we allow the result to count as the ultimately determining factor.'[6] This result is, of course, the fact that there will be no nuclear war. Kuitert calls this a roundabout way, but that is something that we learn from the realism of experience. In the world as it in fact is—what Scripture calls 'this world'—it is the right of the most powerful that prevails. Even though an evangelical protest is diametrically opposed to such a political Darwinism and Machiavellianism, Christians are bound, in their efficient political activity, to take it into account. Even in the medieval world, which was dominated by the Christian Church, things were not radically different. We have always to be extremely suspicious of 'power.'

Efficient activity in this case means, of course, acting in such a way that there will in fact be no nuclear war. The apparently despairing aspect of this problem is, however, this: One group (including the Christian members of it) maintains that (in view of the fact that there are nuclear weapons) the intended result, in other words, the prevention of war, can only be efficiently assured by the possession of nuclear weapons, at least if there is a balance of power between both potential parties opposing one another. The other group (again including the Christians who belong to it), on the other hand, claim that it is this system of deterrents in itself and therefore the very possession of nuclear weapons which forms the greatest danger of nuclear war and that this danger increases in probability as the number of States possessing those weapons grows (although the political assumption is always made that one's own leaders have more common sense than the leaders of other States).

Neither of these two affirmations can at present be verified, because the only atomic bombs that have in fact been used were dropped at a time when only one country possessed them and the enemy country was therefore defenseless. What, however, are we to say if both countries are more or less equal in strength? Which of the two would venture to use a nuclear weapon? The fact is that neither side of this dilemma can as yet be proved true or false. The critical question, then, is: How can the result (the fact that there will be no nuclear war) be discounted as the ultimately determining factor? Or is an attitude of resignation the only possible one—an attitude of waiting until nuclear war comes or does not come—in order to see which of the two affirmations is really valid? Surely something is not right here!

The Praxis of the Gospel Translated into Political Action

First in our modern bourgeois society in the West and then also in the countries of the Eastern Bloc, religion has been relegated to spheres in which it is unable to oppose the State's policy of safety and its resulting economic conflict. The Gospel has, in other words, become interiorized and excluded from the sphere of public political activity.

Society cannot be traced back to the sum total of individual actions, nor can the individual be traced back to the sum total of social relationships. Societies—and this includes sovereign States—have always developed into what they are at a given time and they have usually developed, what is more, in a way that neither side concerned has foreseen, intended, planned or carried out. Many social processes have relative autonomy with regard to the people who set them in motion and shape them. They have a structured course of development. Nonetheless, it is human beings who, for example, wage war and they do so by their actions. These structures also form the personality structure of the individuals in any given society.

This cultural and anthropological situation throws some light on the question why a mere appeal to people's consciences or to their good will and even bearing witness evangelically in the form of proclamation so often simply rebounds from the wall formed by those tough structures. This happens above all in the case of the modern 'structurally a-theistic' social structures that are to be found in all spheres of public life: economics, politics, armed military defense, the law and the natural and human sciences. What, then, is the task confronting the Christian who does not want to live apart from 'this world' in a sacred ghetto?

What made the Jews say about Jesus: 'He taught them as one who had authority' (Matt. 7:29)? The answer to this question can be found in the whole of the New Testament: In the way in which he turns to man, Jesus makes it immediately clear what he is talking about and also proves it to be true. He does not, for example, say to Zacchaeus, the little man in the tree: 'God loves you,' as the modern fundamentalist posters displayed in railway stations and elsewhere in the Netherlands would have us believe. On the contrary, he goes to Zacchaeus' home, eats and drinks with him and proves by his action and by his concern for his fellow-man the truth that God loves him.

Jesus' message was therefore so integrated into his active and communicative appearance that his proclamation and the praxis of his life interpreted each other mutually, with the result that together, proclaiming and acting, they also changed situations in the concrete and he was able, in this world, to anticipate the completion of the kingdom of God. Bearing witness evangelically is therefore only a part of a concrete evangelical activity in the world and only that whole radiates power and achieves something in this world. The same also applies to Christians in their *sequela Jesu* or following of Jesus. The community of believers is not only required to make a confession, but also to have a praxis that is in accordance with the kingdom of God, although that praxis must be within the conditions of 'this world.'

In modern situations, in which man has come to believe that society in the concrete is not an 'order established by God' or purely the result of human planning, but also a system resulting from actions that are both intended and not intended, this connection between bearing witness evangelically by proclamation and the Christian praxis of life also has a political dimension. In addition to an interpersonal turning towards one's fellow-men, this 'turning' is also translated into political action and influencing social, political and economic structures in such a way that these structures do not in the long run make one group whole and bring salvation to that group while destroying other groups. This 'turning' also takes the form of working for a good and just society.

The 'peace of God that passes all understanding' (Phil. 4:7) and social peace in the world cannot be divided. Even though one is not identical with the other, they belong together. From the theological point of view therefore, even though it may be in the fragmentary state of 'this world,' there must be an inner and positive link between the 'peace of Christ' and the peace that is built up fragmentarily by human efforts and has to be built up again and again in the social and political sphere.

Not only some specialists in the field of political science but also those who are concerned with peace studies point from time to time (often not without a certain disdain) to 'another faculty' (by which they mean the faculty of theology) when they hear such words as 'the wolf dwelling with the lamb' and 'beating swords into ploughshares' (a way of speaking which certainly does not belong to the language of peace studies). It is true that the theologian cannot (on the condition that he has knowledge of what is being said by those who specialize in peace studies) dispense with this kind of language, the language of faith, but he must also be able to translate it into political action.

There is, after all, a form of theological reductionism, in which the aspect of grace contained in the power of the 'peace of Christ' is set alongside and even above the social, political and economic dimensions of human history, in so far as these achieve greater justice for all people (and, in view of their urgent plight, this means above all the least privileged) using the (non-violent) means of this world. It is true that the grace of the peace of Christ always transcends the forms in this world in which it appears, but it is equally true to say that that grace can only be found in the historical forms of this world, both in the forms in which political and social peace is extended throughout the world and in the inner 'peace' of man's heart. Such inner peace, however, in 'this world' takes the form of the broken state of inner grief caused by hostility between individuals, groups and nations killing and threatening to kill each other because of a desire to possess and retain. This inner peace therefore also directs the Christian's attention to the social, political and economic aspects of his world that are in need of change, salvation and reconciliation.

The transcendence of God and of faith in God cannot therefore, even in the case of the peace promised in the Gospel, be used as an excuse for political neutrality or for making a merely moral protest against the politics of power in this world. The peace of Christ calls on Christians to develop and follow a theology of political praxis. The Christian cannot reduce the social and political reality of the world to its purely social and political components. There is much more involved than just this— man and his whole humanity in relationship with God are at stake. The Christian's political praxis, directed towards the building up of a society that is fitter for people to live in and is therefore free from war and the threat of war, is undoubtedly the social and political content of his Christian hope in terms of a historical praxis of peace.[7]

His policy of peace can therefore not be confined simply to appealing to and proclaiming evangelically the 'peace of Christ' and to condemning the nuclear arms race in the abstract. It calls also for many different political and practical translations of the Gospel of peace at the level of his own human history and that of his fellow-men. I will try to summarize what this means in the concrete in the concluding paragaphs of this section of my article.

Christians should avail themselves of the findings of recent peace studies and make a (non-ideological) analysis of the concrete structures of society in which 'war' appears as a phenomenon with many causes. In this, they should take into account the fact that modern sovereign States are becoming increasingly dependent on each other, with the result that the sovereignty of each State is at the same time becoming more and more limited. In addition to this, they should also bear in mind that the survival of a 'State' is, like its origins, very much of a chance event in history and therefore a matter of relative importance only.

It is also necessary for Christians to analyze the fact that this increasing 'world integration' is able to break the autonomous rationality of war. But the same phenomenon also implies a much greater concentration of power.

Together with others, Christians can also exert an influence on sovereign States with regard to their ideology of the policy of safety by voting and by their attitude towards the defense budget and taxation for defense projects. It is also very important for this ideology of the policy of safety to be analyzed. The questions that have to be asked in this context are: Whose safety is involved? What is the State trying to make safe? And, most important of all, at whose cost?

An evangelical proclamation of the Gospel of peace that is at the same time wise will always point to the political dimension of being a Christian. The Christian also has to be educated as a Christian to work for peace, and catechesis at all levels has always to be concerned with the political dimension of faith. Finally, peace studies can also play an important part in forming the Christian's evangelical imagination, so that he can, together with others, develop new strategies. There is no doubt that the traditional models of thought have failed here.

This brings me to my last question: Will Christians, because of the evangelical demand (aided by the evangelical imagination), work positively, in their (always limited) political activity, for a strategy consisting of steps towards unilateral (nuclear) disarmament? Another contributor to this issue of *Concilium* thinks that this will not happen. It is, of course, true that men and women, including those who are Christians, are very divided in this question and often very emotional. I respect this difference of opinion.

A Risky Trust in Unilateral Nuclear Disarmament?

According to Jesus, a Christian may not enter into a pact with 'this world' and this teaching of Jesus and the whole of the New Testament becomes even more urgent in a world that is prepared to destroy one side completely in a limited or a total nuclear war (although we know from history that war becomes all the more probable as long as it remains limited; this is something that certain people think is possible in the case of a nuclear war). On the basis of this evangelical teaching, I feel obliged, as a Christian, to ask this question: Can the vicious circle of the (nuclear) arms race be broken in any way other than by the 'virtuous circle' of steps towards unilateral (nuclear) disarmament?

This risky trust in unilateral disarmament seems to me to provide an extreme possibility, but at the same time it would appear to be the only concrete possibility for anyone who really believes in Jesus as the Lord of history. All other means seem doomed to fail, even in principle, and we cannot wait until the world's goods are more justly distributed among people. It is, I believe, only on the basis of this risky trust that we can make an appeal to the mysticism of Christian surrender. Christians have, after all, learned from the fate of their crucified Lord that unarmed and disarming love is able to lead others to hit back in aggression (because the inner impotence of those others' outward policy of power is revealed in an irritating way by this love).

Do Christians really want to share in this possible fate? Or would they prefer to join in the game played by 'this world' or at least leave it as it is in a spirit of resignation? I believe that there are limits to the Christian's loyalty to the State in its policy of power and safety. This is something that we can learn from the New Testament. Leaving aside the details of a Christian strategy, I think that Christians should, in their political praxis, risk taking steps towards unilateral nuclear disarmament and that Church leaders should have the courage to point to the way of this evangelically 'risky trust' as one that we believers ought to follow. It is better for us to be martyrs because we refuse to help to prepare for a possible nuclear war than for us to be victims of such a war because we fail to oppose it actively. In martyrdom, the Christian thinks of himself and of others who also refuse to play the game. In becoming a victim, he thinks above all of the others who end as martyrs in a nuclear war.

I have, now at least, come to the conclusion that the way in which this evangelical decision, translated into a political course of steps towards unilateral nuclear disarmament, should be worked out in further detail cannot be formulated either directly or indirectly on the basis of the Gospel itself. It is simply not possible to derive even indirect criteria which will lead to a consensus of opinion among Christians from the Gospel concerning the concrete strategic details of the (necessary) steps that should be taken in the direction of unilateral disarmament. For this reason, the political work involved in unilateral disarmament has, I am now convinced, to be left to professional politicians, including Christian politicians who (are expert in the matter and who) are prepared to use their evangelical imagination in order to think of concrete political programs.

Political programs of this kind can never be completely covered by official pronouncements made by the churches as a detailed Christian translation of the evangelical demand for unilateral disarmament. In order to avoid any misunderstanding, perhaps I should express this idea in a more concrete way: The Gospel cannot provide either a direct or an indirect answer that is really meaningful to us in the twentieth century as to how these steps towards unilateral nuclear disarmament should be taken in detail, that is, whether we should aim to make Europe a nuclear-free zone or whether we should work towards establishing a nuclear-free zone in our own country or whether any other option should be our immediate aim. Because of this, our Church leaders should be more than simply cautious before giving concrete guidelines here. This free political activity, however, is the inevitable consequence of an evangelical policy of peace which requires Christians to seek for politically meaningful and detailed possibilities by which steps may be taken in the direction of unilateral nuclear disarmament, which is an extreme and an urgent possibility which we should venture to trust.

If sovereign States and their ideological policy of safety are subjected in this way to the criticism of the Gospel and if Christians recognize from this the limits of their loyalty to the State to which they belong, then they will also be able to acknowledge the limits of their loyalty to that State's alliances within the Gospel. What is more, when these limits have been reached, Christians will therefore be able to act accordingly, although they will no doubt be aware of the fact that, in 'this world,' they must expect persecution and imprisonment, as the early Christians did. The ultimate question, then, is not whether Christians are decadent and afraid of nuclear war, but rather whether they are ready to be martyred for 'man's affair,' which is God's affair. It is only if they are prepared for this that 'God's affair' can really be made credible in the eyes of the world.

Translated by David Smith

NOTES

1. See, for example, J. Blank *Orientierung* 46 (1982) 14–15, 157–163; 19, 213–216; 20, 220–223; A. Alföldi *Studien zur Geschichte der Weltkrise des 3. Jahrhunderts nach Christus* (Darmstadt 1967); *Der gerechte Krieg: Christentum, Islam, Marxismus* (Frankfurt 1980) ed. R. Steinweg; *Das Evangelium des Friedens* (Munich 1982) ed. P. Eicher; R. Spaemann *Zur Kritik der politischen Utopie* (Stuttgart 1977) pp. 77–103.

2. Erasmus *Querela pacis undique gentium eiectae profligataeque. Ausgewählte Schriften* ed. W. Welzig (Darmstadt 1968) 5, pp. 359–451.

3. P. Juganaru *L'Apologie de la guerre dans la philosophie contemporaine* (Paris 1933); M. Walzer *Just and Unjust Wars. Amoral Argument with Historical Illustrations* (New York 1977); D. Senghaas *Friedensforschung und Gesellschaftskritik* (Munich 1970); R. Aron *Penser la guerre* (Paris 1976) I and II; H. Schrey 'Fünzig Jahre Besinnung über Krieg und Frieden' *Theologische Rundschau* 43 (1978) 201–229 and 266–284; 46 (1981) 58–96 and 149–180. See also E. Schillebeeckx, T. Beemer and J. A. van der Ven 'Theologen over kernontwapening' *Tijdschrift voor Theologie* 21 (1981) 3; *Wetenschap en vrede* (24 in the series published by the Centre for Peace Studies, Nijmegen) 7 (1982) 3.

4. See M. D. Chenu *La Doctrine sociale d l'Eglise comme idéologie* (Paris 1979); *Kirche und Kernbewaffnung* ed. H. O. Kirckhoff (Neukirchen and Vluyn) 1981.

5. B. Paskins and M. Dockrill *The Ethics of War* (London 1979) pp. 61ff.

6. H. Kuitert in the Dutch daily paper *Trouw* (28 and 30 September 1982).

7. E. Schillebeeckx 'Op zoek naar de heilswaarde van een politieke vredespraxis,' 'Theologen over kernontwapening' in *Tijdschrift voor Theologie* cited in note 3, 232–244.

13

Offices in the Church of the Poor

1984

The Church as the People of God: 'The Community of God'

A great deal has happened in the Church and its many different forms since the appearance of the French original of Yves Congar's *Lay People in the Church* in 1953.[1] The author's purpose when he wrote this book was to break through the then current practice of equating the Church with the hierarchy. Some of the basic ideas contained in his book found their way into the final edition of the Dogmatic Constitution on the Church, *Lumen Gentium*, of Vatican II. A whole chapter on the people of God, the Church, was inserted into that document even before the question of offices was mentioned in that context. In it, the Church—the people of God—was called 'priestly, pastoral and prophetic' and was seen as sharing as a whole in the threefold ministry of Jesus as the Christ. The 'community of Christ' is therefore, as the community joined to Jesus, the leader of the 'messianic people' who are filled with the Spirit, itself the subject of prophetic, pastoral and priestly activity, whereas offices are within this whole—and presupposing this priestly substance of the people of God—a diaconal or 'ministerial' concentration of what is common to all believers. They are a ministry for the benefit of that priestly people of God, the Church. As derived from the priestly character of Jesus Christ and his messianic community, the Roman Catholic Church was also eventually not wrong to call the official ministries for the benefit of the priestly community of Christ 'prophetic, pastoral and priestly.' This was, however, a one-sided development, even though it was historically and theologically quite legitimate.

Before, during and for some time after the Second Vatican Council, there was a great deal of discussion about a 'theology of the laity.' On closer inspection, however, it emerged that many forms of that theology of the laity were unconsciously based on the same 'hierarchical' premises. Attempts were made to give the concept 'laity,' which was still seen as 'non-clergy,' a positive content and the fact that this positive content had already been provided by the Christian meaning of the word *christifidelis* was often overlooked. The distinctive aspect of the lay person was defined as his (or her) relationship with the world. That of the member of the clergy was seen as his relationship with the Church. This meant that both the ecclesial dimension of the *christifidelis* and his relationship with the world were distorted. The member of the clergy thus became the 'apolitical man of the Church,' while the layman became the 'politically committed' man of the world who was hardly committed at all to the Church. The ontological status of the 'new man' who had been reborn through baptism in the Spirit was therefore, according to this view, not recognized in his (or her) own distinctive value, but only seen from the point of view of the status of the clergy. But that is not a status at all, but a ministry for the service or benefit of the Church, a 'church-functional' ministry. The 'ontological' status obtained through baptism in the Spirit was therefore misinterpreted, whereas the office was raised to the level of a status with serious ontological connotations.

The mediaeval concept 'non-clergy,' layman, continued to have an influence here. The 'lay person' was equated with the 'idiota,' the uneducated, poor and carnal man, *vir saecularis*, the man of the world (because no thought was given either in the Church or in society to women at that time). Apart from such 'powerful laymen' as emperors and princes, who were in any case hardly regarded as 'laymen' and were indeed sacrally anointed, laymen were above all stupid and obedient people, subjected to the *maiores*, the educated. This social situation also had a theological substructure. Jurists and even theologians divided the Church community into two genera, *ordines* or statuses: the *ordo clericorum* (to which the *ordo monachorum* was to some extent assimilated) and the *ordo laicorum*. This division into orders or statuses also had serious social and even ethical implications: 'duo ordines, clericorum et laicorum; duae vitae, spiritualis et carnalis'[2] or, as this idea was expressed elsewhere: the basis of the Church consisted of 'carnal and married people' and the top of the Church of 'consecrated (celibate) clergy and religious.'[3]

I know that this has to be taken with a grain of salt. But it is true to say that this pyramidical hierarchical structure of the Church community, which was partly inspired by the social status symbols of the waning Graeco-Roman Empire, was powerfully influenced from the sixth century onwards by the neo-Platonic works of Pseudo-Dionysius.[4] Pastoral and sociological differences in the Church were given a theological infrastructure in the light of this neo-Platonic vision of the world and the various ministries in the Church were 'hierarchicized,' that is, they became gradually descending realities of decreasing value. The higher level, in other words, came to possess in an eminent manner what the lower level possessed as poor-relief and limited power. The official functions of all the 'lower' ministries could be found in absolute fullness at the highest level, which had since time immemorial been, historically speaking, the episcopate. In this way, in accordance with an authentically neo-Platonic view of the world, all power came 'from above.'

This 'hierarchicization' of the top of the Church, however, led to a devaluation of the laity at the base of the pyramid and lay people became simply objects of priestly pastoral care. In principle, the clergy, with the episcopate enjoying the highest *status perfectionis*, realized in a perfect manner a religious pattern of life and were in perfect union with God. Ordinary believers, on the other hand, could only experience and achieve that religious way of life and unity with God indirectly and imperfectly—in obedience to the *maiores*. It has to be said quite bluntly that this neo-Platonic hierarchical view of the Church is nowadays quite untenable. It is also diametrically opposed to the New Testament vision of the Church.

The New Testament Vision of the Church and Its Ministries

This in no way implies a form of biblicism, suggesting that we should nowadays try to imitate the undifferentiated forms of organization in the early Church in the present-day organization of the Church and its offices. It would be hermeneutically impossible to justify such a step. I therefore recognize in this case, on the one hand, the significance of the New Testament as a normative model and, on the other, the power of the rest of the history of the Church to inspire our present understanding of faith. I do not accept any form of biblicism, whether it points to the left or to the right. What I am concerned with is the historical mediation—the social and historical context that exists here and now in the world and the Church.

Men's experience of God's care for them as revealed in Jesus' message and way of life was the origin of the first wave of the Jesus movement, which was initiated above all by Hebrew-speaking (or Aramaic-speaking) Jews who had become Christians and who were waiting for the Lord Jesus to come to judge the world. In the New Testament, however, it was above all those sections of the early Christian Jesus movement consisting of Greek-speaking Jews in the Diaspora who had been converted to Christianity who were given a hearing. It was among them that the Judaeo-Christian movement became a Church with a universal mission. Their faith, the structure of their Church and their mission were not directly based on experience of the historical Jesus (whom they had never met). These were based rather on their baptism in the Spirit (later called 'baptism and confirmation')—their baptism 'in the name of Jesus,' also known as baptism-anointing. The God of those Christians was (and is) the God who did not abandon Jesus, but made him a 'life-giving spirit' (1 Cor. 15:45b). Christians who were baptized in him were therefore *pneumatici*—men and women who were 'filled with the Spirit,' even though this prophetic power of the Spirit was manifested more in one Christian than in another and differently in different Christians. That is why it was said by members of the second or third generation of Christians that the Church was 'built upon the foundation of the apostles and prophets' (Eph. 2:20; 4:7–16) and why Paul was able to speak within the one brotherhood of many different charisms.

That community of faith was an 'egalitarian' brotherhood and sisterhood, a *koinonia*, assembly and coming together of partners who had been made equal in and through the Spirit:

> For in Christ Jesus you are all sons of God . . .
> For as many of you as were baptized into Christ
> have put on Christ.
> There is neither Jew nor Greek,
> there is neither slave nor free,
> there is neither male nor female;
> for you are all one in Christ Jesus
> (Gal. 3:26–28)

This passage is a pre-Pauline baptismal tradition—a solemn declaration made over newly baptized Christians. As there is now a fairly universal consensus of opinion regarding this among exegetes, there is no need for me to justify my use of it here.[5] This baptismal tradition moreover goes back to the early Christian *pneuma* Christology and ecclesiology. The linguistically striking expression 'there is neither male nor female' (not, it should be noted, 'there is neither man nor woman') is an implicit reference to the Septuagint translation of Gen. 1:27 ('male and female he created man'). According to this way of thinking, Christian baptism in the Spirit is the eschatological restoration of an order of creation of equality and solidarity that was at that time (and is still today) experienced both historically and socially as disturbed: 'a new creation' (Gal. 6:15).

Baptism in the Spirit, then, does away with historical and social discriminations and inequalities. The victims of discrimination mentioned in this passage are, first, the heathens (discriminated against in favor of the Jews), secondly, slaves (discriminated against in favor of free men) and, thirdly, women (discriminated against in favor of men). (This Judaeo-Christian list could easily be extended nowadays.)

All historical and social antitheses are done away with in principle by Christian baptism and initially in the Christian community of faith itself. Baptismally, this is, of course, a performative, not a descriptive way of speaking, in other words, a way of speaking that expresses the hope of the Christian community, a hope that has to become a reality in that community of God as an example of how to live together. There should be no relationships of subjection between 'master' and 'subject' and no forms of discrimination within the Church at least. All three synoptics state very emphatically that the way in which authority is exerted in the world 'shall not be so among you' (Mark 10:42–43; Matt. 20:24–28; Luke 22:24–27).

The New Testament vision of 'offices in the Church' is therefore determined by this principle. The early Christian 'egalitarian' *pneuma* ecclesiology does not in any sense exclude authority and leadership from the Church, but it does exclude authority exerted 'in the manner of the world.'

Office or rather offices did not develop in the early Christian churches as has been said so often as the result of a historical change from charism to institution. On the contrary, they came about as the result of a change from the many charisms shared by all Christians to a specialized charism possessed by only a few. From the sociological and from the ecclesial point of view, this is a case of differentiation of system. The charism of the many different ministries, which had its origin in the very varied power of the baptism in the Spirit of all members of the Christian community living from the Spirit, gradually became not so much swallowed up by as certainly concentrated in a specifically ecclesial office, especially in the post-Pauline communities. It is in fact possible to say that the fullness of the original baptism in the Spirit gradually became fragmented—a distinction was made between 'baptism' and 'confirmation' and between 'baptism' and 'office.' This was an ecclesial differentiation of system and it was justified both sociologically and theologically. The early Church was, after all, looking for the most suitable structures for itself. We should not therefore project later church structures back into the New Testament in order to deprive the Church's office of every new possibility of adaptation in the present-day Church.

What this development, which can be analyzed both sociologically and theologically, can teach us, then, is that the 'ontological status' of baptism in the Spirit continues to be both the bearer and the matrix of the Church's office. These relationships should not be turned upside down.

Specialization by a few (or, expressed in the language of the Church, the vocation of a few) in doing what is common to all is a reality that is taken for granted in every group, whether it is sociological or (in the case of the Church community) ecclesial. It is moreover clear from social and historical analyzes that whenever there is no specialized concentration of what concerns all members of a group, only very little of what is common to all is achieved in the long run. Ambrosiaster, the anonymous patristic theologian, had precisely this intuition, when several centuries later he observed the difference between the still quite vague divisions in the structure of the early Christian community and the institutional offices that had been firmly established later according to a Church order that had been set up in the meantime.[6] The danger inherent in this kind of development, however legitimate it may have been, is that this charism concentrated in the Church's office may swallow up the Spirit active elsewhere in (and even outside) the Church and therefore 'quench the Spirit' (see 1 Thess. 5:19) in the community as a whole. The pneumatic and charismatic dimension of the *ecclesia* should not be derived from the official Church ('official' in both senses of the word). The latter is rooted in the baptism in the Spirit of all Christians who enter the 'apostolic community,' the *christifideles,* and must be seen to be thus rooted. In the opposite case, believers are no longer subjects of faith and the expression of faith. They are, in a word, no longer subjects of the Church.

The term 'apostolicity' has been used in this context. It has at least four different aspects. The first is the fundamental apostolicity of the local communities as 'built upon the foundation of the apostles and prophets' (Eph. 2:20), who founded and inspired the first Christian communities. The second aspect is the apostolicity of the *id quod traditum est,* the *paratheke* or entrusted pledge, the apostolic tradition to which the New Testament as the original document belongs. The third is the apostolicity of the *ecclesiae* or communities of faith themselves, which were directly or indirectly brought into being by the apostles and prophets and normalized by what was 'handed down.' Part of this aspect is the communities' obedience in faith to the Gospel and their consistent *praxis* of the Kingdom of God—what is known as the *sequela Jesu* or following Jesus. Finally, there is a fourth aspect: the apostolicity of the Church's offices in the already established churches—the so-called 'apostolic succession.'

Apostolicity, then, is a concept which is rich in content and cannot be simply reduced to the fourth aspect, apostolic succession. There are many different factors in the growth and preservation of the traditional process of the Catholica. The visible Church communities came about as communities of men and women with a common destiny who had lived in the tradition of Israel and, within it, especially in the tradition of Jesus of Nazareth, confessed as the Christ, the Son of God and Lord. On the basis of this, these communities confessed the same faith (although they used different modes of expression), celebrated their shared destiny and finally let their conduct be governed by the guideline of the praxis of the Kingdom of God, a kingdom of justice and love in which Jesus had preceded them and set the example.

There are therefore many traditional factors keeping the Church on the right course: the foundation of the communities by the apostles and prophets, the traditional content of faith, the confession of faith and especially the *regula fidei*, the praxis of believers and indeed the whole life of the many *ecclesiae*, including especially their baptism and the Eucharist, and finally specific official ministries of many different kinds, differentiated in confrontation with social and cultural contexts and contexts within the Church itself. In the faithful and living preservation of the original evangelical inspiration and orientation, offices are an important factor, but only one such factor. The four aspects of apostolicity are, moreover, and always have been in a state of constant interaction with each other.

'What you have heard from me before many witnesses entrust to faithful men who will be able to teach others also' (2 Tim. 2:2). At the deepest level, the *apostolicum* is the Christian confession of faith and the community of faith based on that confession. Office-bearers place the whole of their ministry at the service of that community. The gradual historical development by which the Church's office acquired a central and fundamental importance and the devaluation of baptism in the Spirit that accompanied this development were in the course of the Church's history to reveal all kinds of detrimental side-effects. This situation also led to the development of what was until recently the 'classical' pattern: first, of teaching (by the Church hierarchy), secondly, of explaining (by the Church's theologians) and thirdly, of obedience and listening (by the believers, known as the laity) to the Church's teaching (as explained by the theologians). Where in this classical pattern is the reality of the *christifidelis?* Believers are no longer seen in this paradigm, ecclesially at least, as subjects, but are reduced to the level of objects of priestly activity. An attempt was made during the Second Vatican Council to break through the ideology of this paradigm, but the very divergent views of the Church held by the bishops led in the end to a compromise solution.

The result of this development, which had already commenced in the later patristic period, was that all the charisms of the Spirit were concentrated in and sometimes even annexed by the specific office of the Church and then also narrowed down and embedded juridically in that office. What had in the New Testament been an official diaconate, a ministry and a serving love arising from the wealth of all believers and given to increase the wealth of all was then expressed in terms of power (*potestas*) and, what is more, of two categories of power: the power of ordination and the power of jurisdiction.

In its Dogmatic Constitution on the Church at least, the Second Vatican Council avoided as far as possible using the term *potestas* and spoke of *ministeria* and *munera* (although there was, theologically speaking, a rather ambiguous distinction between these two terms). In any case, in *Lumen Gentium*, office is seen as ministry within and for the Church in the world. To begin with, the Council broke through the medieval and later juridicism that surrounded the Church's offices by minimizing the distinction between the power of ordination and that of jurisdiction and by shading their meaning at least by affirming that jurisdiction (which, from the point of view of the Church is certainly concerned with the inner bond between the community and office) is fundamentally and essentially already given in its sacramental basis (the sacrament of ordination).

Nonetheless, Vatican II sometimes situated the 'representation of Christ' in and through the Church's office in the one holding office as a person and not formally in the act itself of the exercise of office[7] (as Thomas, who was more modest in his claims, had done). This clearly points to a surviving confusion between two levels: the ontological level of baptism in the Spirit, which makes us a 'new creation,' and the church-functional level of office—a function, nonetheless on a real, sacramental basis. This second level presupposes the first and deeper level of baptism in the Spirit, precisely in order to be what it in fact is. Representation of Christ in the Church does not occur simply on the basis of office, which is only a typological, diaconal concentration and crystallization of the universal charism of the Spirit or a specialization at the church-functional level of the official ministers who have been called, given a mandate and sent by the Church and the Spirit dwelling in the Church. It goes without saying that this diaconal ministry has to be associated with a Christian ethos and spirituality of office—what may even be called a 'mysticism' of office. This is, after all, almost the only aspect of offices discussed in the New Testament. The mystical profundity of the apostolic ecclesial communities that 'live from the

Spirit' should never be undermined or neutralized by contrasting it with a more intense mystification of office and the persons of those holding office.

There is, then, in the great tradition of the Catholica, a subtle distinction between baptism and office, between the universal priesthood of all believers and the official priesthood. This distinction is, however, tilted in favor of the baptism in the Spirit of all believers and not in the other direction. It is in baptism that Christians share ontologically in the threefold ministry of Jesus. Office, on the other hand, is a (sacramental) function or, as the Second Vatican Council calls it pleonastically and rather hesitantly in the Decree on the Priesthood (*Presbyterorum Ordinis*, 2) a 'ministerial function.' It is a ministerial specialization, a typological representation of the same threefold ministry of Christ and the whole of his Church. The three characters (baptism and confirmation and the sacrament of ordination) have frequently been presented as an increasingly full and more intensive share in Jesus' threefold ministry, each one representing a hierarchically higher step. This view was not held in the Middle Ages, but theologians in the baroque period saw the matter in this light, forgetting that baptism (and confirmation) was at a completely different level from office—a much deeper level, baptism being the reality that bears the others up. For this reason, it is sometimes also the basis of what the Church (rather juridically and even in a kind of *Deus ex machina*) calls the *supplet Ecclesia*. It is also the basis of extraordinary ministry in exceptional circumstances.

This unsound mystification of office and those holding office in the Church was reinforced by certain statements made by the French *Ecole de spiritualité*. Despite many excellent pronouncements about office. John Eudes, for example, could say: 'The Son of God makes you (= priests) sharers in his quality as mediator between God and men, in his dignity as the sovereign judge of the world, in his name and ministry as the redeemer of the world and in many other excellences attributed to him.'[8] The reason for this extremely 'mystifying' elevation of office and those holding office (which is unknown in the writings of Augustine or Thomas Aquinas, for example) can be found in the fact that this school departed from the whole of Catholic tradition and saw Jesus' priesthood as directly based not on his humanity, but on his divinity. John Henry Newman protested against this view in the nineteenth century in connection with the less 'mystifying,' but otherwise very similar views expressed by Cardinal Manning.[9] If, on the other hand, we do what Thomas, for example, did and see Jesus' priesthood as directly based on his humanity, the Church's priesthood is given a more modest significance, which is in no way less authentically Christian and sacramental. It is somewhere at this point that the crisis of the present-day priesthood is to be found.

Offices in a Social and Historical Context

This mystification of the priesthood, together with an undervaluation of the new way of being a Christian would seem to be the main reason why many believers are wary of approaching the question of offices in the Church from a social and historical point of view. We have, it is true, to speak not only in sociological language, but also in the language of religion and theology about the Church's offices. There is, however, often an unacceptable dualism in this case. What can be made sociologically and historically intelligible is distinguished by many believers and even separated from what is experienced, correctly, by the 'community of God' as God's call and grace. Such Christians react, when they are confronted with sociological and historical data concerning office, by saying: 'Good, but the Church's office is more than that. It is not simply a sociological or historical phenomenon.' This may, again correctly, be a protest against a reduction of office to a purely sociological reality, but it is equally possible to reduce office theologically by looking for the aspect of grace that is present in office alongside, above or behind its social and historical forms. In such cases, two separate aspects are recognized that can only be approached from different points of view and can only be discussed in two different language games (namely the language of science and that of faith). This is correct, but the next step is to project these two aspects (that have been separated in the abstract) as such, that is, to project them as conceptually separate on to the screen of reality and, what is more, to do this at one and the same level. The result of this is that they are considered together, thus creating the greatest possible difficulties. There is, after all, no revelatory surplus alongside or above the concrete forms of office. To believe this would be a form of supernaturalism or dualism.

In this matter, we are concerned with one and the same reality. The form of office that has developed historically and can be analyzed sociologically is precisely what the believer experiences and what he expresses in the language of faith as a concrete form of the Church's response to God's grace—the form of a fortunate, a less fortunate or even a pastorally wrong response in the Church to God's grace and the signs of the times. This particular aspect cannot be interpreted sociologically or historically. Yet the dualism favored by so many Christians results in an attempt to make the Church's office immune from socio-historical and historical criticism. This is unwise both from the

ecclesial and from the pastoral point of view and it cannot be justified theologically.

This brings me to the concluding section of this article, in which I
deal with office in the socio-historical context of a Church present
among the poor, oppressed and suffering people. I have given this section the same title as the article itself.

Offices in the Church of the Poor

The Socio-historical Context

Forms of theology of office and practices of that office in the Church
never come about in a vacuum. There is the area of the *ecclesia* itself
and there is also the socio-historical and the socio-political area of
society in which the churches live and develop their offices. It often
happens that many different offices come about in a conflict for competencies and in a complicated process of role formation within a group
and therefore as part of differentiation of system and in the long run
also as a later theological justification of historically acquired positions
of authority. In the first century, for example, there was (in addition to
a peaceful co-existence) conflict between the 'prophets' and the 'presbyters' and between the offices of men and those of women and later, until
the fourth century, there was also conflict between presbyters and
deacons. In the middle ages, there was conflict for competencies
between those responsible for diocesan and parochial pastoral care
and those responsible for abbatial pastoral care. Later still, there was
conflict between monks who were priests and canons regular and finally
conflict between the mendicants, whose pastoral care was supradi-
ocesan and those whose pastoral work was traditional, diocesan and
parochial. The same fluctuations appeared in the theology of office,
that of the 'victors' in these conflicts eventually becoming the dominant
theology. (I am unfortunately not able to go more deeply into this here.)[10]
This process is still continuing today, when we are aware of role conflicts
in the Church between the 'traditional priests' and the 'pastoral workers'
who are not ordained but who are the ones who are really inspiring the
Christian communities.

The Iglesia Popular

The 'people's Church' has, in the understanding of Latin American
theologians, a special meaning that is frequently misinterpreted. On
the other hand, however, the term can certainly give rise to such misun-

derstandings. In the first place, after the experience of Nazism and fascism in the West, we are all justifiably suspicious of anything that smacks of the 'people'—the *Volk*. This is, however, quite alien to the thinking of the liberation theologians of Latin America, although, in view of the world-wide significance and importance of their theology, it might perhaps be better for them to avoid using terms with unfavorable connotations (which are, it hardly needs to be said, not intended by the theologians themselves). I know from my own experience that language can easily give rise to emotional theological connotations. For the sake of the matter itself—the 'people's Church'—it might be advisable to review the use of language, although this may sound like pedantic advice to Latin American theologians by a European theologian.

The Spanish word *pueblo* means 'people,' but it also has at least two special shades of meaning which are not in themselves to be found in other living languages. *El pueblo* is the people (a) in the formal sense as a collective reality that is a factor acting in history and (b) the term also refers formally and in the concrete local situation to the majority of the people, in other words, to the poor in that locality or country. Used in this second sense, it has something in common with one of the meanings of the biblical concept *anawim*, 'the poor of the country.' The term *el pueblo* therefore has biblical credentials and 'the poor' are those people who have no voice or rather who have a voice, but a one which is not heard and which others often do not want to hear, because what it expresses for them is an accusation, the 'complaint of the people' rising up to heaven, and it is a voice that is heard by God, a God who sooner or later will call on a new Moses to set his people free.

The 'people's Church,' then, is a Church of the poor masses, a Church that looks after the poor and at the same time is the collectivity of the poor, who are, as the poor, the 'subject of being the Church,' compressed together in an '*oikoumene* of suffering ones' gathered around the Lord. There is certainly a 'performative' element in this Latin American way of speaking about the 'people's Church,' implying that the official Church is not (although it ought to be) a 'Church of the poor' and that it is often not on their side, but on the side of the powerful and therefore (although this is not the intention) in fact against the poor. The official Church is therefore also partisan. There is also an echo of already fulfilled hope in the term 'people's Church,' a suggestion that manifestations of the 'Church of the poor' are already clearly present here and there, manifestations that are increasing in number and can no longer be checked. This Church of the poor already has its own martyrs and martyrdom has since time immemorial been the 'seed' of Christian faith.

In so far as I have been able to ascertain, Bishop Romero never used the term *iglesia popular* in his sermons and writings. He probably deliberately avoided the term in order not to give rise to misunderstandings. All the same, he was very concerned to express the conviction that the Church, as inspired by the Gospel, should take root and find its focal point in the poor, to whom the Gospel was, in an Isaian manner, proclaimed and who were themselves becoming proclaimers of the Gospel—subjects of being the Church and of the Church's priestly, pastoral and prophetic ministry. What we have here, then, is the formation in a socio-historical context of a Church community that is in no way alien to the spirit of the New Testament. It cannot be disputed, of course, that a certain separation has come about in this situation, not in itself between the people and the bishops (as has been suggested in certain quarters), but certainly between the poor and the rich. But then Paul himself criticized not the poor, but the rich in a similar situation, when he asked: 'Do you despise the Church of God and humiliate those who have nothing? What shall I say to you? Shall I commend you in this? No, I will not!' (1 Cor. 11:22).

The Church's new Code of Canon Law repeats the very fortunate statement of Vatican II, speaking of the local churches, of which the one Catholic Church consists (can. 368) and saying that the 'one, holy Catholic and apostolic Church of Christ' is really present and active in the local churches (can. 369). The universal Church, then, is also present and living in a Church of the poor. The official ministries have therefore to be carried out in the concrete in these local churches within a clear context and in the light of the great Christian tradition. It is simply not possible for theologians or sociologists to ascertain by study and reflection the concrete form that the offices in a Church of the poor will take. This can only be done in a permanent process of theological reflection about what is in fact taking place in the building up of communities in the already existing local churches. Inspired by the Gospel, leaders arise naturally, take initiatives and fulfil what is known in the Christian tradition as the ecclesial meaning of 'office.'

The only question that remains to be answered is: Should there or should there not be ordination? The southern countries differ from the northern ones here. In northern Europe, we are concerned with a pure theology of office, but theologians in the countries of the South tend to solve this problem pragmatically and are only concerned that what is necessary for the evangelical vitality of Christian communities should take place. In my opinion, both points of view go back to similar although divergent theological concerns. The pragmatic theologians believe that the existing threefold division of the Church's office (episcopate, presbyterate and diaconate) can be left as it is (in view of the attitude of those in authority in the Church) and they are therefore not really interested in any sacramental 'merging' or *ordinatio*. In my opinion, it would be ecclesiologically wrong to do what has sometimes been done in Europe, namely to identify 'ordination' with clericalization and on the basis of this identification encourage an attitude of awe in the presence of every ordination.

The theoreticians' attitude towards this pragmatic view is that the threefold division of office that has existed since time immemorial does not in any sense stand in the way of new forms of office that may eventually emerge. No one will of course object to the phenomenon of as many Christians as possible committing themselves to the building up of the Church—that is, after all, the task of all Christians. It is also not a phenomenon that will do away with the specific sacramental aspect of office in the Church. I am personally therefore in favour of a suitable form of ordination (a laying on of hands accompanied by a special *epiclesis* that is specific to office) for those who have in recent years emerged as 'animators' of these ecclesial communities of the poor.

Translated by David Smith

NOTES

1. Y. Congar *Jalons pour une théologie du laicat* (Paris 1953; 2nd edn. with addenda 1964).

2. Stephen of Tournai (d. 1203) *Summa*, Prologue.

3. *Decretalia* VII, 12, q. 1; ed. Friedberg I, 678.

4. A. Faive *Naissance d'une hierarchie. Les premières étapes du cursus clérical* (Paris 1977).

5. G. Dautzenberg 'Zur Stellung der Frauen in den paulinischen Gemeinden' *Die Frau im Urchristentum* (Freiburg 1983) pp. 182–224 and especially pp. 214–221; E. Schüssler Fiorenza *In Memory of Her. A Feminist Theological Reconstruction of Christian Origins* (New York 1983) pp. 205–218.

6. Ambrosiaster *Ad Ephesios* 4, 12. 1–4 (CSEL Ambrosiaster III, 81, 99).

7. See especially P. J. Cordes *Sendung zum Dienst: Exegetisch-systematische Studien zum Konzilsdebat 'Vom Dienst und Leben der Priester'* (Frankfurt 1972) especially pp. 202 and 291–301.

8. Quoted by P. Pourrat *Le Sacerdoce: doctrine de l'Ecole Française* (Paris 1947) pp. 44ff.

9. J. H. Newman *Select Treatises of St Athanasius* (Oxford 2nd edn. 1888); H. E. Manning *The Eternal Priesthood* (London 20th edn. 1930).

10. See for a more complete analysis of this history my new book *The Church with a Human Face: A New and Expanded Theology of Ministry* (New York, 1985).

14

The Teaching Authority of All:
A Reflection about the Structure
of the New Testament

1985

There is something illogical and even contradictory about speaking about a '*magisterium*' of believers. There may be at least confusion with regard to the double level at which authority can be exercised. Therefore, in order to prevent misunderstanding and possibly a slipshod use of language, I shall at the very beginning of this article make a distinction between authority in the Church in the sense of the community of faith in matters of faith and the teaching authority of the official Church. In other words, the distinction is between the teaching authority of all and the teaching office of only a few—those who have been given a mandate by the community of faith itself in the power of the Spirit dwelling in it in the name of Christ. The teaching authority of believers, which is difficult to define, in the matter of the doctrinal expression of faith is at a different level from the authority, which can be juridically more sharply defined, of the official office-bearers—the authority, in other words, of the world's bishops in unity with the pope or 'Peter with the Eleven' and preferably never without the Eleven.

Both forms of authority in the Church have a mutually normative, critical and complementary function with regard to the recognition in faith of the Church's content of faith as the fruit of God's activity. I hope that this will be demonstrated elsewhere in this number. As a systematic theologian, I shall only analyze here (in accordance with the plan of this number) what can be learnt from the internal structure of the story of the canonical Bible in connection with the authority of believers in the matter of faith and ethics, as a reflection of Jesus' authority in the community of faith of the Church.

Jesus in the Reflection of the Church's *Sequela Jesu*

Not only the Old Testament but also Jesus' own disciples are co-determinative for an understanding of Jesus, just as the second and third generations of Christians are also co-determinative for an understanding of the authority of the earlier 'apostles and prophets' on which the Church is, according to Eph. 2:20, built.

The New Testament provides us with the story of a Jew who appeared in our human history and who was confessed after his death by fervent followers as 'Christ, God's only Son, our Lord.' In that story we read how certain people reacted to that historical appearance of Jesus and how they, as a result of this, began to lead a new life. We also read how other people reacted equally radically in their encounter with him or on the basis of hearing about him and rejected him and even got rid of him by executing him. Through the New Testament, then, we can, as in a reflection, discover in essential features who Jesus was, how he lived and what motivated and inspired him. It was, after all, him whom these Christians wanted to imitate and whom others wanted (in defense of their own status) to destroy. We have no writings from his own hand and no direct 'documents' by him. It is only in the reflection provided by his followers that a portrait of Jesus has been handed down to us. The Church's *sequela Jesu* is the only document that Jesus has left us. It is *par excellence* the 'icon' of Christ in our midst.

The later followers tried to understand for themselves what Jesus meant for his first disciples. They did this in order to know what he meant and could mean for their own lives here and now. The story of the first and already richly varied process of imitation ended, together with the process of interpretation implied in it, at least gradually in what we call the 'New Testament.' What emerges from the New Testament stories is that what resulted from Jesus' historical life is of such a nature that it led people either to imitate him radically or to reject him violently. His appearance was special and challenging. 'Who do you say that I am?'—this question has a theologically significant meaning. This is the vision of the canonical New Testament itself.

We can moreover say without hesitation that the entire history of Christianity consists of a never-ending process of imitation and interpretation, in which Christians, confronted again and again with different situations and problems in the Church and within changing cultural environments, have been concerned, in faith and in faithfulness to the tradition of faith as well as in a critical manner, with what previous generations of Christians have handed down to them. What emerges from a diachronic comparison between the interpretative activity of Christians in the different periods in the life of the Church community or the gathering together in faith around Jesus Christ is what Christian identity is. This is clear despite all the differences in experiences and theoretical expressions.

What strikes us again and again in the New Testament is the essential relationship between the person of Jesus and his message of the approach of what Jesus called the 'kingdom,' the 'rule' or the 'government' of God. There is an inner bond between the message and the one who proclaims it, just as there is an inner connection between that message and Jesus' consistent dealing with it. With his person, his message and his way of life, Jesus vouches for God's liberating and reconciling love of man—a love that opens the way to communication.

Something very important is revealed in this, Jesus' message of and about God is, in the light of his experience of God, so integrated into his active, liberating association with his fellow-men—an association that opens the way to communication—that his proclamation and the praxis of his life interpret each other. At the same time, they also act together to change and renew the prevailing situation and man, setting both it and him free to serve other men in solidarity and love. A striking example of this is Zacchaeus, who, after his liberating encounter with Jesus, let the poor share in all his possessions (which had not been obtained fairly). It is clear from this that our knowledge in faith of Jesus' own mode of being and his way of speaking and acting cannot be dissociated from a knowledge of others' reaction to this. Jesus proclaims the reality of God as salvation for men, who then experience salvation profoundly in contact with him. In his existence as a man, he affirms God through his human activity as the reality that saves and liberates people.

Jesus' identity has therefore to be read from and in the salvation that was, thanks to him, made a reality in other people. It is in the conversion and renewal of such people in and through contact with Jesus that who he is and what he does is revealed. This is why the testimony borne by the New Testament and that borne by all people forms an essential part of the answer to the question as to who Jesus was and who he can be for us today. This testimony therefore has a share in the authority of Jesus and cannot be dissociated from that authority. The *sequela Jesu* (which cannot be separated from an accompanying spontaneous or explicit 'process of interpretation') of Christians throughout the centuries and even now is the historical mediation between Jesus' time and that of our own contemporary generation. It is in the form of this testimony borne again and again in time by believers that Jesus' authority radiates as in a reflection. It is in this that believers can take it or leave it if they wish in the Church—in the power of the Spirit.

The same structure can be found in the resurrection of Jesus and in the faith of Christians in that resurrection. These are two different but inseparable realities. God authenticates the person, the message and the way of life of Jesus over the break of his death in his resurrection as the new eschatological saving act of God, brought about in Jesus himself. He places his seal on it and through it contradicts what people have done to Jesus and are still doing—and also what other people have done and are still doing (in an exemplary way in him). But here too the principle is in force that the 'in himself' and 'for us' cannot be separated. Jesus' own resurrection, his sending of the Spirit, the emergence of the Christian 'community of God' that 'lives from the Spirit' and the New Testament testimony, although they are in no sense identical, define each other. And it is only within this mutual definition that anything can be said about Jesus of Nazareth and that he can be confessed as the Christ. It is *in* the community of faith, then, that the crucified but risen Jesus appears. The authority of Jesus becomes transparent in the authentic *sequela Jesu* of the community of the Church—in the footsteps of Jesus.

A Reflection in the Third, the Fourth and . . . the Thousandth Generation

The experience of God's care for people, which emerged from the message and the way of life of Jesus, was the origin of the first wave of the Jesus movement that was kept up everywhere by Hebrew (Aramaic) speaking Jews who had become Christians. They waited patiently for the coming of Jesus as the judge of the world. In the New Testament, however, it was in fact above all those segments of the early Christian Jesus movement, consisting principally of Greek-speaking Jews of the Diaspora who had been converted to Christian faith, which provided the environment within which the Judaeo-Christian movement became a universal missionary Church.

For these Christians, the foundation of their faith, their building up of the Church and their mission was not directly an experience of and an encounter with the historical Jesus (whom they had never met). That foundation was their baptism in the Spirit—their baptism in the name of Jesus. The God of these Christians was—and is—the God who did not abandon Jesus at his death, but made him a 'life-giving Spirit' (1

Cor. 15:45). Christians who are baptized in him are therefore themselves *pneumatici*. This was the view that the earliest Hellenistic Jewish Christians in Jerusalem, the circle gathered around Stephen, had of the Church. It was not long before they were driven out of Jerusalem. Many of them emigrated to Syria via Samaria, going especially to Antioch, where they founded the Church's first great missionary community— the Church of Antioch. After his conversion, Paul was among those who were taught by them.

This pneuma-Christological view of the Church was very widespread in the early years of Christianity. We have, however, only an indirect knowledge of this image of the Church from the New Testament— through Paul and Paulinism, through Luke's Acts of the Apostles and through certain traditions in the gospel of Mark and a few other New Testament texts.[1]

The key-words used in this Christian missionary movement and its theology were solidarity and equality of all Christians 'in the Spirit' (Acts 2:17–18; 2 Cor. 5:17), living 'by' or 'in the Spirit' (Gal. 5:25; 6:1) and the 'new creation' (Gal. 6:15; 2 Cor. 5:17). The source of this ecclesiology was baptism in the Spirit, the foundation of the whole of the life of the Church. Paul, whose view of the Church was the same, was to criticize the pneumatic movement for denying the resurrection. But what was really at stake was not so much the resurrection as such as a special form of 'present' or 'already realized' eschatology. This meant that Christians lived through their baptism in the Spirit as people who were already redeemed in a 'new world' and 'in the fullness of time.' For this reason, they did not concern themselves with the 'old world' and some of them did not even want to work any more. The old world had become irrelevant for them. Within the community of their companions in faith at least, they were already living in the new world and were not at home at all, in fact were completely alienated in the everyday world outside.

There are several passages in the Acts of the Apostles that are very suggestive in connection with this early Christian view of the Church (see Acts 19:1–7; 18:24–19:1). There were some of Jesus' disciples who had been baptized by John the Baptist, but who were nonetheless very well 'instructed in the way of the Lord' (Acts 18:25). They were apparently acquainted with the so-called logia tradition concerning Jesus. But they had not even heard of the Spirit! One of them was Apollos and typically enough he came from Egypt. He must have received 'baptism in the Spirit,' since this was the basis of all pneumatic and even all ecstatic experiences in the community. He was not yet acquainted, however, with the pneuma-Christology of this pre-Pauline and to a great extent already Pauline form of Christianity. The contrast between 'baptism with water' and 'baptism with the Spirit' can be found

from the time of the Q tradition (Matt. 3:11; Luke 3:16) at all levels of
the New Testament (Mark 1:8; John 1:26, 31, 33; Acts 1:5; 11:16; 1
Cor. 13:13). According to Acts (2:17–21), the prophecy of Joel refers to
the whole Christian community, all baptized Christians forming one
prophetic and pneumatic people of God and their community being one
of equal partners without domination (Gal. 3:27–29), but with leadership.

This pneuma-Christological Wisdom-messianism is summed up very
well by Paul: 'Christ (is) the power of God and the wisdom of God' (1
Cor. 1:24), but it goes back to pre-Pauline traditions. Another text is
'Your life in Christ Jesus, whom God made our wisdom' (1 Cor. 1:30).
Hence the Antiochian name of 'Christians' (Acts 11:26) for people who
are *in* Christ—in Jesus, who is himself full of Pneuma and is in fact
'Pneuma' (1 Cor. 15:45). 'No one can say "Jesus is Lord" except by the
Holy Spirit' (1 Cor. 12:3). This Wisdom-Christology is also at the heart
of all the Wisdom hymns referring to Jesus that are quoted by Paul
and in Paulinism (see, for example, Phil. 2:6–11; Col. 1:15–20; Eph.
2:14–16; 1 Tim. 3:16; Heb. 1:3; 1 Pet. 3:18, 22; see also, in male Logos
terms, John 1:1–14). Christ or Messiah Jesus, Wisdom Jesus and Logos
Jesus—in all their Christianity, these are all typical expressions of
Hellenistic Jews who have become Christians. Christology is in them
re-grafted Jewish messianism—grafted, in other words, on to Jesus.

The whole of the Mediterranean coast was buzzing with *pneumatici*
at that time. These were for the most part religious fanatics of various
kinds from the East. Jewish Christians were also expressing their own
Christian experiences in experiential terms taken from the contemporary context of the surrounding culture. They, however, saw this as
firmly based on the 'paschal' Pentecostal experience of baptism in
the Spirit.

Paul, who had also become a Christian, was confronted above all by
this form of early Christianity. It was with good reason that even post-
Pauline traditions still speak about the Church as *built on* 'apostles
and prophets' (Eph. 2:20). All the same, Paul had to correct this tradition
in a number of ways. He had emphasized the 'already,' but still had to
stress most of all the 'not yet' of redemption. By stressing this, he was
correcting the present eschatology of these Christians and bringing the
irrational and ecstatic elements in their pneumatic movement back to
reasonable proportions. (There is evidence of this in 1 Cor. 14:40.)

Despite their experience of living in a 'new world,' then, these enthusi-
astic members of Christian communities had to be brought back to the
everyday world.

Paul placed these Christians in that world in a manner that was
guaranteed to reinforce the system—the slave was a 'free man' in the

Church, but in worldly society he remained a slave. In so doing, he did not have the critical function that Christians had to exercise in the 'old world' in mind. In the Church, a woman might not be in any way subject to a man, but 'in the world' male privileges continued to be valid. These and similar admonitions made by Paul were inspired by pastoral missionary motives. He saw the Gentiles as 'potential Christians' and it was therefore quite wrong to scandalize them in any way. Kerygma and dogma were not involved here—only contextual pastoral strategy, with the result that these are not obligatory norms for contemporary Christians.

The 'power of the Spirit'—this key-word in the early Church expresses a fundamental conviction of those generations of Christians. The 'Great Church,' by canonizing many different Christian texts, made a connection between this pneuma-Christology, via the logia tradition, and the historical Jesus. In this way, it prevented pneumatology from losing its Christological basis and therefore from becoming a superficial and general religious movement without a messianic or Christian basis.

Non-Functional Authority

When Barnabas and Paul were sent by the community at Antioch, the leaders there were 'prophets and teachers (*didaskaloi*)' (Acts 13:1–3). It is clear from documents up to and including the third century that 'teachers of faith' could be either ordained or non-ordained. They undoubtedly had great prestige in the Church. They had not been made teachers by a Church mandate. On the contrary, they had become teachers on their own initiative on the basis of clearly recognizable gifts of the Spirit—as Tertullian says, 'Frater aliquis doctor, gratis scientiae donatus.'[2] At the beginning of the third century, the *Traditio* of Hippolytus refers to *doctores*. These are either clergy or laymen. It was sufficient to be baptized in the Spirit to be able to teach faith and the gift of the spirit was in certain believers more effective than in others. It is clear from the history of the layman Origen, who was later obliged to let himself be ordained priest, as Eusebius narrates,[3] and Jerome[4] shows that from the very beginning 'laymen' were *doctores* or teachers of faith in the Church, but that the bishops took over all teaching in the middle of the third century, with the result that there was at that time only a question of *sacerdotes doctores*.[5] The history of the lectorate as an ordained office is confirmation of the growing clericalization of the 'teaching authority' in the Church.[6] That teaching authority was narrowed down at that time exclusively to the teaching office.

It was not until the High Middle Ages that a clear distinction was once again made between the 'teaching authority' of the *doctores* and the 'teaching office' of the pope and the bishops. The latter was called the *cathedra pastoralis*, whereas the former was known as the *cathedra magistralis*. Mediaeval theologians regarded themselves as *doctores* and as such as independent of the Church's authority. In fact, these *doctores* were priests, but their teaching authority was not based on ordination or on a Church mandate. It was based on their university qualifications.

Although a non-official teaching office had clearly been accepted once more in the Church, another process of narrowing down of the 'universal teaching authority of believers' had also just as clearly taken place. That universal teaching authority had in fact been narrowed down intellectually to the caste of scholars in accordance with the pseudo-Dionysian and hierarchically feudal model, as defined by Thomas Aquinas. 'Divine revelation,' Thomas says, 'reaches the lower orders according to a definite order of precedence through the mediation of those in a higher position, . . . as is clear from Dionysius. And therefore, for similar reasons, the interpretation of faith must be communicated by those who have attained majority (*maiores:* those in a higher position) to those in a lower position.'[7]

According to Thomas, priests are the masons of a cathedral, their bishops are the work superintendents and theologians are the architects.[8] On the other hand, he also said that a simple old woman (and why not an old man?) could have a deeper insight into faith than the greatest theologian. Despite his feudal way of thinking, he laid great stress on the *cognitio per modum connaturalitatis*, knowledge of faith on the basis of a deeply Christian and ultimately holy way of life.

It was only when the Ancien Régime came to an end that the *doctores* with the privileges that they enjoyed for themselves and their wives and children, if they were married, lost their status. Since then, it has been quite exceptional for 'lay' people to make their own contribution to the illumination of faith by being called to be 'teachers of the Church,' as is the case with Teresa of Avila and Catherine of Siena. These peaks that have been recognized by the official Church, however, undoubtedly point to what is somehow fundamentally present in all baptized persons—the fact that there is a teaching authority in the Church outside the teaching office and the theological authority of scientifically trained men.

Since the Enlightenment, however, 'authority' has been identified in a more one-sided way with authority on the basis of intellectual knowledge and partly as a result of this the term *magisterium* has been reserved exclusively for the *official* authority in the Church, especially from the nineteenth century onwards. The old Greek word-play about *pathein* (to suffer) and *mathein* (to learn) disappeared from the scene. Recently, however, we have come once again to recognize that the authority of reason has to subject itself to the criticism of the 'authority of suffering humanity.' Enlightened reason has initially to establish itself with regard to the non-functional authority of suffering man. If this does not take place, there is always a danger that 'leaders'— theologians and office-bearers—will behave like ayatollahs. That is why the model of the contemporary forms of liberation theology is so attractive. Those theologies express the implicit Christology and theology that exists in a people that is surrounded by suffering, the members of which are moved by an evangelical impulse for the sake of their brothers and sisters. Suffering and a situation of concrete distress provide the basis for a memory of the Jesus Christ of the Bible to lead to a definite Christian praxis. A consensus comes about among those believers, who are the subjects of their own expression of faith. In this, all that theologians do is to *help* those people.

In the past, it was often 'religious geniuses' who influenced the consensus prevailing among the believing people for long periods in the Church's life. Augustine, Athanasius, Thomas Aquinas and Luther were precisely such geniuses. Now, however, something else is happening. In addition to academic theology, there is also a theology of the basic groups. God's revelation is an event that is independent of people and their historical experiences, but it is nonetheless experienced by people and expressed in the form of a cumulative tradition of experience and interpretation. And it is precisely as something that is expressed by people that God's revelation is dependent on the culture, time and place in which it is expressed.

This is particularly significant in our present situation in the world and the Church. All kinds of new forms of non-academic theologies have arisen recently—a phenomenon to which J.-B. Metz has already referred. These ways of doing theology do not find their immediate context in university circles, but in various movements and in the life and praxis of different communities of faith, in other words, at the 'base.' No connection is made in this new form of theology between 'theology and university.' The connection is between theology and a Christian community of faith—in other words, Church—however academic, that is, sound and solid, this form of doing theology may be.

This phenomenon does not, in my opinion, make so-called academic theology superfluous. What it does is to deprive academic theology of its earlier claim to an almost exclusive right and probably also of its claim to be the primary type of theologizing. It is becoming rather a 'subsidiary' type of theologizing, which includes within its way of looking at things critically from a greater distance the primary type of theology, that is, the non-academic type of community theology. The *university* continues to be the right context for this secondary type of theologizing, while the immediate environment of the non-academic forms of theology, whatever shape they may take, is the *Church community* (in a very contextual setting).

Academic theology has the task of *integrating* the new experiences and the new praxis and reflections of local communities and basic groups into the whole complex of the 'Church's memory' and into the great reserves of experience and faith of the entire Church. It therefore at the same time prevents these new experiences, in which a new and increasing 'consensus' is manifested, from remaining merely sporadic or from tending to disintegrate the Church. In this way, academic theology 'mediates' the rich traditions of the Church's experience throughout the centuries down to the basis and at the same time prevents that basis from becoming cognitively isolated as a sect. It is even enriched itself as academic theology by these new experiences, reflections and forms of consensus that are made manifest in this so-called non-academic theology.

The great Christian tradition, then, is enriched by the creation of new traditions. In our own times, it is above all the basic groups that are becoming more and more the active subjects of the expression of faith. There is, of course, no doubt that the emergence of a new consensus in this is selective. There are also no experiences of faith which represent in themselves and in their expression at a given moment in the present the fullness of the Judaeo-Christian tradition, and this is a criticism that the official Church often makes of the basic groups. In doing so, however, it frequently forgets that even the official tradition of the Christian deposit of faith is also selective and in addition to this often intellectualistic. There is and there always has been a difference between the scale of values established in the 'hierarchy of truths of faith' by the official Church and that held by the Church of the people, because their context of life is so different and especially their context of suffering, distress and need. Believers themselves are in the best position to express this. Ordinary believers have a spontaneous sense of the 'coming of the *eschaton*' and know that it has to be connected positively with their own activity. For that reason, the field of Christian activity is usually the place where Christian consensus comes about in the clearest way.

Elsewhere in this number of *Concilium*, the reader will find a description of how both the teaching authority of believers and that of the theologians who are close to them as well as the authority of academic theologians (who are to some extent at a greater distance from believers, but are not without some internal participation in their activity) are in a situation of interaction with regard to the teaching authority of the teaching office of the Church, which in *very exceptional and definite cases* is gifted with the *same* 'infallibility,' that is, stability of the exchange rate, as that with which the whole Christian community of faith is gifted.[9]

What emerges clearly from this is that the *teaching office* in the Church can be defined from the vantage-point of the 'teaching authority of all believers,' normalized by the 'Word of God' to which the teaching office is also subject and not vice versa. That was even the view of the highly disputed First Vatican Council. The Dogmatic Constitution *Lumen Gentium* of Vatican II *expressed* and *discussed* the 'people of God' (although it did not let that people *speak for itself)* even *before* it spoke about the official leadership and official authority in the Church. By doing this, it reinstated the New Testament and an early Church view to a position of honor. It has also proved to be an enormous advance from the ecumenical point of view. The obvious conclusions for the *Church as an institution* have, however, not yet been drawn from this, with the result that the teaching authority of the community of faith even now is treated with only scant justice and sometimes even suffers from the power of office in the Church. From the ecclesiological point of view, this is not in any sense a normal situation.

Translated by David Smith

NOTES

1. The following bibliography is far from complete: J. Ash 'The Decline of Ecstatic Prophecy in the Early Church' *Theological Studies* 37 (1976) 227–252; M. E. Boring *Sayings of the Risen Jesus. Christian Prophecy in the Synoptic Tradition* (Cambridge 1982); Y. Congar 'Pneumatologie ou "Christomonisme" dans la tradition latine?' *Ecclesia a Spiritu Sancto edocta (Mélanges théologiques G. Philips)* (Gembloux 1970) pp. 41–63; G. Dautzenberg *Urchristliche Prophetie. Ihre Erforschung, ihre Voraussetzungen im Judentum und ihre Struktur im ersten Korintherbrief (BWANT* 104) (Stuttgart 1975); J. Hermann *Kurios und Pneuma. Studien zur Theologie der paulinischen Hauptbriefen* (Munich 1961); H. Kraft *Die Entstehung des Christentums* (Darmstadt, 1981); E. Schüssler Fiorenza *In Memory of Her* (New York 1983); D. Wallace-Hadrill *Christian Antioch. A Study of Early Christian Thought in the East* (Cambridge 1982).

2. *De praescr. haer.* XIV, 1; see III, 5.

3. *Hist. Eccl.* VI, 3; VI, 15; VI, 19, 3.

4. *De Vir. Ill.* XXXVI.

5. T. Schaeffer *Das Priester-Bild im Leben und Werk des Origenes* (Frankfurt 1978) pp. 103–115.

6. A. Faivre *Naissance d'une hiérarchie. Les premières étapes du cursus clérical* (Paris 1977) pp. 153–170.

7. *ST* 2a. 2ae. q.2, a.6.

8. *Quodlib.* 1, a.14. See also R. Guelluy 'La Place des théologiens dans l'Eglise et la société médiévale' *Miscellanea historica in hon. A. de Meyer* (Louvain 1946) pp. 571–589; H. Grundmann 'Sacerdotium, Regnum, Studium' *Archiv für Kulturgeschichte* 34 (1951–1952) 5–21.

9. Vatican I, Denz.-Sch. 3074.

15

The Role of History in What Is Called the New Paradigm

1989

The paradigm vogue in the natural sciences began to fascinate theologians at a moment when the discussion round Thomas S. Kuhn had ebbed away and when almost anything began to be called 'paradigms' (theories, hypotheses, axioms, laws, postulates and basic assumptions), while conversely a more precise understanding and use of models and paradigms was being achieved.

The Present-Day Use of Models

Apart from what could be called 'methodical models' (for example, the literary-historical method and the structuralist method in exegesis), some clarity has now been reached with respect to 'theoretical models' as used in the empirical sciences. From the literature dealing with the theory of science after Kuhn, a meaningful and operational definition can be distilled, on the basis of which one can verify how far theology also thinks in models. As a result of this discussion, a model appears to be an incomplete and insufficient design, which, on the one hand, *represents empirical observation,* and, on the other hand, *interprets the theory:* (*a*) in order to explain the empirical data; (*b*) in terms of a theory (in the making), and (*c*) in the service of the formation of theory. Consequently, in the empirical sciences theoretical models form a link between empirical observation and theory; for that reason they touch on both empirical observation and theory.

The link between empirical observation and theory is seen as necessary in order to translate the (highly formalized) language of coherence characteristic of theory into a language of correspondence. The researchers themselves through models make the theories refer to empirical observation. But we must not forget that all this takes place in the context of a polemic in the theory of science about the primacy of either theory or the so-called 'hard facts' (or experience, which itself is already 'laden with theory'). In sciences dedicated to the investigation of laws, like the natural sciences, this thinking-in-models was at times even seen as setting a standard for all other sciences. As a result Christian theology, which speaks of the unrepeatable uniqueness of Jesus of Nazareth, confessed as the Christ, and which at the same time was making serious efforts in academic circles to be accepted as a 'science,' sometimes got into trouble through this emphasis on a standard model. Meanwhile we were taken by surprise when the so-called structuralistic phenomenology (in particular, as proposed by Roman Jakobson) proffered the thesis that the universal is to be found not only on the side of theory, but on that of experience: the universal is co-experienced, in the sense of 'observed.'

What can theology do with this limited and more sharply defined concept of paradigm and model? It is a fact that on the analogy of this empirical use of the category 'model' too, theology thinks in models. There is for example the Anselmian, Germanic-feudal 'model of a legal order,' used to shed light on Christian soteriology. The model originates in feudal punitive practice. As with every model, it allows of alternative models and is essentially incomplete and insufficient. It is better, therefore, not to speak of a 'theory of satisfaction,' but rather of a 'model of satisfaction.' In fact this model put paid to a patristic model which saw salvation as a 'ransom from the power of the devil,' in which sinful man had been able to find a sort of alibi. If, then, the Council of Trent mentions the word '*satisfecit*' (DS 1529), it speaks of real salvation in Christ, but through a model. As a result it is not the model which is 'dogmatized,' but only something which has occurred in the history of Jesus' life and which through this model is being put into words. This thinking-in-models is important because it enables us to make a conscious distinction between the substance of faith and the model in which the faith is put into words. Theologians often confuse 'the thought' with 'thinking-in-models.'

In this way we can also speak of the 'two-natures model' in christology which, as a model, is naturally incomplete and insufficient: other models remain possible. Another example is the 'original sin model,' and so on. On the analogy of this thinking-in-models in the empirical sciences, theology employs models just as much. To understand this is an advantage, but at the same time it should warn us, for thinking-in-models is not without its own dangers.

All the same, I get the impression that at this congress the problem concerning models and paradigms presents itself at a completely different level from the one just mentioned, in which case we cannot look for any help from the empirical, and in particular the natural sciences.

So-called 'Epochal Ruptures'

Karl Rahner and Bernhard Welte talked a considerable time ago of what they called 'epochal ruptures.' They did not elaborate these categories. In my view the *Annales*-school of French historiography can provide theology with more light on this matter than Kuhn. In addition to a short-term or 'ephemeral' history of facts there is a 'structural' and 'conjunctural' history. The conjunctural history embraces larger periods, branches out further, penetrates deeper, and is more comprehensive; a cultural conjuncture lasts a long time. On the other hand 'structural history,' in spite of being history, passes very slowly. It is characterized by an age-long duration which is almost identical with stagnation, and yet it moves.

The conjunctural history (which I compare to what Rahner and Welte have called the 'epochal level') is very important for theological thinking. This cultural conjuncture provides the framework within which the history of facts, which took place in a determined period, can be interpreted. Precisely this conjunctural history shows a resemblance to what at this congress is called 'paradigm.' A conjunctural epoch has its own conjunctural horizon of understanding and gives rise to models of understanding in order to be able to situate and comprehend events. Such was the case in feudal times with the Anselmian model of a 'legal order' in christology. In a particular conjunctural culture this sharpens people's capacity to discern certain problems.

Sometimes the conjunctural epoch changes, as a result of a variety of factors. At first it remains unnoticed, but at last a conscious change is made to a new cultural horizon, with its own new models. People's eyes start to see different problems. In such a case we talk about a 'paradigm shift.'

Nevertheless, it is the 'structural level' of history which is the most fundamental and the least changeable. This structure makes it possible that interpretations from different conjunctural horizons of understanding can still be made accessible once more to people who live in another cultural epoch. This enables us, for example, to understand biblical models, like those of Chalcedon, today too, even if we use other models.

It does mean, however, that if we transfer the Chalcedon model to our own cultural conjuncture, we run a serious risk of misunderstanding such a model from a different cultural conjuncture. Consequently interpretation, when we come down to it, is something of a culture-shock. A particular conjunctural horizon of understanding sees as fundamental certain questions which we, in a different cultural epoch, experience as peripheral. Each epoch also has its blind spots, and this gives rise to 'forgotten truths' which will once more become relevant in a different conjuncture. The emphasis on horizons and models (within the structural and conjunctural history and also within the fluctuations inside cultural conjunctures) provides us indeed with the possibility of re-interpreting, for example, the model of Chalcedon for other times and other places.

Theology as a Hermeneutical Enterprise within a Practical-Critical Intention and as a Criticism of Ideology

The above-mentioned distinction between structural and conjunctural historical periods is, theologically, all the more important because the specific culture is what Christian faith in fact is modeled on; it is also that through which the Christian faith is assimilated in a living way, and, finally, it is in this that the faith is lived specifically by people here and now. This social and cultural mediation and incorporation of the faith causes problems for believers when the social and cultural patterns and their categories of experience and thought undergo drastic changes.

The Christian faith's tradition of experience and interpretation is a tradition of *meaning* with *liberating force*. It opens a horizon of possible experience for us today also. What we are dealing with here is not primarily a theoretical disclosure of meaning, but first and foremost a *narrative* revelation of meaning, which nevertheless was already being accompanied by at least an initial theological reflection even in the Old and New Testament.

A Hermeneutical Enterprise

We are facing a very delicate problem here. On the one hand, the gospel in its fundamental tendency and power is transcendent and universal and, in that sense, 'transcultural,' by which I mean that it is not limited to *one* culture. On the other hand, precisely this universal and 'transcultural gospel, which challenges all people and cultures, can only be found in the forms of *particular cultures* (the Jewish, Judaic-hellenistic, Hellenistic, Carolingian, Celtic, Roman, African, Asian . . . cultures)—never above or outside them; one never comes across a 'peeled substance' of faith; there is no way of stripping off the skin and getting down to the essence of the gospel. Only in the concrete and in the particular can the gospel be the revelation of the universality of God and his salvation. In that sense, the expressions of faith in the Bible and church's traditions depend on context and culture; they are localized and particular, while they nonetheless keep referring to the universal message of the gospel. The point at issue is *the historical identity* of what is permanent, *precisely in* what is *transitory* because of its contingent character.

If, then, we speak of two poles, these must lie in the cultural forms of the past (first pole) and in the present-day cultural forms (second pole) of *the one substance of faith,* which itself is the *source,* both of the past and of the contemporary expressions of the faith. It is not a question of applying a normative Bible to a 'theologically free' situation; in the Christian tradition of faith the *past situation* has already been accounted for; and in the *present-day situation* God's saving presence is just as creative and liberating as in the past. The distinction between, on the one hand, source (the Bible) and, on the other 'situation,' which can only be understood as 'context,' is inadequate and even misleading.

Cultural forms are constitutive mediations of the explicit message of revelation. God's revelation in Jesus is an event *independent* of men and women and their experiences and history; but it is experienced and put into words in the form of a religious tradition of accumulating experiences and interpretations by human beings. By being experienced and expressed by human beings, this revelation receives a historical seal, *dependent* on the place and time when the discussion takes place. It is this that makes this revelation communicable. For the personal and collective experience of faith and of eschatological salvation in Jesus by the first disciples could be mediated in a communicable way to contemporaries and further generations, because those first disciples described their experiences *by means of a commonly shared* (semiotic) *system of communication* (in conjunctural cultural forms). 'Correlation' cannot really be used to express this adequately. It is better to speak of 'the encounter of cultures,' a 'culture-shock,' or confrontation of cultures that draw their vitality from the Christian gospel and acclimatize it in their own cultural forms.

As a consequence of this, it will be obvious that for us a 'Christian identity of meaning' cannot be found on the level of the Bible and the Christian tradition, *as such;* and therefore it cannot be found in a material repetition or repristination of the past. But it cannot be found either on the level of the situation, past and present, _as such_ (whether in a biblicist or in a modernist direction). This identity of meaning can only be found _on the level of the corresponding relation between the original message (tradition)_ and _the always different situation_, both in the past and in the present. The fundamental identity of meaning between subsequent periods of Christian understanding of the tradition of faith does not concern the corresponding _terms;_ it concerns the corresponding _relations_ between the terms (message and situation, then and now). So there is a fundamental unity and equality, but this bears no relation to the terms of the hermeneutical equation, but to the _relation_ between those terms. The relation of equality between these _relations_ carries within itself the Christian identity of meaning. At stake is a proportional equality. Thus we never get a straight look at the Christian identity of meaning; moreover, this identity can never be fixed once and for all. Although in their divergent interpretation of the one gospel all these historical-cultural mediations do not contradict each other, we cannot either harmonize them all on one even level. Their unity is a unity in depth. It is a process of an always new 'cultural incorporation' of the gospel's transcultural substance of faith, which itself can never be found or received outside a particular cultural form. At stake is the Christian identity _in_ cultural ruptures or shifts and not an identity through what formerly was called, purely intellectualistically, 'homogeneous continuity' (which for that matter cannot be proved historically). The Christian _perception_ of meaning takes place _in_ a creative process of _giving_ meaning: a re-reading of the tradition from within new situations. Interpretation produces new traditions, in creative faithfulness. This is what it means to hand on the tradition of faith in a living way to future generations.

The 'common Christian element' (Christian identity) in the mediation of different cultural worlds like those of Jesus, Paul, Augustine, Pope Gregory, Thomas Aquinas or Bonaventure, Bellarmine, Luther or Calvin, Teresa of Avila or Bishop Romero, is to be found in one and the same fundamental view of God and humankind in their mutual relation, although that same vision and its corresponding life styles appear in forms which differ from each other historically and culturally, even geographically and psychologically, and also according to social class participation. But these limits (which may give a distorted picture) were always, and still are, crossed and transcended in a specifically Christian manner.

Hermeneutical Theology in an Anti-Ideological Perspective

The tradition of faith which discloses meaning is at the same time a call for a clearly determined personal and communal praxis of liberation. In the last analysis it is a question of two stories converging: the story of the Christian tradition of faith, and the personal and communal story of our lives.

Jesus' gospel of the kingdom of God is so much integrated in his acts of communicative and liberating association with human beings, that this preaching and the praxis of his life interpret each other mutually, while together they change the heart and the given situation. In his human existence Jesus affirms, through his liberating human activity, God as saving reality. Consequently, we cannot reduce theology to a purely theoretical interpretation of the Christian past. There is dialectical relation between the past, the present and the future yet to be made. Its relation to praxis ('*sequela Jesu*') is essential to theological theory itself. The purely theoretical approach forgets that there may be ideological elements contained in both the Christian tradition (in the massive way it has been handed down to us), and in the present-day situation in which we live.

By 'ideology,' I understand in the first instance something which in itself is positive but which can degenerate. In a positive sense I call ideology a totality of images, representations and symbols which a particular society creates in order to justify its identity. Ideology is the reproduction and confirmation of one's own identity through 'founding symbols.' However, this ideological function of identification and safeguarding of one's own identity can develop into something diseased, resulting in various negative forms of 'ideology,' which have been analyzed in divergent ways by Karl Marx, Freud and Nietzsche, and after them by many others. The function of ideology becomes 'pathological' especially insofar as that legitimization is distorted, manipulated and monopolized by the ruling or dominating people in society. But because a group cannot provide a false view of itself *unless* it was previously constituted at the level of symbolic structure, the unfavorable meaning of ideology is not the original one. Precisely because every society possesses a symbolic structure, these symbols can also become mendacious and diseased. In this sense, *any* complex of thought can become ideological, in the second and derived sense.

With hermeneutics which is critical of ideology (in the derived sense) I mean to unmask the naive idea that *being* and *language* (= thinking and speaking) are always congruent as far as their contents go, in spite of all the conceptual inadequacy already recognized by the classics. Thinking and speaking are also dependent on all kinds of private and group interests. Very often concepts and theories are used to justify and safeguard systematically certain social interests and positions of power.

Often enough, too, the history of theology is the history of the victors and the powerful, by whom possible alternatives to the gospel have been pushed into the background or even silenced altogether, having suffered defeat at the time (although, this cannot last forever, for forgotten truths do tend to come to the surface again). Without a de-ideologizing intention, every form of theoretical hermeneutical theologizing could miss its proper target in two directions:

(a) on the one hand the theologian would in such a case unconsciously adapt the Christian tradition of faith, through a false 'aggiornamento' or timing with modernity, for example with our western technocratic consumer society, privatized and geared to the a-political individual, and with its modern faith in progress. This theology would deprive the Christian faith of its liberating power, also in respect of the repressive aspects of our modern societies. In such a case Christian faith is adapted to the categories of experience and thought of what is called 'modern men and women,' without an attempt to analyze those categories critically;

(b) on the other hand, a theologian would also fail in his mission in respect of past traditions of faith. For these, too, do not come to us in pure evangelical form, but in categories of experience and thought belonging to many cultures and cultural periods, which also should be examined for their ideological elements. The danger lies in this: that under the pretext of the gospel or church's tradition we would posit obsolete and ideologically loaded concepts as normative for the Christian and theological understanding of the faith, thus curtailing Christians unduly in their evangelical freedom.

The New Paradigm? Or New Paradigms?

An analysis of the various—Synoptic, Pauline, Johannine, Petrine, Asia Minor, etc.—traditions in the New Testament makes it clear that, even within what is globally one and the same, albeit varied, conjunctural-cultural period, Christians express their faith within divergent paradigms and models. Striving for one and the same paradigm (in a kind of ideal 'theological consensus') would lead to an impoverishment of the gospel's very message, too rich to be contained within one paradigm. 'Do not extinguish the Spirit!'

On the other hand, history can teach us that a humanism which (in any society) is founded exclusively or at least predominantly on science and technology and on concentrated economic powers (our present-day situation) poses the threat of inhumanity to human beings and their society. If religion here has its irreplaceable word to say, this must be a religion concerned for human beings in the world, a religion which begins from faith in a liberating God who is interested in humanity and its history and, as a consequence of this, in human individuals in their specific historical and social context. Can there be any other humanism than the humanism of God himself, a God concerned for humanity, who wants people to be concerned for humanity as well? A humanism neither dogmatic nor threatening, but more universal and more humanist? But if the religions and the Christian churches want to proclaim this message with any credibility, they should begin by confessing that they have often obscured and even mutilated the face of God's humanity. Where religion or science is made absolute rather than God himself, not only the image of God but humanity itself is disfigured: the *ecce homo* on the cross and on the many crosses which men have set up and keep setting up. Theology has also played its part here in the past. But whatever one thinks of contemporary theologians, one thing should be granted them: by means of a historical praxis of commitment to mysticism and politics they are trying to discover the human face of God, starting from there in order to revive hope in a society, a humanity with a more humane face.

In the Jewish-Christian tradition God is experienced as a God who is concerned with humanity, as the promoter of good and the enemy of evil—as pure Positivity, albeit non-definable even in his own positiveness by human knowledge. The biblical vision of the coming of God's kingdom or rule envisages a humanity in which there are no more exploiters and no more exploited humanity, no more individual or structural servitude and no more slaves.

Our time imposes on us the task of stressing two things at the same time, both of which we need to realize as an authentic two-in-oneness. Precisely in Jesus Christ the unmistakable two-in-oneness becomes manifest in one indivisible personality. On the one hand Jesus identifies himself with God's concern; spirituality (theology) is concerned with God. On the other hand he identifies himself with humankind's concern; spirituality and theology are concerned with human beings and the life that they live; theology serves humanity. Finally, in Jesus these two concerns seem to be simply one concern: humanity's concern is God's concern and God's concern is also humanity's concern. Precisely because it expresses this through the central idea of Jesus' message, the Kingdom of God among men and women, present-day Christian contextual theology (and spirituality) can be recognized.

If one can speak about 'the new paradigm' (theology after Auschwitz, and theology after a Christian history of domination and victors), it would be this: the recognition that the contemporary context for talking meaningfully about God is the context of humankind's need for liberation, emancipation and redemption. In our times, an authentic faith in God only seems to be possible in the context of a praxis of liberation and of solidarity with the needy. It is in that praxis that the idea develops that God reveals himself as the mystery and the very heart of humanity's striving for liberation, wholeness and soundness. The concept of that mystery, which is at first concealed in the praxis of liberation and of making whole, is only made explicit in the naming of that concept in the statement made in faith that God is the liberator, the promoter of what is good and the opponent of what is evil. The discovery that God himself is the very heart and the mystery of all liberation gives rise to praise and thanksgiving and to liturgical celebration of God the liberator, even before we are completely liberated.

This means that mysticism (understood as an intensive form of prayer) and politics (understood as an intensive form of social-political involvement) are each bound to be at the heart of the other. Critical memory of the past, consciously believing in and belonging to the Christian faith's tradition of experience and interpretation, is not only a liturgical confession but, in two-in-oneness, a political act.

If, therefore, we are able to speak about *the* paradigm in today's situation, *it will be the paradigm of 'humanity,'* the paradigm of the (undefinable) cry for the humane, open to God's future which transcends human history. A religion which in fact has a dehumanizing effect, in whatever way, is either a false religion or a religion which understands itself wrongly. This criterion of humanizing proclaimed by Jesus, this concern for the humanity of humankind, is not a reduction or evacuation of religion; it is the first condition for its human possibility and credibility. It is of this God, and no other, that Jesus Christ is 'the great symbol': 'the image of the invisible God' (Col. 1, 15; see 2 Cor. 4, 3–4).

If living human beings are the fundamental symbol of God (*imago Dei*), then the place where human beings are dishonored and oppressed, both in the depth of their own hearts and in an oppressive society, is at the same time the privileged place where religious experience becomes possible in a lifestyle which seeks to give form to that symbol, to heal and restore it to itself: to express its deepest truth.

Nevertheless, an active search for the incomprehensible mystery of the ultimate *humanum*, which always takes place within a particular cultural, social and even geographical context, in fact merges into the mystery of 'the suffering righteous messianic prophet,' Jesus, 'the Holy and Righteous one' (Acts 3, 14), rightly called 'Son of God.' It is here that the power (*dynamis*) of defenseless and disarming love is revealed: suffering *through* and *for* others as an expression of the unconditional validity of a praxis of doing good and opposing evil and innocent suffering.

That seems to me the new paradigm—the words *of old:* 'I have seen the affliction of my people in Egypt, and I have heard their cry because of their taskmasters; I know their sufferings, and I have come down to deliver my people' (Ex. 3, 7–8).

'He is'; the same and the one God who is concerned with humanity calls us to the same solidarity with suffering humanity (see Ex. 3, 14). The new paradigm is the Newness of the Gospel itself *within* humanity's changed conjunctural culture and situation.

Translated by Margaret Köhl

16

The Religious and the Human Ecumene

1989

The history of humankind in past and present is marked by religious wars and the violence of religions. The coexistence of religions does not seem in fact to be favorable for the promoting of humanity, for the movement toward living together in community worthy of humanity. This is indeed a highly paradoxical situation, especially for Christians, for Vatican II declares solemnly the Christian church to be "the sign and the instrument . . . of the unity of all the human race" (*Lumen Gentium*, 1). But try saying this in Northern Ireland, where for years Christians have been doing everything to make one another's living impossible, in the most literal sense of the word. Or, look at Iran and Iraq, Lebanon, the Golden Temple of the Sikhs, and so on. If paying homage to the highest human values becomes imperialistic, such praise deteriorates into the worst enemy of concrete human dignity!

Gustavo Gutiérrez has brought the church "as sacrament of the world" into connection with "the option for the poor."[1] I should like to elaborate on that vision here.

The Plurality of Religions and Christianity

The history of humanity presents us with a collection of divergent ways of life, a multicolored proposal of "ways of salvation": monotheistic Judaism, Christianity, and Islam; Hinduism and Buddhism; Taoism, Confucianism, and Shinto; animism; African and Amerindian ways to salvation and blessing. We call all of these "religions"; that is, we are convinced that there is an essential agreement among all the divergent

249

phenomena. That is why they are designated by a single concept: religion.

Likewise, *Nostra Aetate* (1), a declaration of Vatican II, says that persons "look to the various religions for answers to those profound mysteries of the human condition which today, even as in olden times, deeply stir the human heart." In other words, by offering a message of salvation and by showing a path to salvation, religions respond to a fundamental question about life. In a similar key, modern sociologists (such as H. Lübbe) say much the same thing, albeit in very general terms but nonetheless correctly, talking about religions as "systems of orientation to the ultimate" or "systems of dealing with contingency": comprehensive systems that give meaning or systems that help us to come to terms spiritually, emotionally, and especially existentially with our vulnerable, precarious existence in an ambivalent society.

However, students of culture and philosophers of religion have some misconceptions about all of this—in the dual line of either an essentialist or a nominalist approach via "general terms" ("universals") to what is meant by "religion."

In my opinion, we can say this better with a term of Wittgenstein: that there exists among the many religions "family resemblances." Then there is really no talk of one or more "common characteristics," or of "ideal types." Phenomena that show resemblances and are on that basis designated with the same term ("religion") are (just as the members of a family, so Wittgenstein would say) each really unique in their specific combination or configuration of characteristics. But on the basis of "family resemblances" they still can be compared with one another despite their uniqueness. As a socio-cultural phenomenon and system of meaning, Christianity is also a religion alongside other religions: one out of many.

And here the difficulties begin. How can religions as religions "live together" with another, despite their conflicting pretensions? We stand here before a particularly difficult and delicate problem regarding the question of how religious persons from a variety of religions might coexist.

For themselves, Christians find their only rescue in Jesus confessed as the Christ. Therefore they have kept asking (out of their own vision and orientation in life) in the course of history how non-Christians could work out their salvation. For their confession of Jesus' uniqueness was not merely an expression of a subjective conviction. According to Christian confession, that vision has to do with something real: that is to say, *it is true* (although it is an affirmative of faith and not a scientifically provable and verifiable truth; thus it can never be used in a discussion as a weapon against non-Christians).

On the basis of that faith conviction in Jesus' universal redeeming activity, Christians had to ask the question sooner or later about the possibility of salvation for non-Christians. This happened indirectly from the very beginning of Christianity: already the Second (or New) Testament says that God desires the salvation of "all" (1 Tim. 2:4), and that God wills it in a realizable manner, adapted to the situation of given individuals (even if they do not know Christ). The actual thematization of this problem—how individuals "could become blessed" if they had never come to know Jesus Christ—began especially in modernity and really only in our own time to become a fundamental and even crucial theological problem.

For we as Christians are confronted with biblical texts that do not fit easily with this problem and for which we must account. Jesus surely preached the reign of God as a reign of justice, peace, and wholeness of creation for all persons. But according to the witness of the New Testament, Jesus himself stands in a constitutive or essential relationship to this universal reign of God for all humanity. Christians say with the Bible that "there is one God, and there is one mediator between God and men," Jesus Christ (1 Tim. 2:5); "and there is a salvation in no one else, for there is no other name under heaven given among men by which we must be saved" (Acts 4:12). The Johannine Jesus also says: "I am the way, and the truth, and the life; no one comes to the Father but by me" (John 14:16). "For so the Lord has commanded us, saying, 'I have set you to be a light for the gentiles, that you may bring salvation to the uttermost parts of the earth.' And when the gentiles heard this they were glad" (Acts 13:47). Also a Paulinism directed in a different fashion but just as Christian, says: "For as by a man came death, by a man has come also the resurrection of the dead. For as in Adam all die, so also in Christ shall all be made alive" (1 Cor. 15:21–22). What happened to Jesus is a fact "once for all" (Heb. 9:12). That which has taken place holds for all nations, peoples, and cultures; it is universally relevant in time and space; it has world-historical significance. The post-Pauline tradition even says: "He is the image of the invisible God" (Col. 1:15). A similar sound is heard in all the gospel traditions. "He who sees me sees him who sent me" (John 12:45). The essential bond between the coming of the reign of God for all people and Jesus the Christ is confessed in all levels and traditions of the New Testament, also by the first Hebrew-Jewish interpretation of Jesus of Nazareth.

Those are texts that we cannot circumvent or dilute or act as though they were not there. Moreover, that would not be honest; a selective elimination of parts of the scriptures is also hardly an honest solution. To be sure: all these statements are statements of *belief,* of course; they interpret a confessing discourse, in no way a scientific-objectivizing or propositional and thereby verifiable discourse. But this latter has in no way an exclusive claim on truth. We cannot, however, disregard these absolute statements from the New Testament, or render them harmless by reducing them to exaggerated, elegant flourishes of rhetoric, such as when lovers say to one another "you are the most beautiful and the only one in the world." That is meaningful language, but it holds only for the two lovers, even though outsiders understand clearly its meaning. It is a sensible use of language.

Confessional language of faith, to be sure, also has something to do with similar expressions of someone's complete devotion to a loved one. It indeed says something also about one's subjective stance and complete surrender to another person. But confessional language is not exhausted by that. A certain confessional language also says something about that very person, about reality, a reality that actually calls forth this complete and radical surrender, and is worthy of it, precisely because it is real. Although the immediate basis for such language may lie in a personal or collective experience, that experience also mediates something more profound. The ultimate ground of Jesus' uniqueness spoken of in the scriptural quotation is, according to the New Testament witness, "for in him all the fullness of God was pleased to dwell" (Col. 1:19); or, according to the so-called Apostles' Creed, "He is the Christ, God's only beloved Son, our Lord."

The scriptural quotations refer clearly to Christian consciousness, that Jesus of Nazareth was considered by Christians as the definitive and decisive revelation of God, who nonetheless "desires all to be saved and to come to the knowledge of the truth" (1 Tim. 2:4), also therefore even if they have not come to know Jesus Christ. Whether that revelation then is normative for other religions is the next consideration. For all kinds of ambiguities can come about here if we use the word "normative" or "criterion," because those words are used extensively on the level of "scientific objectivity," whereas the assertion that in Jesus God's definitive and decisive revelation takes place is an affirmation of faith, something that is not accessible or evident on a scientifically objective basis.

In connection with the uniqueness of the Christian church, one can ask good and bad questions. And in the past many bad questions were asked, so that the answer to them shares in the meaninglessness of the question. In the history of the Christian churches it was generally accepted until recently that Christianity was the bearer of absolute truth. "In fact," the Christian churches have so comported themselves in the course of the ages. A proper claim to universality was twisted imperialistically into an ecclesiastical claim of absoluteness, to a monopoly or exclusive claim to truth. This imperialism became the cause of religious wars and of persecution.

A Brief Overview of the Contemporary Theological State of the Question, Especially in Catholic Theology

Vatican II broke with this imperialism of truth. In broad lines, that was clearly a new path away from the previous centuries-old tradition. However, it was not a radical break, because both the First and Second Testaments and church traditions also recognized good things in the other religions.

Already before Vatican II Karl Rahner and other theologians went further than the already broad statements of this council.[2] They not only recognized the possibility of individual salvation of the adherents of other religions, but also ascribed to those religions themselves—as such, therefore as institutions—salvific value. They, too, were "ways of salvation" to God, institutions of salvation (something that Vatican II, despite urgings from theologians, did not yet dare to say). Even the already open statements of the Second Vatican Council in *Lumen Gentium, Nostra Aetate,* and *Ad Gentes* did not go so far, at least not expressly. It seems also that implicitly for the philosopher of religion from Bonn, Hans Waldenfels, that modern position (inspired by Rahner) goes too far, when he writes that if non-Christians likewise find their salvation, "that happens not *in spite of,* but in each case *in* their religion. The formula *through* (or through the mediation of) their religion is one Christians should rather avoid," he adds explicitly.[3] For myself, I do not understand this hesitation toward religion as a social system so well; apparently he fears that this touches a seed of the truth in the old claim to absoluteness of the "imperialist" Christianity.

One does have to concede with the theologian Max Seckler that the salvific value of all religions cannot be posited merely abstractly and globally.[4] One will have to look very concretely at each religion, one by one, regarding their own values and the image of humanity and the world implicit within them. How do you want to be and how do you see your own humanity? Although it was (unavoidably) schematic, Vatican II tried to express the proper value of Judaism, Hinduism, Buddhism, and Islam, and finally this council speaks in *Lumen Gentium,* chap. 16, even of the possibility of salvation of agnostics and atheists. With this we are already close by my personal theological position, which basically affirms the following: before one can speak historically of religions, there was the reality of God's saving activity in profane history: "outside the world, there is no salvation." God brings about in world history salvation through human mediation *and* persons bring about calamity. Religions are latecomers in the history of salvation coming from God in our profane history.

In recent years some have gone even further. Thus the philosopher of religion Heinz Robert Schlette reverses the categories used earlier: for him, Christianity is not the "normal" or "ordinary way to salvation" to God; the other religions are that. Christianity is the "exceptional" or "extraordinary" way to God.[5]

With this we are still not through the bend in the road. Recently the American Catholic theologian Paul Knitter went even a step further than Schlette: he denies any form of claim to universality of Christianity.[6] In our times there indeed reigns among Christians a certain new form of modern "indifferentism," and some theologians have made themselves spokespersons for it: all religions are of the same value. Of course they are not, for even their visions about humanity are rather divergent, and a religion that, for example, sends the eldest son to death is certainly not of the same value as a religion that expressly forbids it. Criteria of humanity apply here too!

Even though one's own religion is involved in every comparison of religions with one another, one ultimately cannot avoid the truth question. But the truth question presents itself within a "hermeneutical circle." The question is not whether there are many open questions here that cannot be solved speculatively, and moreover whether one is asking the right question and not the wrong one (which can never be resolved). The question of truth with regard to one's own religion in no way need be discriminatory in itself vis-à-vis other religions. No single religion exhausts the question of truth. Therefore *in religiosis* we must put behind us both absolutism and relativism.

Our times have "liberated" themselves in many points from the peculiarly modern claim to truth and universality since the Enlightenment. Logically and practically, plurality has gained priority over unity. The ancient and neoplatonic Greek ideal of unity is in no sense still a norm for modern and postmodern persons. The claims made by a Jewish, Christian, and Muslim monotheism on all persons is perceived by many (or some) as something totalitarian. Some see in this the reason for the move of many Westerners to Asian religions. The statement "all religions are equal" is understandable to postmodern sensibilities, even though that statement is cheap and, to my mind, fundamentally wrong.

The question rather is whether monotheism with its claim to universality cannot be a critique or a challenge to those sensibilities. Current sensibilities are not normative in themselves either! The universal claim to salvation of Jesus and the human reason that remembers the suffering of humanity can also deliver a critique of that liberal pluralism of our time. For there is also a cheap form of toleration—indifference: *laissez faire, laissez passer*—I don't care! This is an attitude without the courage of the witnessing blood of martyrs.

To be sure, Christianity has often expressed its own truth, universality, and uniqueness (which are undeniable) as a claim to absoluteness, by means of which all other religions were considered inferior, whereas the good that was to be found in them was assumed to be present in Christianity itself in a preeminent fashion. One discovered "Christian values" in the other religions, but robbed them of their own identity by the fact. The consequence of this religious and cultural "imperialism" was that the modern history of colonialism and of mission has been in good measure also a time of oppression of foreign cultures and religions, both during and not less than before from the time of the abstract Enlightenment.

But Asia and practically all countries where Islam reigned shut themselves off from Christianity; these universal religions had their own claim to absoluteness. Because of that in the public forum of the West, Christianity came to be considered more and more as one religion among many and moreover, historically, as a religion under which many non-Christian cultures and other religions had suffered severely. This climatic change in Western thinking was paired with a privatization of Christianity as religion: in one's own heart one could quietly praise Christianity as the one true religion, as long as it had no consequences for others and for the bourgeois public forum. At the moment Christianity is not dropping its claim to universality, but is letting both its exclusivist and inclusivist claim to universality go. "Exclusivist," in the sense of "only Christianity is a true religion," and "inclusivist" insofar as there is truth and goodness immanent in other religions, with their adherents being "anonymous Christians." In both cases this discriminates against non-Christians and this therefore is improper.

New Theological Perspective

Given this prehistory, we shall have to seek in any case a direction that avoids both absolutism and relativism. To ask the truth question regarding Christianity, and simultaneously with that the question whether it is possible for Christians to live together with members of other religions and with atheists and agnostics, in no way presumes, as had been thought earlier, the superiority of Christianity in the sense of how can Christians, who as members of a particular religion consider themselves superior to other religious persons, live together with non-Christians? Rather, the question is about a Christian identity that respectfully acknowledges others' religious identity and allows itself to be challenged by other religions and challenges them in return on the basis of its own message. In short, we are being confronted with other questions than were asked in the past, questions that are more productive and fruitful for all parties concerned.

We are therefore asking other questions, even if it remains binding for Christian believers that they find salvation "only in the name of Jesus of Nazareth." And in this Christian perspective questions arise about whether and how, for example, can one be a Christian as a Hindu? In other words, is there a Hindu version of being Christian? This is not a question of a speculative approach to one another's religions, but of a probably centuries-long experiment to come to a "common experience." Only a common experience can lead to a consonant hermeneutical interpretation. That common experience is by no means here yet. Therefore it seems to me that the question is whether the pluralism of religions is a *factual* phenomenon that should be overcome as quickly as possible, or a *foundational* phenomenon that asks for a continuing humane coexistence. The consequences of this are rather important for one's own vision of the ecumene of the world religions and ultimately for world peace, which, through religious intolerance and through the pretensions to exclusive or inclusive claims to absoluteness, has been put severely to the test in the course of time and today in many countries through religious wars.

My concern here directly is the identity and therefore the proper self-definition of Christianity, in which this religion sees how it is to be situated vis-à-vis other religions: on the one hand, without absolutism or relativism; on the other, without discrimination or feelings of superiority.

Phase One: The Historical Contingency or Limitedness of Jesus of Nazareth

In contrast to the earlier claim to absoluteness of Christianity, determined as it was by the regnant *Zeitgeist* of that time, lies the positive acceptance of the diversity of religions, which is, to my mind, inherent in the essence of Christianity. The problem is not so much that posed at the level of an earlier consciousness of the problematic: Is Christianity the one, true religion, or is it (in a more moderate version) a better religion than all the others? In these comparisons the concept "religion" is borrowed from the religion of the one doing the comparison (whatever religion that might be). For Christians, therefore, it is Christianity. Rather, the problem is this: *How can Christianity maintain its own identity and uniqueness and at the same time ascribe a positive value to the diversity of religions in a nondiscriminating way?* When posed in this way, it is not the common elements in the many religions, but precisely their respective differences that form their uniqueness and particularity, that is relevant for Christianity. If this is the case, one needs to indicate a basis in Christianity itself for this new Christian attitude of openness and nonintolerance toward other world religions.

This basis lies, to my mind, in Jesus' message and praxis of the reign of God, with all their consequences. For Christianity is in its particularity and uniqueness as a religion essentially bound to an insuperable "historical particularity" and thus to regionality and limitation. Thus Christianity, too, like all religions has boundaries: limited in forms of expression, and also in ways of looking at things and in concrete praxis. Christians sometimes have difficulty looking at this reality rationally. But this limitedness belongs to the essence of Christianity (even expressed especially when Christians use their "incarnation model" in their theology—which remains in this tradition the dominant paradigm).

The special, particular, and unique character of Christianity is that it finds the life and essence of God precisely in this historical and thus limited particularity of "Jesus of Nazareth"—confessed as the personal-human manifestation of God. Thereby is confessed that Jesus is surely a "unique" but nonetheless "contingent" manifestation (that is, historical and therefore limited) of the gift of salvation coming from God for all persons. Whoever ignores this fact of the concrete, particular humanity of Jesus, precisely in his geographically limited and socio-culturally recognizable and limited quality as "human," makes of the individual Jesus a "necessary" divine emanation or consequence, whereby indeed all other religions disappear into the void. This seems to be essentially in conflict with the deepest sense of all the christological councils and creeds, and finally with the very being of God as absolute freedom. Jesus' humanity is devalued in that vision to a (docetic) phantom humanity, while trivializing on the other hand all non-Christian religions. Nevertheless Christians have in the course of time absolutized without remainder precisely this historical and limited particularity of Christianity. This rang in the historical misery of empirical Christianity in opposition to the original evangelical authenticity.

However, the revelation of God in Jesus, as the Christian gospel proclaims it, does not mean that God absolutizes a historical particularity (be it even Jesus of Nazareth). From the revelation in Jesus we learn that no single historical particularity can be called absolute and that therefore, because of the relativity present in Jesus, every person can encounter God outside Jesus, especially in our worldly history and in

[handwritten marginalia: Jesus reveals a theocentr.? vision -creator God -redeemer / a voila truly in particular]

the many religions that have arisen from it. The risen Jesus of Nazareth keeps *pointing beyond himself to God.* One could say: God points via Jesus Christ in the Spirit to God as creator and redeemer: to a God of *all* persons.

The particularity of Jesus, which defines the origin, particularity, and uniqueness of Christianity, implies therefore that the differences between the individual religions remain and are not erased. The manifestation of God in Jesus does not close out "religious history," which is evident from, among others, the rise of Islam as a post-Christian world religion. And no one, not even in Islam, can deny that new world religions can and will arise after Islam. Despite all critical questions that can be addressed, certain contemporary neoreligious movements can support this hypothesis.

It is clear that there are convergences and divergences between all religions. Differences, however, are not to be judged in themselves as deviations that should be worked out ecumenically, but as positive values. God is too rich and too supersubstantial to be exhausted *in fulness* by one distinct and thus limited religious tradition or experience. Surely, according to the Christian view of things, "the whole fulness of deity dwells in" Jesus. New Testament texts witness to that for Christians (Col. 2:9; 1:15; Heb. 1:3; 2 Cor. 4:4). But it is precisely in "bodiliness"—or "this dwelling (of God's fulness) in Jesus' *humanity*"—that the *contingent* and *limited* form of Jesus' appearance in our history is drawn. (Otherwise one should proclaim the docetism condemned by all Christian churches—that is, that the divine could only appear in a phantom humanity in Jesus.)

As a result of all this we can, may, and must say that there is more (religious) truth present in *all the religions together* than in one individual religion, and this holds also for Christianity. There exist because of that "true," "good," and "beautiful"—astonishing—aspects in the manifold forms of coming to terms with God present in humanity, forms that have not found and do not find a place in the specific experience of Christianity. There are divergent authentic religious experiences that Christianity has never thematized or brought into practice precisely because of its historical particularity. Probably (I say it cautiously, but assertively) because of the specifically personal accents of Jesus himself, Christianity cannot thematize these experiences *without undoing those particular accents of their jesuanic sharpness and ultimately of their specific Christianness.*

From all this I learn that (also in Christian self-understanding) the plurality of religions is not an evil that needs to be overcome, but rather a fructifying richness to be welcomed by all. This does not deny that the historically irresolvable plurality of religions is nurtured and fed interiorly by a unity within our history that is explicitly no longer thematizable and practicable: the very unity of God (confessed by Christians as a trinitarian one), insofar as this transcendent unity is reflected in the immanent family resemblances among the religions, something that gives us permission to give the unitary name of "religion" to all these divergent religious phenomena!

The particularity, identity, and uniqueness of Christianity vis-à-vis those other religions resides in the fact that Christianity is a religion that connects the relationship to God to a historical and thus highly situated and thereby limited particularity: Jesus of Nazareth. This is the uniqueness and identity of Christianity, but at the same time its unavoidably historical boundedness. Clear with this is that the God of Jesus (based on Jesus' parables and praxis of the reign of God) is a symbol of openness, and not of being closed. This gives a positive relationship of Christianity to other religions, at the same time nonetheless maintaining the uniqueness of Christianity and ultimately honoring the Christian loyal affirmation of the positive nature of the other world religions.

The truth question is not evaded by this, but what is true here is that no one holds a lease on the truth, and that no one can claim the fulness of God's richness for themselves alone. This insight, somewhat new for Christians, flows from the fact that we are also asking new questions now that could not have been asked earlier, purified as we are by past (and still new!) meaningless religious wars and unfruitful discrimination. In doing this we do not proclaim the cheap modern liberal principle that all religions are equal, or all are equally relative, or even equally untrue (as the atheists maintain).

Christology is an interpretation of Jesus of Nazareth: it states that Jesus is redeemer of all persons and is in that sense the universal redeemer. But that which redeems, which mediates liberation and redemption, is not the interpretation, but the means of redemption itself. In *Jesus: An Experiment in Christology,* I already referred to the fact that we are not redeemed by the christological titles of Jesus, but through the means of redemption itself, Jesus of Nazareth, in whatever framework of language that means is experienced and expressed. That is to say: "Jesus" redeems us, not "Christ," a christological title coming from a certain culture and often not usable in other cultures. Moreover, redemption in Christ is only unique and universal insofar as what happened in Jesus is continued in his disciples. Without a relationship to a redemptive and liberative practice of Christians, the redemption brought about at one time by Jesus is suspended in a purely speculative, vacuous atmosphere. The credal exclamation, "Jesus is Lord" (Rom. 10:9) does not of itself bring redemption, but rather "he who does the will of my Father" (Matt. 7:21). One has to follow the path Jesus did; then Jesus' way of life takes on concretely a universal meaning (Matt. 25:37–39, 44–46). An actual, albeit fragmentary, making persons whole is also the best proof of liberation!

The claim that Jesus is the universal redeemer implies that we are beginning in our history to bring forth the fruits of the reign of God. This christology receives its authenticity from the concrete praxis of the reign of God: the history of Jesus' path through life must be continued in his disciples; only then is there meaningful talk of the uniqueness and particularity of Christianity. There is also a coredemptive function of the "body of Christ," specifically, the historical Christian community. The path through life, following after Jesus, is marked by two essential characteristics: the way of denial of any messianism of power, coming from a seigneurial-human interior freedom (resisting oppressive powers is the basis for the human voluntary commitment to poor and oppressed persons: a solidarity of love), *and* this path includes the *via crucis*, the cross. Jesus was indeed the expected messiah, but he was that in an "unexpected way," perceived only by a few. In this is the uniqueness of Jesus; the "proof" is this: throughout the centuries Christians have witnessed to this path through life by going through him to a witnessing martyrdom. "In my flesh I complete what is lacking in Christ's afflictions" (Col. 1:24), as it was expressed in ancient times. Resistance and surrender. This brings us to the following concretization or second phase, without which that first phase of reflection remains still abstract.

Phase Two: The Universal Right of the Poor

The *universality* of Christian faith means that the Christian faith community is an open community. Sadly enough, the institutional church has had the inclination to universalize precisely its nonuniversal, historically inherited peculiar characteristics bound to a certain culture and time, and to impose them uniformly upon the entire Catholic world: in catechesis (think of the "universal catechism"), in liturgy and church order, also in theology and until recently even in a uniform language (Latin). Universality—in Greek it is called "catholicity"—means rather that the Christian faith places itself open (critically) for each person, for each people and each culture. "Universal" means: what holds equally for all. That universal must incarnate itself then in all and in each one, without exhausting all the potentialities and virtualities of the universal in those given incarnations. Thus, in the contemporary context of aching structural world poverty, the universal openness and universal invitation of the gospel message receives a socially very concrete dimension and a new location, as it were. In that way especially Latin American, but also African and Asian forms of liberation theology inspire me.[7]

In the West we used the concept "universality" often in an abstract and nonhistorical fashion, in the sense of "valid for all persons." In itself, a correct usage! But, we said rather nonchalantly that something is valid for all persons while forgetting that humanity is divided concretely into "poor" and "nonpoor" persons, and that what was valid for the nonpoor, historically and concretely was not valid for the poor and oppressed. Structurally they are excluded. Talking about universality is therefore only meaningful and concrete if, in our fundamental theological concepts, we express at the same time the distinction between nonpoor and especially the structurally poor. It is not a matter of speaking of a pastoral predilection of the church for the poor in the sense in which the duty to universal love always means a preferential love for certain individual persons, as the church also can speak of pastoral priorities—for example, in connection with the church's option for youth. No, the option for the poor is a *datum of revelation*. The basis for that option is the Christian faith in the God of Jesus Christ, who himself gives witness to this partisan option. That option for the poor is thus a question of Christian orthodoxy; it touches all the belief statements of the Christian credo. The option for the poor, the indigent, and the oppressed is a partisan, free choice of the God of Jesus of Nazareth, as well as an option for the not always in fact "nonpoor," socio-culturally, psychologically, and religiously marginalized persons. The incarnation of God in Jesus of Nazareth is not a "becoming human," but an identification of God in Jesus with the poor, oppressed, and finally executed innocent individual, for whom Jesus stands as a model. Only within this perspective can we now speak of the concrete universality of ecclesiastical Christianity, insofar as it walks in the footsteps of Jesus.

It is therefore a matter of a "concrete universality" through which Christian believers take upon themselves the aspirations of those who are deprived of their rights in this world and are in solidarity with the cry for justice of the poor and disenfranchised. The cause of justice is the cause of all. Freedom, the rights of humanity, are there for all; and if this is not the case (in other words, if there are only rights for those who demand them), there are no human rights! If rights are valid only for a part of humanity, this part of humanity would thereby legitimate and sanction the lack of rights. In the measure that the church chooses the side of the poor and those deprived of rights and is in solidarity with human rights, it takes up that concrete universality, for the "Catholic universality" is not only a given from the very inception of Christian faith, it is a contextual charge to be achieved historically.

In the contemporary socio-political and economic time-bind of structural deprivation of rights for the majority of humanity, not only the *caritative diaconia universalizes* the Christian gospel among all people (as Mother Teresa benevolently practices it), but also the *political diaconia* that wishes to remove the causes of this structural deprivation. It thereby recognizes the universality of human rights and human dignity, and does not cover up poverty theologically and prolong it ideologically. The active presence of the Christian churches with poor and deprived persons, adding its voice to the cry for redemption of the oppressed, has therefore a universal meaning: a *meaning for all*—also for the rich and powerful as a summons to solidarity. The transformation of the world toward a higher humanity, toward justice, peace, and wholeness of creation belongs therefore essentially to the "catholicity" or universality of Christian faith, and this is a nondiscriminatory universality par excellence.

That Christianity is a universal message to all people means therefore that Christianity is only universal if Christians are concerned to reach all of humanity in its being lacerated into "poor" and "nonpoor." "To the poor is preached the good news": that is the essence of the Christian gospel! And this message is also practiced toward the poor (without Christians being able to view this as a Christian exclusive right or monopoly). The sending of Christians in solidarity to the poor in all the world belongs then also to the essential aspects of what we now call "mission." For Christians it comes down to this: by Christian praxis—in the footsteps of Jesus—to witness to the one whom they confess as their God: the God of Israel, father of Jesus Christ, who is called a defender of the poor, creator of heaven and earth, who cannot be claimed by any single religion for itself. But then we must keep clearly before our eyes with this the peculiar accent of Jesus' conception of God (if we wish to preserve the evangelical accents).

Critique of certain images of God, especially of conceptions of God that threaten our humanness, is also an essential aspect of the evangelical message of Jesus of Nazareth; it is even a focus in that message. And it was from a religious source and, for that matter, from a Christian insight of faith (otherwise therefore than in the Enlightenment) that God is personally involved with persons in their history, that Christianity is, from a theologal or mystical source, originally and simultaneously an impulse toward liberation and emancipation. On the basis of Jesus' message, parables, and his praxis of the reign of God, we see how the biblical concept of God is essentially bound up with a praxis of persons who liberate their fellow human beings, just as Jesus did before us. Precisely because in the course of church history the bond weakened and was even forgotten, and God was thereby "objectified" as the capstone and guarantor of all human knowledge, order, and behavior, and thus was declared the legitimation of the status quo—an enemy of any change, liberation, and emancipation, therefore—the crisis of the Enlightenment was historically not only possible, but even "unavoidable."

This all had, on the other hand, the consequence that in Enlightenment deism (and in its direct and indirect aftereffects) the biblical "calling upon God" disappeared and left only a secularized and diminished liberation and emancipation process—a diminished freedom movement. From a Christian point of view it is, however, a matter of an unbreakable connection between revering God (let us say: prayer and mysticism) *and* emancipatory liberation in the fullest and multifaceted sense of this word—in that a theologian such as Gustavo Gutiérrez goes ahead of us all with conviction!

This mystical and liberating message, accompanied by a consonant evangelical praxis, following after Jesus, proclaiming loudly to all who will hear, is the good right of Christianity. But Christians must remember in this a word of the prophet Amos: "Did I not bring up Israel from the land of Egypt, and the Philistines from Caphtor and the Syrians from Kir?" (Amos 9:7). Suffering humanity is evidently *the* chosen people of God. If that is so, living together with the "human ecumene," seen religiously, and the "ecumene of suffering humanity," is indeed possible.

Translated by Robert J. Schreiter

NOTES

1. Gustavo Gutiérrez, "Twee perspectieven op de kerk. Sacrament van de wereld—keuze voor de armen," in Hermann Häring, Ted Schoof, and Ad Willems, eds., *Meedenken met Edward Schillebeeckx* (Baarn: H. Nelissen, 1983), pp. 221–45.

2. Karl Rahner, "Christianity and Non-Christian Religions," *Theological Investigations,* vol. 5, pp. 115–34; see also "Church, Churches, and Religions," ibid., vol. 10, pp. 30–49; "Anonymous Christianity and the Missionary Task of the Church," ibid., vol. 12, pp. 161–78; "Jesus Christ in the Non-Christian Religions," ibid., vol. 17, pp. 39–50; "Über die Heilsbedeutung der nichtchristlichen Religionen," *Schriften zur Theologie,* vol. 13, pp. 341–50.

3. Hans Waldenfels, "Der Absolutheitsanspruch des Christentums und die grossen Weltreligionen," *Hochland,* 62 (1970) 202–17; "Ist der christliche Glaube der einzig Wahre? Christentum und nichtchristliche Religionen," *Stimmen der Zeit,* 112 (1987) 463–75.

4. Max Seckler, "Theologie der Religionen mit Fragezeichen," *Theologische Quartalschrift,* 166 (1986) 164–84.

5. Heinz Robert Schlette, *Toward a Theology of Religions* (New York: Herder and Herder, 1966); idem, *Skeptische Religionsphilosophie* (Freiburg: Herder, 1972).

6. Paul Knitter, *No Other Name? A Critical Survey of Christian Attitudes toward the World Religions* (Maryknoll, N.Y.: Orbis, 1985).

7. Among those to be cited are Gustavo Gutiérrez, Leonardo Boff, and others. For Africa and Asia, especially Jean-Marc Ela, *African Cry* (Maryknoll, N.Y.: Orbis, 1986); Aloysius Pieris, *An Asian Theology of Liberation* (Maryknoll, N.Y.: Orbis, 1988).

Table of Original Publication

1. "The Church and Mankind," in *The Church and Mankind* (*Concilium* vol. 1 [1965]).

2. "The Magisterium and the World of Politics," in *Faith and the World of Politics* (*Concilium* #36 [1968]).

3. "Some Thoughts on the Interpretation of Eschatology," (*Concilium* vol. 1, no. 5 [1969]).

4. "The Problem of the Infallibility of the Church's Office: A Theological Reflection," in Edward Schillebeeck and Bas van Iersel, eds., *Truth and Certainty* (*Concilium* vol. 3, no. 9 [March 1973]).

5. "Critical Theories and Christian Political Commitment," in Norbert Greinacher and Alois Müller, eds., *Political Commitment and the Christian Community* (*Concilium* vol. 4, no. 9 [April 1973]).

6. "The Crisis in the Language of Faith as a Hermeneutical Problem," in Johann Baptist Metz and Jean-Pierre Jossua, eds., *The Crisis in the Language of Faith* (*Concilium* vol. 5, no. 9 [May 1973]).

7. "The 'God of Jesus' and the 'Jesus of God,'" in Edward Schillebeeckx and Bas van Iersel, eds., *Jesus Christ and Human Freedom* (*Concilium* vol. 3, no. 10 [1974]).

8. "Questions on Christian Salvation of and for Man," in David Tracy, Hans Küng, Johann B. Metz, eds., *Toward Vatican III: The Work that Needs to be Done* (New York: Seabury and *Concilium*, 1978).

9. "The Christian Community and its Office-Bearers," in Edward Schillebeeckx and Johann-Baptist Metz, eds., *The Right of the Community to a Priest* (*Concilium* #133 [1980]).

10. "Secular Criticism of Christian Obedience and the Christian Reaction to that Criticism," in Christian Duquoc and Casiano Floristán, eds., *Christian Obedience* (*Concilium* #139 [1980]).

11. "Christian Identity and Human Integrity," in Jean-Pierre Jossua and Claude Geffré, eds., *Is Being Human a Criterion of Being Christian?* (*Concilium* #155 [1982]).

12. "Eager to Spread the Gospel of Peace," in Virgil Elizondo and Nolbert Greinacher, eds., *Church and Peace* (*Concilium* #164 [1983]).

13. "Offices in the Church of the Poor," in Leonardo Boff and Virgil Elizondo, eds., *La Iglesia Popular: Between Fear and Hope* (*Concilium* #176 [1984]).

14. "The Teaching Authority of All—A Reflection about the Structure of the New Testament," in Johann-Baptist Metz and Edward Schillebeeckx, eds., *The Teaching Authority of Believers* (*Concilium* #180 [1985]).

15. "The Role of History in what is Called the New Paradigm," in Hans Küng and David Tracy, eds., *Paradigm Change in Theology* (New York: Crossroad, 1989).

16. "The Religious and the Human Ecumene," in Marc H. Ellis and Otto Maduro, eds., *The Future of Liberation Theology: Essays in Honor of Gustavo Gutiérrez* (Maryknoll, N.Y.: Orbis Books, 1989).

Index

Abraham, 4
Adam, 3, 17
Ad Gentes (Vatican II), 253
Adorno, Theodor, 72-73
Albert the Great, 144, 175
Alexander III, Pope, 143
alienation, human, 97
Ambrosiaster, 216
Anselm, 238-39
anthropodicity, 72
anthropological constants, 113-21
apocalyptic, 51
Apollos, 229
apostolicity, 216-17
Aquinas, Thomas, 2, 18, 65, 144, 148-49, 181, 186, 218, 232-33, 242; on humility, 175-77
Aristotle, 61, 168-70, 173, 175
Athanasius, 233
Augustine, 61-62, 138, 142, 145, 172-74, 176-77, 219, 233, 242
authority, 232

baptism, 14, 214-16, 228-29
Barnabas, 132, 231
basic communities, 127
Bay, M., de, 61
Becker, K. J., 141
Bellarmine, Robert, 242
Berger, R., 141
Bernard, 174, 176
Bérulle, Pierre de, 147
bishops, 138, 140, 151
Bloch, Ernst, 72-73, 110
Bonaventure, 144, 242
Bosco, Don, 33

Calvin, John, 64, 242
canon of Scripture, 93
cathedra, magistralis and *pastoralis*, 232
Catherine of Siena, 232

Catholicism, 64
celibacy, 148
Celsus, 172
Chalcedon, Council of, 133-34, 142-43, 240
character, sacramental, 144-46, 151, 219
Christianity, anonymous, 14; implicit, 11, 13; as superstructure to normal life, 1
Church, 2, 8, 10, 13, 56-57, 153; as fellowship, 18-20; New Testament vision of, 213-19
Cicero, 168
Cleanthes, 170
Clement of Alexandria, 139
Clichtove, Josse, 147-48, 165n61
collegiality, 137
communion of saints, 3
Complaint of Peace (Erasmus), 200
Congar, Yves, 211
creation, 192-93
"critical communities," 75, 78, 80
Cyprian, 137, 140

Daniel, 50
Darwinism, 119, 203
deprivatization, 80
Descartes, René, 63, 177-78
Dessauer, F., 114
Deutero-Isaiah, 50
dialog, 28
Didache, 139
Droste, 141
Durandus of Saint-Pourçin, 145
dynamism, 157

emancipation, 71-74
Enlightenment, 74, 178-79, 181
Epictetus, 172
epiclesis, 136, 150
Erasmus, 148, 200
eschatology, 49-53

eschaton, 50-53
Eucharist, 128, 131, 137, 144, 151, 155-56
Eusebius, 231
existentialism, 111

faith, 119
Feuerbach, Ludwig, 119
Frankfurt school, 74-75
freedom, human, 97
Freud, Sigmund, 243
Freudianism, 52
future, 48-49

Gadamer, H.-G., 90
ghetto language, 85-89
God, of Jesus, 100-102; as Promise, 191-94
grace, trinitarian, 16
Gratian, 142
"great refusal," 73
Gregory IX, Pope, 145, 242
Groethuysen, B., 179
Gutiérrez, Gustavo, 249

Habermas, Jürgen, 72, 74-75, 77-79, 90
Harnack, Adolf von, 91
heaven, 53
Heidegger, Martin, 65
heresy, 158
hermeneutics, 48
Hippolytus, 135-36, 138, 231
history, 45, 53
Horkheimer, Max, 72-74, 80
Hugh of St. Victor, 142
humanism, 245
humanity, 187-89, 194
humility, 172-73

ideology, 86
Ignatius of Antioch, 140-41, 194
illegality, temporary, 154
Illuminism, 65
indefectibility, 57
infallibility, 62-65
Innocent III, Pope, 143
Irenaeus, 5

Isidore of Seville, 134
Israel, 3-4, 6, 100

Jakobson, Roman, 238
James, 132
Jansen, Cornelis, 61
Jansenists, 61-62
Jerome, 127, 135, 231
Jesus Christ, 2, 4-5, 8, 52, 55, 93, 101, 103, 130-31, 204, 259 as God, 102-7; as lord of all history, 85; as political figure, 76
Jesus: An Experiment in Christology (Schillebeeckx), 259
Joel, 230
John, 132
John (evangelist), 167, 251
John XXIII, Pope, 201
John the Baptist, 229
John Eudes, 219
John Paul II, Pope, 201
Jüngel, J., 76
just war, 200

kairos, 6
Kant, Immanuel, 73, 178-79
Kasper, Walter, 63
kingdom of God, 101, 130, 188, 194
Knitter, Paul, 254
koinonia, 3, 7, 13, 19, 214
Kolakowski, L., 78, 90
Kuhn, Thomas S., 237, 239
Kuitert, Harrie, 202
Küng, Hans, 58, 63

laity, 212
language of faith, 83-84, 86, 89-91; and remembrance of the past, 91-94
Lateran Councils, 142-44, 147
laymen as Eucharistic leaders, 141-42
Lay People in the Church (Congar), 211
Lévinas, E., 116
Lévi-Strauss, C., 59
liberation, 189-91

liberation theology, 261
Lonergan, Bernard, 58
Lübbe, H., 250
Luhmann, N., 90
Luke, 103, 229
Lumen Gentium (Vatican II), 149, 211, 218, 235, 253
Luther, Martin, 64, 148, 233, 242

Maag, V, 50
Machiavelli, 200
Machiavellianism, 203
magisterium, binding power of, 25; and political matters, 25-39
Manning, Cardinal, 219
Marcus Aurelius, 171-72
Marcuse, Herbert, 72-75, 77, 90
Mark, 167, 194, 229
Marx, Karl, 74, 119, 243
Marxism, 52, 72, 76
Maximilian, 200
Mazzi, Don, 75
metanoia, 91, 100-101, 106
Metz, J. B., 34, 35, 90, 107, 181, 233
Moltmann, Jürgen, 49, 108
Moses, 3
Mystical Body of Christ, 17

neo-Platonism, 213
Newman, John Henry, 219
Nicaea, Council of, 136
Nietzsche, F. W., 180, 243
Noah, 3-4
Nostra Aetate (Vatican II), 250, 253
nuclear armament, 199, 201
nuclear disarmament, 207-9

obedience, Christian, secular criticism of, 167-75, 177-80
Oelmüller, W., 90
office(s), and the universal Church, 152; in the Church, 220; in the Church of the poor, 221-24
office-bearers, 127-28, 131, 133
On the Church in the Modern World (Vatican II), 26-39

order, Church, 152-54, 157, 159
ordination, 134, 136, 147, 150
Origen, 18, 172-73, 231

Pacem in Terris (Paul VI), 25
pacifism, 199-209
Paul, 6, 10, 16, 103, 132, 139, 155, 214, 229-31, 242, 251
Paul VI, Pope, 25, 201
Paulinus of Nola, 134
Paulism, 229-30
Paupert, J. M., 34
Peter, 6, 7, 132, 194
Pius X, Pope, 148
Pius XI, Pope, 148
Pius XII, Pope, 148
Plato, 169-70, 172
pluralism, 122
Populorum Progressio (Paul VI), 25
pre-Church, 13
priest(s), 138; image of, 148-49; ordained by need of the community, 133-35; shortage of, 128, 155-56
privatization of office, 146-47
Procksch, O., 50
Protestantism, 64
protology, 49
Psalms, 50-51
Pseudo-Dionysius, 213, 232

Quesnel, Pasquier, 61

Rad, G, von, 50
Rahner, Karl, 17, 51, 239, 253
rationalism, 65
redemption, 91
religion(s), 179-80, 249-50, 253
resurrection, 51
revelation, 55-56, 60
Ricoeur, Paul, 34, 60, 67, 78, 90
Romero, Oscar, 222, 242
rule, 100-101

sacerdotalism, 137-38
sacrament, 150-51
salvation, 1-3, 6, 9, 51, 95, 98, 107, 109-10, 189-90;

Christian, 123-26; non-
religious, 190-9
Schlette, Heinz Robert, 254
Schlier, H., 16
Schneider, T., 119
Schultze, R., 141
Seckler, Max, 253
Seneca, 170
sequela Jesu, 128, 130, 204, 216,
243; of the Church, 226-28
Siger of Brabant, 177
sin, 11; original, 66, 78
Socrates, 168
Sölle, Dorothee, 75
soteriological language, 91
Spinoza, Benedict, 178
Stoicism, 169-71, 174
structuralism, 111
suffering, 194-96
Summa Theologiae (Aquinas), 175

teaching authority, *in* the Church,
and *of* the Church, 225-28
Teresa, Mother, 262
Teresa of Avila, 232, 242
Tertullian, 141-42, 200, 231
theodicy, 72
theology, 180
Traditio Apostolica (Hippolytus),
135-36, 231

transcendence, 46
Trent, Council of, 66, 129, 143,
147, 154, 238
truth, 60

utopia, 34-35, 37, 121

Vass, G., 59
Vatican I, Council, 62-64, 68, 235
Vatican II, Council, 20, 65, 147,
149, 152-54, 155, 158-59,
211-12, 217-18, 223, 249-50,
253
Vincent de Paul, 33
Vincent of Beauvais, 146
Vögtle, A., 6
votum ecclesiae, 18
Vziezen, T., 50

Waldenfels, Hans, 253
Weber, Max, 74
Welte, Bernhard, 239
Wittgenstein, Ludwig, 86, 186,
250
world, 11

Zacchaeus, 204, 227
Zealots
Zizoulas, J. D., 150